THE FIRST DAYS OF SCHOOL

HARRY K. WONG   ROSEMARY TRIPI WONG

Harry K. Wong Publications

Executive Producer: Rosemary T. Wong
Graphics: IPC Graphics and Printing; Carolyn Phelps Clark,
    Barbara Day Zinicola, and Shery Welti
Illustrations: Heidi Heath Abreu
Editor: Bruce Emmer

Harry K. Wong Publications
1030 W. Maude Ave., Ste. 507
Sunnyvale, CA 94086

ISBN: 0-9629360-0-6
Library of Congress Card Catalog Number: 91-90960

Printed in Korea

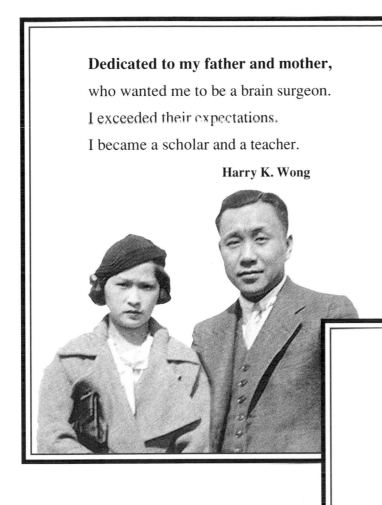

Dedicated to my father and mother,

who wanted me to be a brain surgeon.

I exceeded their expectations.

I became a scholar and a teacher.

Harry K. Wong

Dedicated to Mr. Frederick McKee,

my first principal, whose evaluation

of me said I needed better "classroom

management" skills: Thank you

for telling me I needed to improve my

skills. I did. It worked!

Rosemary Tripi Wong

For Whom Is This Book Written?

***The First Days of School* is written to help all teachers "jump-start" and begin school successfully.** This book is the result of the myriad ideas and techniques that have been shared by the legions of educators who have interacted with us. We thank these people for their contributions, and now we share them in return.

This Book Is Written for All Educators

EXPERIENCED TEACHERS: To hone your competence.

PRESERVICE TEACHERS: To help you plan your career.

NEOPHYTE TEACHERS: To give you a good start.

NEW TEACHERS: To help you stay on track.

MENTOR TEACHERS: To help you advise all teachers who seek your help.

ADMINISTRATORS: To use in your staff development.

IN-SERVICE COORDINATORS: To use as a foundation in your induction and in-service programs.

COLLEGE PROFESSORS: To use as a basic text for your preservice teachers.

Alicia Escobar still grimaces when she recalls her introduction to teaching last September.

"I had the key to this room in June. I cleaned the room inside and out. I knew every corner."

But the novice teacher hadn't a clue on how to plan lessons or organize her paperwork.

"I was overwhelmed; I didn't know where to start."

"Teams Help Coach Rookie Teachers,"
San Jose Mercury News,
February 13, 1989.

Looking Ahead

One important moment please!

Before you start planning the first days of school, take a quick look at what's ahead for the decade of the 1990s.

✓ Fifty percent of the teachers teaching in 1995 will have been in the classroom five years or less.

✓ Of the teachers teaching in the year 2000, 75 percent will have been trained after 1990.

✓ Up to 40 percent of the new teachers will leave teaching within their first seven years.

The message is clear. The entire teaching profession will all but turn over during the 1990s.

✓ **If you are a new teacher:** You have a magnificent future awaiting you, with teaching positions and educational opportunities galore. Prepare yourself for these possibilities.

✓ **If you are an administrator:** This is the chance of your educational lifetime to affect reform within 10 years. Help your new teachers start with the best in-service development possible. They are the future of education and humanity.

✓ **If you are a veteran teacher:** This is your chance to leave a legacy to education. Use your expertise to help the new teachers entering the profession. Be a mentor and a positive role model.

The message is also clear. **Do not be one of the 40 percent who will leave the teaching profession discouraged, overwhelmed, and abandoned.** Use *The First Days of School* to help you become a super successful teacher.

Teaching

The art of teaching is the art of assisting discovery. ♥ You can teach a lesson for a day but if you teach curiosity, you teach for a lifetime. ♥ It's too bad that the people who really know how to run the country are busy teaching school. ♥ When truth stands in your way, you are headed in the wrong direction. ♥ When teaching the love of truth, never lose the truth of love. ♥ Teacher's task: take a lot of live wires and see that they are well-grounded. ♥ The mediocre teacher tells, the good one explains, the superior one shows, the great one inspires. ♥ Nothing improves a child's hearing more than praise. ♥

calligraphy by M.E. King

Five Units at a Glance

Contents

UNIT D   **Third Characteristic — Lesson Mastery**

The effective teacher knows how to design lessons to help students reach mastery.

UNIT E   **Future Understandings — The Professional**

The teacher who constantly learns and grows becomes a professional educator.

How to Use This Book

> *The First Days of School* is not a novel, so you will probably not read it in sequence from beginning to end.
>
> *The First Days of School* is more like an automobile owner's manual. You will be able to turn to the right section to solve a problem if something doesn't work right.
>
> Every effort has been made to make this book user-friendly. Familiarize yourself with the parts of this book.

American Library Association

The term user-friendly implies that whatever you use will be nonthreatening.

Step 1. Look at "Five Units at a Glance" on page vii and note the framework of this book. For general understanding, read Units A and E. If you want specific techniques, read Units B, C, and D.

Step 2. Read the "Table of Contents." This will give you a quick overview of the organization and chapters of the book.

Step 3. Thumb through the book and note that each chapter has a "Key Idea" that states the purpose of the chapter. If this is where you want further information, read the chapter for the accompanying text and techniques.

How to Get Quickly to the Meat of This Book

If You Want to Know	Read the Key Idea for Each Chapter
How to motivate and inspire your students	Unit B (page 34)
How to manage a classroom that is uncontrollable	Unit C (page 80)
How to have your students do their assignments and pass their tests	Unit D (page 196)
How to understand why you are teaching in the first place	Unit A (page 2)
How to cope with the years still ahead of you and retire with dignity	Unit E (page 270)

Have You Ever Watched a Slow Reader Read?

Slow readers start at the beginning and read every word, one by one, in the order in which they occur, at the same slow rate of speed. They are slow not necessarily because they cannot read but because they do not know how to read effectively—that is, with speed and efficiency.

Intelligent, effective readers—like you—scan, browse, overview, organize, survey, . . .

This process is called SQ3R:

Survey
Question
Read
Recite
Review

That is how *The First Days of School* should be read. It's not necessary to read it from cover to cover. Browse through this book to familiarize yourself with its structure so that you can refer to the right parts for help when you need help.

Now please go back and do **Steps 1 to 3** in "How to Use This Book" on the previous page.

Why You Need This Book

> **If you are going to be a teacher, you've got to know how to teach.**

Experienced teachers know that what you do and what you say in the first few seconds of the first day of school can make or break you. That is why you need this book, because you've got to know what you are doing. *The First Days of School* **will bring positive results to your teaching and from your students.**

Since there are no foolproof plans or models for successful teaching, you need this book all the more. This book does not contain A PLAN. Nor is this A MODEL.

Do not call this the Wong model.

The First Days of School will help you start the school year properly so that the remainder of the school year can run smoothly. This book has been written to **HELP** you formulate your own plan, your own model.

Innumerable ideas, techniques, and skills can help you improve your performance as a teacher. Here are some ways that *The First Days of School* will help you:

- ✓ You will have FEWER PROBLEMS in the classroom.
- ✓ You will PRESENT YOURSELF POSITIVELY to your students.
- ✓ You will feel LESS STRESS.
- ✓ You will feel BETTER about your CAPABILITIES in the classroom.
- ✓ You will be much SOUGHT AFTER and ADMIRED.
- ✓ You will be RESPECTED as a professional.
- ✓ You will have greater STUDENT SUCCESS.
- ✓ You will be a SUPER SUCCESSFUL TEACHER.

Best wishes as you master The First Days of School!

The Key Word Is *Help*

This book will only help.

There is no teacherproof method of education.

There is no one way to teach.

There are no pat answers, quick fixes, or foolproof plans for teaching.

There is no way to reduce teaching to a simple and predictable formula.

To do so would "de-skill" and deprofessionalize education.

What you need to do is continually try and learn.

What This Book Will Teach You

> **If you dare to teach, then you must dare to learn.**

You want results? You've got them! This book is teacher-specific and excellent for getting results.

This book has nothing to do with educational reform. No controversial, cutting-edge, sacrilegious, or outrageous ideas are proposed. All the ideas and techniques explained in this book are used by hundreds of thousands of teachers. They are tried and true, fundamental, basic things that good teachers know and practice to get results in the classroom.

We haven't invented any of the ideas and techniques featured here. They have simply been gathered over years of watching good teachers and reading about effective teaching and then adapted to our particular classroom setting.

Certain basic classroom techniques can help you manage a classroom for high-level student success. Here are some techniques you will learn from *The First Days of School*:

✓ How to have your CLASSROOM PREPARED for instruction

✓ How to establish CREDIBILITY with your students

✓ How to have a DISCIPLINE PLAN that works

✓ How to have PROCEDURES and ROUTINES that cause a classroom to run smoothly

✓ How to have students who will work together in COOPERATIVE LEARNING

✓ How to maximize ACADEMIC LEARNING TIME

✓ How to give ASSIGNMENTS that are clear and concise

✓ How to write a CRITERION-REFERENCED TEST

Welcome to the world of lifelong learning!

The Key Word Is *Free*

This book is long on practical techniques.

It has just the right amount of research and common sense.

Implementation of the techniques suggested costs no extra money.

Learning the techniques suggested requires no extra in-service training.

You can do everything on your own time and at your own pace.

Money and materials cannot buy an ideal learning environment.

Only you can provide that environment.

◆ ◆

UNIT A

Basic Understandings – The Teacher

The successful teacher must know and practice the three characteristics of an effective teacher.

◆◆◆

UNIT A

Basic Understandings — The Teacher

*The successful teacher must know and practice
the three characteristics of an effective teacher.*

❖❖

Key Idea: Your success during the school year will be determined by what you do on the first days of school.

The First Days Are Critical

> **What you do on the first days of school**
> **will determine your success or failure**
> **for the rest of the school year.**
> **You will either win or lose your class**
> **on the first days of school.**

The first days of school can make or break you. Based on what a teacher does or does not do, a teacher will either have or not have an effective classroom for the rest of the year. What happens on the first days of school will be an accurate indicator of your success for the rest of the school year.

Douglas Brooks, in his article "The First Day of School,"[1] discovered two things:

1. Very few teachers receive any instruction on what to do on the first day of school.

2. Very few teachers get any experience or training during student teaching on what to do on the first day of school.

---

[1]Brooks, Douglas M. "The First Day of School." *Educational Leadership*, May 1985, pp. 76-78.

Nearly every teacher goes out to teach with no instruction or knowledge and no experience on what to do on the first day of school. **Yet there is overwhelming evidence that the first two to three weeks of school are critical in determining how well students will achieve for the remainder of the year.**

The first two or three weeks? How about the first two or three days? The first two or three minutes! The first two or three seconds!

> **Student achievement at the end of the year is directly related to the degree to which the teacher establishes good control of the classroom procedures in the very first week of the school year.**

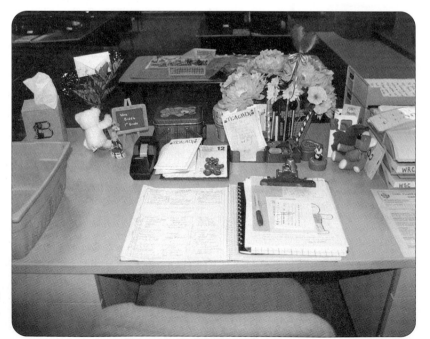

This teacher is ready on the first day of school.

The effective teacher establishes good control of the class in the very first week of school. Control does not involve threats, intimidation, or dictatorship. Control means that you know (1) what you are doing, (2) your classroom procedures, and (3) your professional responsibilities. It is urgent also that your students know that you know what you are doing.

You must have everything ready and under control when school begins. **Your success during the school year will be determined by what you do on the first days of school.**

Effective People Know What They Are Doing

How often have you walked out of a bank, office, restaurant, or repair shop with a smile, and someone asks, "Why are you smiling?" And you reply, "I like to go in there because they know what they are doing. They do things right. They have everything under control."

People who do things right are **EFFICIENT**. And people who do things right over and over again, consistently, are considered **EFFECTIVE**.

> **The efficient and effective teachers know what they are doing and do the right things consistently.**

Effectiveness has to do with **DOING**. To be effective, you must be doing something, constantly working toward improved performance.

Notes from The First Days of School

EFFICIENT:
Doing things right

EFFECTIVE:
Doing the right things consistently

EFFICIENT: Doing Things Right

"My, he's an efficient waiter!" This may refer to a waiter who fills your water glass without your having to flag him down and ask for it. He does things right, so that you get efficient service and enjoy your meal.

"She is an efficient teacher!" This may refer to a teacher who knows how to take roll without wasting classroom time so as to move on to the lesson for the day.

EFFECTIVE: Doing the Right Things Consistently

"She runs an effective office!" This refers to someone who does the right things or makes the right decisions repeatedly so that the office is effectively run.

"He is an effective teacher!" This refers to a teacher who does the right things consistently so that the teacher has an affect on the lives of his students.

The Effective Teacher Knows What to Do

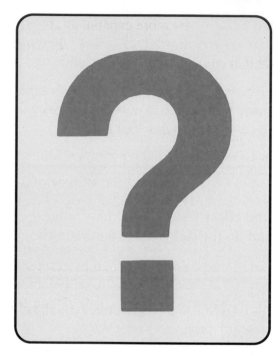

✓ Do you know what to do on the first days of school? (See page 3.)

✓ Do you know how and when to take roll? (See page 130.)

✓ Do you know how to quiet a class in 15 seconds or less? (See page 183.)

✓ Do you have a discipline plan—not rules, but a plan? (See page 144.)

✓ Do you know how to get a class to work cooperatively? (See page 245.)

✓ Do you know when to ask questions during a lecture, movie, reading assignment, or classroom activity? (See page 29.)

✓ Do you know how to give an assignment that will increase the rate of students who will do the task? (See page 214.)

✓ Do you know on what day to write a test? (See page 230.)

✓ Do you know how to grade and record tests with a minimum of effort? (See page 244.)

✓ Do you know how to have students pass in papers in a matter of minutes and without the students' punching each other in the back during the process? (See page 191.)

Effective Teachers Affect Lives

Teachers who are efficient and effective are more capable of affecting the lives of students than teachers who are not efficient and effective. Perhaps you have heard the definition of education, as written on the notepad to the left.

For instance, what is the difference between a student who is tardy and a student who is not tardy? Between one who turns in the homework and one who does not? Between one who studies for the test and one who does not?

It is not height, age, sex, race, religious affiliation, or socioeconomic background.

It is behavior or attitude. You change or affect the attitude of a student, and you suddenly have a student who is not tardy, does the homework, and studies for the test.

You were hired to affect or touch lives. You were hired not so much to teach third grade, history, or physical education. You were hired to influence lives. You touch the life of a student, and you will have a student who will learn history, physical education, even science and math, clean all the erasers, staple all the papers, and turn cartwheels to please you.

The beginning of school is the most critical time of the school year. **What you do in the first days of school to affect the lives of your students will determine your success during the rest of the school year.**

Education is not teaching people what they do not know;

Rather, education is teaching people to behave as they are not already behaving.

The effective teacher affects lives.

The Effective Teacher

1. **Establishes good control the first week of school.**

2. **Does things right, consistently.**

3. **Affects and touches lives.**

Key Idea: The effective teacher must be proficient in the three characteristics of an effective teacher.

The Effective Teacher

The Three Characteristics of an Effective Teacher

1. An effective teacher has positive expectations for student success.

2. An effective teacher is an extremely good classroom manager.

3. An effective teacher knows how to design lessons for student mastery.

The Three Characteristics of
an Effective Teacher

It's no mystery. The characteristics of an effective teacher are known, and successful teachers have practiced and learned how to be effective.

You can learn to be a very effective teacher.

Every one of us is both a student and a teacher.

We are at our best when we each teach ourselves what we need to learn.

Ways to convey positive expectations are discussed in detail in Unit B.

Positive Expectations

Positive expectations, also called high expectations by some people, should not be confused with high standards. Having positive expectations simply means that the teacher believes in the learner and that the learner can learn.

The belief in positive expectations is based on the research that whatever the teacher expects from the learner is what the learner will produce. If you believe that a student is a low-level, below-average, slow learner, the student will perform as such because these are the beliefs you transmit to the student. If you believe that a student is a high-ability, above-average, capable learner, the student will perform as such because these are the expectations you transmit to the student.

It is essential that the teacher exhibit positive expectations toward all students. It can only benefit both the teacher and the student, as well as the total classroom environment.

Classroom Management

Classroom management consists of practices and procedures that a teacher uses to maintain an environment in which instruction and learning can occur. For this to happen, the teacher must have a well-ordered environment.

The management techniques that a teacher must use in the first days of school to get the students to develop good classroom habits are discussed in detail in Unit C.

Jane H. Smith
Principal, Haughton High School

High Academic Standards In A Controlled Environment

210 E. McKinley Dr.
Haughton, LA 71037   (318) 949-2429

The standards this principal has set for her school are reflected on her business card.

> **Well-ordered Environment + Positive Academic Expectations = Effective Classroom**

A teacher must foster an environment in which students are involved in and cooperate in all classroom activities. The teacher must also establish a productive working environment. **The effectiveness of such an environment is the result of how well a teacher manages a classroom.**

How to design lessons to reach mastery is discussed in detail in Unit D.

Lesson Mastery

Mastery is the student's demonstration that a concept to be learned has been comprehended or a skill can be performed to a degree of proficiency as determined by the teacher.

When a home is built, the contractor receives a set of blueprints from the architect. The blueprints specify the degree of competence that will be acceptable. The inspector who periodically checks on the construction always looks at the blueprint first and then checks the workmanship to see if the work has been performed to the degree of competence specified.

Teaching is no different. To teach for mastery, an effective teacher must do two things:

1. Know how to design lessons in which a student will learn a concept or a skill.

2. Know how to evaluate the learning to determine if the student has mastered the concept or the skill.

Student success in the subject matter of the class will be the result of how well the teacher designs lessons and checks for mastery.

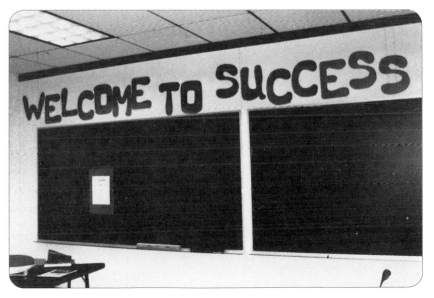

The classroom of Roberta Ford, middle school English teacher and Colorado teacher-of-the-year, is structured for success.

The Effective Teacher

1. **Exhibits positive expectations for all students.**
2. **Establishes good classroom management techniques.**
3. **Designs lessons for student mastery.**

Key Idea: The beginning teacher must perform the full complement of duties while learning those duties.

Entry into the Teaching Profession Is Sudden

The First Year of Teaching Can Be Frightening

1. Teacher education will not have prepared you.

2. Student teaching will not have prepared you.

3. You will be expected to perform immediately.

Do you remember the first time you went on a roller coaster?

Do you remember the first time you were asked to dance or had to ask someone to dance? How about the first time you had to address a group of people?

Do you remember the first time you dived off the diving board? Or the first time you got behind the wheel to drive?

Each was an exciting, anticipated event, but very frightening at the same time.

Teaching is no different, especially if you are about to teach for the very first time. Yet you can succeed if you are effective on the first days of school.

> The first day of school or a class—even the first few
> minutes—will make or break a teacher.
> It is those first few minutes and first few days of school
> that are the subject of this book.

Teacher Education Will Not Have Prepared You

Teacher education rarely prepares the student teacher for noninstructional tasks. You will have lots of ideas for instructional tasks: bulletin boards, activities, projects, books, and media.

But you will probably have received no training in such noninstructional activities as how to maintain discipline, conduct a parent conference, keep a grade book, act and dress for success, teach procedures and routines, or deal with negative, nonsupportive, and energy-draining students and colleagues.

The schools of education are not to be blamed. No one ever said that education ends with a college degree. The best teachers are also the best students. Good teachers are continually improving themselves by going back to college; joining professional organizations; attending conventions, conferences, and workshops; paying attention at in-service meetings; and working cooperatively with others on the staff to improve student achievement.

Selected Professional Educational Organizations

Each publishes a journal and holds meetings. Many have state and local branches. Consult with your mentor for addresses.

American Alliance for Health, Physical Education, Recreation, and Dance
American Association of Physics Teachers
American Council of the Teaching of Foreign Languages
American Home Economics Association
American Library Association
American School Counselor Association
American Speech-Language-Hearing Association
American Vocational Association
Association for Childhood Education International
Association for Children and Adults with Learning Disabilities
Association for Educational Communications and Technology
Association for Gifted and Talented Students
Association for Supervision and Curriculum Development
Comparative and International Education Society
Council for Exceptional Children
Council for Learning Disabilities
Delta Kappa Gamma
International Reading Association
International Society for Technology in Education
Kappa Delta Pi

Lutheran Education Association
National Alliance of Black School Educators
National Art Education Association
National Association for Bilingual Education
National Association for Gifted Children
National Association for Industry-Education Cooperation
National Association for the Education of Young People
National Association of Biology Teachers
National Association of School Nurses
National Association of Elementary School Principals
National Association of School Psychologists
National Association of Secondary School Principals
National Business Education Association
National Catholic Education Association
National Council for the Social Studies
National Council of Teachers of English
National Council of Teachers of Mathematics
National Rural Education Association
National Science Teachers Association
Phi Delta Kappa
Society for Music Teacher Education

Student Teaching Will Not Have Prepared You

S**tudent teaching rarely includes any training in what to do the first day of school.** First day? You probably did not receive any training for the <u>first minutes</u> of class when the students walk in and decide whether or not they are going to be with you.

Your master teacher is not to be blamed. No one ever trained your master teacher in what to teach you. Few teachers took over a class on the first day of school when they were student-teaching. Few student teachers enter teaching with any experience with what to do the first day of school. Typically, the master teacher started the class and then turned the class over to the student teacher. Or the student teacher came to teach for a period of time during the school year.

Thus most student teachers enter the teaching profession with no training and no experience in what to do on the first day of school.

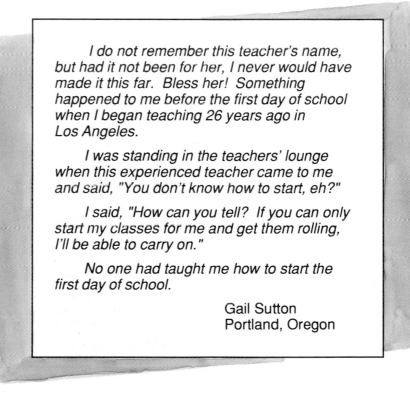

I do not remember this teacher's name, but had it not been for her, I never would have made it this far. Bless her! Something happened to me before the first day of school when I began teaching 26 years ago in Los Angeles.

I was standing in the teachers' lounge when this experienced teacher came to me and said, "You don't know how to start, eh?"

I said, "How can you tell? If you can only start my classes for me and get them rolling, I'll be able to carry on."

No one had taught me how to start the first day of school.

Gail Sutton
Portland, Oregon

You Will Be Expected to Perform Immediately

Unlike the business world, where the newcomer goes through a training or apprenticeship period, gradually gaining knowledge, experience, and responsibilities, this does not happen in the teaching profession.

> **You will be expected to perform your full complement of duties immediately while learning them at the same time.**

In sports you begin as a rookie on the bench, slowly gathering knowledge and experience, working your way, perhaps in a few years, toward a regular starting position.

Have you ever wondered why the same students who seemingly cannot follow directions or accept responsibilities in your classroom are capable when working at a fast-food restaurant of being polite and efficient and of making change with the speed of a math genius? The answer is very simple.

Restaurants like McDonald's and Domino's Pizza have a sophisticated training program to prepare workers before they face the public. Once they are in the public's eye, education continues. Go into the back of a McDonald's or a Domino's and you will see workers looking at video programs, learning and reviewing aspects of their job.

In the trades, plumbers and electricians go into an apprenticeship program, first working as an apprentice, then laboring as a journeyman, and finally qualifying as a licensed tradesman or craftsman.

Because schools spend next to nothing on staff development, successful teachers have learned to invest in their own development by attending meetings and conferences.

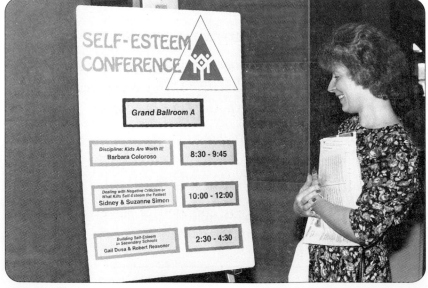

In teaching, however, entry into the profession is sudden. Teachers are not added gradually to a staff from a pool of apprentices as they increase in skill and knowledge.

> **The beginning teacher has the same tasks and responsibilities as the most seasoned teacher on the staff.**

It is ridiculous but true. The beginning teacher must perform the full complement of teaching duties while trying to learn the duties at the same time.

That's like asking a pilot to learn how to fly while taking a planeload of passengers up for the first time. That would be ludicrous in the airline industry, and the public would never tolerate it; yet that is the prevailing practice in education.

Worse yet, you may have negative, energy-sapping colleagues, albeit few, who will tell you that additional learning from journals, workshops, in-service meetings, fellow colleagues, and administrators is a waste of time.

Your First Year of Teaching Can Be a Happy Experience

Your whole life is ahead of you. With 20 to 40 years of teaching to look forward to, you can have a lifetime of happiness and success. **If you want positive results from your life, you must keep certain responsibilities in focus**:

✓ Work in a collegial manner with your colleagues.

✓ Associate with and learn from positive mentors.

✓ Join a professional organization.

✓ Continue to learn through classes, workshops, conferences, in-service meetings, books, journals, tapes, and advanced degrees.

Avoid teachers who constantly complain and make excuses. **Rather, invest in yourself, and start your career as a teacher who is efficient and effective.** You and your students will perform better. Nothing will make you happier than achieving results with a classroom of students.

The first year of teaching need not be frightening. With the right mentor and the right attitude, you can affect your own life in a very positive way as you strive toward excellence.

Excellence
A person's commitment to do a job
more efficiently and better.

This was seen on a third-grade teacher's bulletin board in south Chicago.

You Can Have Any Job in Education in Three to Five Years with a Raise in Salary of 25 Percent or More

Your future in education can be very rewarding, but only the teachers who strive for success will be rewarded. It's no different with students. Only those who work hard and have the most positive attitudes get the best grades. Here are some reasons why the future is good for you.

■ By the year 2000, 75 percent of all the teachers who were teaching in 1990 will have been replaced by newer teachers.

■ Pay raises for teachers will average close to 6 percent per year. Many districts will pay higher in catch-ups, all part of a rising tide of concern over improving our schools. There is also a realization that there will be fewer teachers going into the profession in the 1990s, just as the number of elementary school students will be increasing.

■ All kinds of job opportunities will be available, and not just in the classroom. Many teachers will become administrators or college professors, hold jobs in educational organizations, write textbooks, become consultants, run educational programs for private businesses, open child-care centers, and embark on many other educationally related endeavors.

■ Shaping up our schools will be our toughest task in the 1990s. Expect a longer school day and year, more choices among schools, higher teacher pay, testing of teachers, more focus on math and sciences, and computers in the classrooms.

■ Business will get heavily involved because it MUST. And companies will reeducate workers who didn't learn in the classroom. Private industry will be spending more money on education than public education.

■ **There is a new sense of urgency about our schools, a hopeful sign. And you can play an active role during this time of urgency—and be rewarded for your contribution.**

Education

And Now, a Teacher Shortage

Sunbelt school systems are caught with their rosters short

WANT TO TEACH BUT HAVE NO CREDENTIAL? asks the headline on a poster inside the Los Angeles unified school district's crash recruiting center. "Relax," continues the pitch. "We can help you get your teaching credential while you work full time as a junior or senior high school teacher . . ."

Among the remaining young people who do decide to teach, reportedly up to half quit within five to seven years.

Most threatening of all, perhaps, is the imminent prospect of numerous retirements. The average age of American teachers has risen to an estimated 40 to 43, and in the next five years, 30% to 50%

Because of the need for many more teachers in the future, there will be many opportunities for effective teachers.

The Greatest Threat

The greatest threat to a nongrowing teacher is a teacher who is growing. The stagnating teacher will do everything to discourage and prevent you from growing because your growth is perceived as a threat.

Do not listen to cynical, nongrowing teachers who try to tell you that you are no good unless you stay in the classroom, teaching at the same grade level, using the same textbook, worksheets, and tests.

These are the people who make fun of administrators, schools of education, workshop leaders, conventions, conferences, in-service meetings (they sit in the back rows), and anything and anyone else that wants to help you grow into the great teacher and person you are destined to be.

Find yourself a mentor, a fellow colleague, who will serve as your role model and from whom you can learn and take inspiration and hold up as a symbol of the success you want to be.

The Effective Teacher

1. **Works cooperatively and learns from colleagues.**

2. **Finds a mentor for a role model.**

3. **Goes to professional meetings to learn.**

4. **Has a goal of striving for excellence.**

CHAPTER 4

Key Idea: The teacher is NOT in private practice.

You Are in a Helping Profession

> **Teachers are not in private practice.**
> **We are in the helping and caring profession,**
> **a service profession to help people**
> **enhance the quality of their lives.**

It is essential that you understand your role in the teaching profession. This applies to all teachers, experienced as well as entry-level, first-year teachers.

If you want to choose your own hours and decide what you want to do, how you want to do it, and when you want to do it—go into business for yourself.

If you want to treat people as you please, sell whatever you please, and decide how much profit or loss you are willing to take—go into private practice.

If you want to create materials and keep them private, even copyright them, and do not like to share and exchange materials—go into private practice.

Be a brain surgeon, a self-employed cabinetmaker, or a real estate broker. Open a pizza restaurant, sell Mary Kay cosmetics, or deal in stocks, bonds, futures, and commodities.

You Are Employed by a School District

If you choose to be a teacher, know that you will be an employee of a district or a board of education. As a district employee, you are not allowed to teach only what you want or do as you please.

Palmer v. Board of Education of Chicago (1979)

Probationary teacher Palmer did not want to teach about one of the holidays. She was discharged of her duties. She took the district to court, and the district won.

The effective teacher knows the district's curriculum guide and uses materials that reflect those objectives.

Why? **The district is owned by the local citizens.** It has a set of policies with operational rules and regulations governing the behavior of all their employees and students to protect this ownership.

The district has a curriculum. The district's curriculum was not handed down chiseled in stone. The district's curriculum has been and will be an evolving product, formulated by a district's curriculum committee made up of many of your colleagues.

The district has employees, like you. Your colleagues who helped write the district's curriculum knew what they were doing. They brought years of experience and study with them to formulate the district's mission, philosophy, and curriculum. The board approved their work, and it is the curriculum for the district, of which you are an employee.

This means that when you sign your contract, you are agreeing to teach the district's curriculum as well as to abide by and carry out the district's policies, rules, and regulations.

Do Not Sign a Contract Until You Do These Three Things

1. Ask the administrator hiring you to show and to explain to you the district's (a) philosophy, (b) goals, (c) mission statement, (d) policies, (e) rules, (f) regulations, and, most important to you because you will be teaching it, (g) curriculum.

2. Read whatever else the district has prepared in its guidelines or operations manual.

3. Accept in your own mind and heart that you can live and perform comfortably with the district's role for you.

   If you can't live with the district's expectations for you, perhaps you should go into private practice.

You Will Not Be in One Room Forever

Understand that your first assignment will not be your last assignment. You will not teach the fourth grade or history in Room 10, have only two preparations, and use the McDuffy Reading Series for the rest of your life.

Furthermore, you will be expected to do your job with the same enthusiasm that you expect from your own students. Know that you will be expected, on your own initiative, to serve on committees, confer with parents, and attend meetings, in-service programs, conferences, college classes, and workshops to further yourself and the district's goals.

You are an employee of the district, and as such, expect to be reassigned from time to time. Be a model of adaptability. Just as you expect your students to go into a changing world and adapt, show that you can adapt and excel in a changing world. Finally, understand that you have a role as part of a larger community and society.

Only the Brave Should Teach

Only the brave. Only the brave should teach.
Only those who love the young should teach.
Teaching is a vocation.
It is as sacred as the priesthood; as innate a
*   desire as inescapable as the genius which*
*   compels a great artist.*
If he has not the concern for humanity,
*   the love of living creatures,*
*   the vision of the priest and the artist,*
he must not teach.

Pearl Buck

> ### Understand Your Role
>
> 1. The schools are owned and operated by the citizens of your local community.
>
> 2. Schools are the foundation for transmitting the values and traditions that ensure our life in a free society.
>
> 3. The schools are built for the STUDENTS.

Get to Know All Your Colleagues

Get to know all your colleagues. And listen to them. You will see many who are there to help enhance the lives of the students—not to be in private practice. Many know what they are doing and are happy to help you. Learn from them.

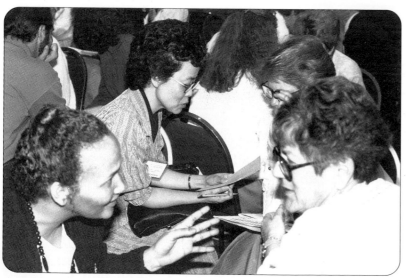

Get to know all your colleagues.
They have much to offer.

Get to know all your colleagues. Watch and listen to them. You will see many who are constantly working with each other (administrators, teachers, paraprofessionals, parents, counselors, secretaries, custodians, food-service staff, bus drivers) to find ways to improve the performance of the students—not to be in private practice. Associate with them.

Get to know all your colleagues. Listen as you interact with many of them socially and professionally. You will discover that most are eager to help, share, and exchange with you—not to be in private practice. Work with them.

The happiest and most successful teachers, administrators, parents, and school board members are there to work WITH YOU to help you become an effective teacher so that you, in turn, can help and teach students.

They say that the three most important words in real estate are *location, location, location.* The three most important words for a teacher are ***listen, listen, listen***.

If you are a beginning teacher, ***listen, listen, listen.***
If you are an experienced teacher, ***listen, listen, listen***.

WELCOME (back) to the helping and teaching profession.

The Effective Teacher

1. **Can explain the district's, school's, and department or grade level's curriculum.**

2. **Realizes that teaching is not a private practice.**

3. **Is flexible and adaptable.**

4. **Listens, listens, listens.**

A child's life is like a piece of paper on which every passerby leaves a mark.
Ancient Chinese Proverb

Key Idea: Effective teachers use proven research-based practices that are employed by thousands of other teachers.

The Research Process

> The effective teacher understands how and why research is done.

When you change a recipe, you are doing research.

Research is the process of critical thinking and solving problems. It is this ability that sets humans apart from all other forms of living things. Research is simply the use of the human mind to search for and seek answers or, as some would say, to search for the "truth."

Research is what a person does to find answers. Research is not something only scientists do. Business people do research; so do baseball players, knitters, plumbers, lawyers, dentists, and homemakers. Students, when they do term papers, do research.

Humans have always been seeking and searching. And that is what research is all about, to search. To search and search and search, over and over again. That is why it is called *re-search*.

During the Renaissance, the process for research became formalized. This process is the same basic process used by a scientist seeking an answer to cancer, a student doing a term paper or project, a lawyer investigating a case, or a homemaker trying to find a better way to make a cheesecake. It is a higher-order thinking process.

The Research Process

Problem:	What do I want to know?
Prediction:	What do I think is the right answer?
Procedure:	How will I solve the problem?
Data:	What will I look for?
Conclusion:	What do the results tell me?

There is no research to support the following model of teaching:
- *Assign chapters to read.*
- *Answer the questions at the back of the chapter or on the worksheet.*
- *Take lecture notes.*
- *Watch a movie or do an activity.*
- *Take a test based on a number of points.*

It May Be Dangerous to Teach as You Were Taught

Since the 1960s, there has been much research in education. Prior to that time, much about teaching, as well as much about running a school, was based on myths, hearsay, and traditions handed down from teacher to teacher or on teachers' recollections of how they were taught when they went to school.

No education professor, administrator, in-service speaker, or teacher at a workshop has ever said that the model of teaching on the scroll is the way to teach.

Unfortunately and erroneously, many teachers tend to teach as they were taught. And most of us were taught by teachers who either were not effective teachers or did not know the current research on effective teaching. Most teachers tend to teach as their academic college professors taught them simply because that was their last and most remembered educational experience.

✓ Academic professors are not teachers. They are researchers who are creating, seeking, and gathering new knowledge.

✓ Most academic professors do not have teaching credentials. They are not certified to teach.

Yet many teachers teach as their college professors, who are noncertified role models, taught them and think that this is teaching.

Not all research is done by college professors in an academic realm or by researchers working for a government agency. Much educational research is done by practitioners, teachers, or administrators, many working on their master's or doctoral thesis, or by people who just like to do research.

An Example of Educational Research That Applies to Every Teacher

John P. Rickards discovered two things:[1]

1. The most ineffective place to print questions is at the end of a textbook chapter.

2. It is an ineffective method to give a student all the questions for an assignment at one time and then ask the student to answer all the questions and to turn them in all at one time.

Rickards found that if you want a student to achieve high-level comprehension, you should intersperse the questions through the text.

You know that this is true from having taken reading comprehension tests. Reading comprehension tests are not written with pages of text followed by a long list of questions. They constantly go back and forth, a paragraph or two of text followed by a few questions.

To put it another way, no doctor asks questions when the patient is dead. A doctor intersperses questions during the treatment of a patient.

Likewise, the effective teacher does not ask all the questions at the end of the discussion, class period, movie, chapter, lecture, or meeting. **The effective teacher who wants high-level comprehension intersperses questions throughout all class activities.** This is what the research tells us.

Stimulating High-Level Comprehension by Interspersing Questions in Text Passages

John P. Rickards

A principal means of influencing reading behaviors is via "orienting directions," which are defined as "verbal stimuli which dispose the reader to respond to certain aspects of the text" (Frase, 1970, p. 338). Although directions of this sort could conceivably take many different forms, it is clearly the case that "questions are one sub-class of events that might be used to insure the occurrence of appropriate learning behaviors" (Frase, 1970, p. 338).

Educational research helps the teacher become more effective in the classroom.

**Effective teachers do what the research tells us is most effective.
Effective teachers use proven research-based practices.
Why would you do otherwise?**

---

[1]Rickards, John P. "Stimulating High-Level Comprehension by Interspersing Questions in Text Passages." *Educational Technology*, November 1976, p. 13.

Researchers Report on Effective Teacher Practices

Educational research is not all theoretical, conducted in an ivory tower. Nearly all educational research quoted in this book was performed by researchers looking at teachers and students in functioning schools and reporting on effective and ineffective practices.

The research states:

✓ **Effective Teachers:** Teachers with effective practices.

✓ **Ineffective Teachers:** Teachers with ineffective practices.

So why are there so many ineffective teachers? Because they are not familiar with or use what the research says are the effective practices. The effective teacher does three things:

1. Understands how research is done.

2. Uses proven research-based practices.

3. Understands that these practices are used by thousands of other teachers and are tried-and-true methods that work.

Effective Teachers Use Proven Practices

It is one thing to know what you are doing. It is another to know how to do it. Most important, you need to know why you are doing what you are doing.

> **People who know what to do and people who know how to do it will always be working for those who know why it is being done.**

Do not teach from hearsay, myths, or prevailing practices. To be an effective teacher, understand that effective school research is based on the reporting of what effective teachers do.

So if you want to be an effective teacher, start the first days of school by using proven research-based practices. These are methods used by hundreds of thousands of effective teachers. You can be one also!

The Effective Teacher

1. **Understands the research process.**

2. **Teaches with proven research-based practices.**

3. **Knows the difference between an effective teacher and an ineffective one.**

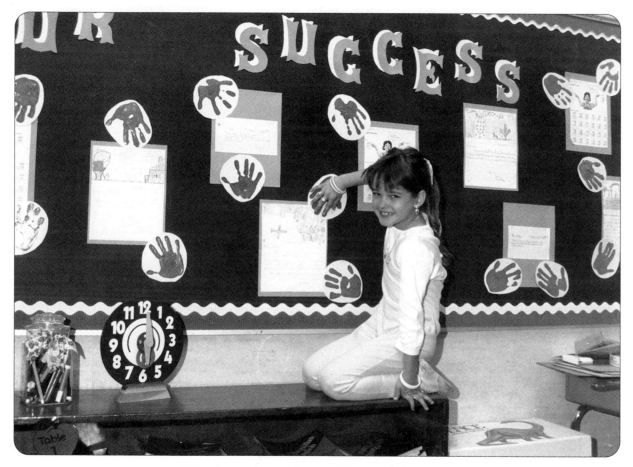

Children are like wet cement. Whatever falls on them makes an impression.
Haim Ginott

UNIT B

First Characteristic – Positive Expectations

The effective teacher has positive expectations for student success.

UNIT B

First Characteristic — Positive Expectations

*The effective teacher has positive
expectations for student success.*

◆◆◆

Key Idea: Your expectations of your students will greatly influence their achievement in your class and in their lives.

Humans Have a Success Instinct

> There is absolutely no research correlation between success and family background, race, national origin, financial status, or even educational accomplishments. There is but one correlation with success, and that is ATTITUDE.

The Two Kinds of Expectations—

Positive or high expectations

Negative or low expectations

All living things live to survive. They spend their entire day, instinctively, seeking food and shelter and escaping their predators.

Humans have a success instinct. This is what makes humans different from all other living things. They want success, and they strive for their success potential. When we see people go through depression, we know that they have not become what they know they can be.

Positive and Negative Expectations

Knowing what you can or cannot achieve is called **EXPECTATION**. An expectation is what you believe will or will not happen.

A San Jose, California, shopping center ran this newspaper advertisement soon after the new school year began. Is this a positive or a negative message to a student?

Positive Expectations . . .

An optimistic belief that whoever you teach or whatever you do will result in success or achievement. If you expect to be successful, you are constantly alert and aware of opportunities to help you be successful.

Examples of Positive Expectations

✓ "We are going to win the league championship."

✓ "I believe that every child can learn and will achieve to his or her fullest potential."

✓ "I am a good teacher, and I am proud that I am a professional educator."

✓ "I am always learning, and that is why I enjoy going to conferences, workshops, and in-service meetings."

Results of Having Positive Expectations

The odds are greater that what you want to happen will happen because you will be expending energy to see that this will be so. You predispose yourself to realize success both personally and with the people you deal with, such as your students.

Negative Expectations . . .

A pessimistic belief that whoever you teach or whatever you do will not happen or will fail. For that matter, why bother to do anything or teach anyone at all? If you expect to fail, you are constantly looking for justification, proof, and demonstration of why you have failed.

Examples of Negative Expectations

✓ "We'll be lucky if we lose by only 10 points."

✓ "I want to teach only the college-bound students. Why do I have to teach these other students?"

✓ "They can't read; they can't spell; they can't sit still; they can't behave."

✓ "In-service meetings are boring; conferences have nothing to offer to me."

Results of Having Negative Expectations

The odds are that what you expect to happen will not happen because you will be expending energy to see that nothing happens. You predispose yourself to realize failure both personally and with the people you deal with, such as your students.

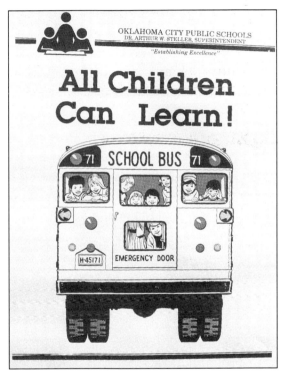

This poster was developed by the
Oklahoma City Public Schools.
Is the message positive or negative?

It takes just as much energy to achieve positive results as it does to achieve negative results. So why waste your energy to fail when that same amount of energy can help you and your students succeed?

Expectations of	Negative or Low Expectations	Positive or High Expectations
Parents	I'll be happy if my children do not become involved with drugs.	I want my children to graduate as the class valedictorians.
Students	This class is boring. Why do we have to study this junk?	My dream and intention is to be a teacher.
Teachers	In-service meetings are so boring. Why do we have to listen to this drivel?	I learn so much and meet so many interesting people at conferences.

Expectations Are Different from Standards

Expectations should not be confused with standards. Standards are levels of achievement. Teachers who practice positive expectations will help their students reach high standards.

Example: This will be an exciting class, and you are going to have the most memorable year you have ever had; as a result, you will do very well.

Teachers who practice negative expectations will prevent students from reaching high standards.

> **Example: "I only give one A each year. I have very high standards" (said in aggrandizement of one's intellectual superiority).**

The Classic Research on Expectations

The classic research on expectations, published as *Pygmalion in the Classroom*, was done in the 1960s by Robert Rosenthal of Harvard University and Lenore Jacobson of the South San Francisco schools.[1] They fed erroneous information to a group of South San Francisco elementary teachers and watched the people make the results come true.

In the spring of the preceding school year, the students at a school (called Oak School) were pretested. When school began that fall, the researchers and the administrators told the teachers that they were special teachers who were to be part of a special experiment.

They were told, "Based on a pretest, we have identified 20 percent of your students who are special. They will be 'spurters' or 'bloomers' and are a designated group of students of whom greater intellectual growth is expected."

The names were really selected at random, but the teachers were led to believe that the status of being special children was based on scores of the pretest, the Harvard Test of Inflected Acquisition.

---

[1]Rosenthal, Robert and Lenore Jacobson. *Pygmalion in the Classroom.* New York: Holt, Rinehart and Winston, 1968.

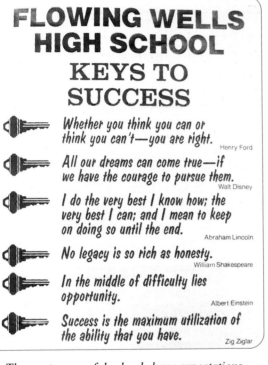

FLOWING WELLS HIGH SCHOOL
KEYS TO SUCCESS

Whether you think you can or think you can't—you are right.
Henry Ford

All our dreams can come true—if we have the courage to pursue them.
Walt Disney

I do the very best I know how; the very best I can; and I mean to keep on doing so until the end.
Abraham Lincoln

No legacy is so rich as honesty.
William Shakespeare

In the middle of difficulty lies opportunity.
Albert Einstein

Success is the maximum utilization of the ability that you have.
Zig Ziglar

The most successful schools have expectations that everyone will succeed.

"As a special reward for your teaching excellence, we are going to tell you this information, but with two conditions:

1. You must not tell the students that you know that they are special.

2. None of us are going to tell the parents that their children are special.

"Thus we expect and know that you will do extremely well with these special students."

Eight months later all the students were tested again and a comparison was made of the designated special students and the undesignated students, as measured by IQ scores. The results showed a significant gain in intellectual growth for the 20 percent who were designated special in the primary grades with no significant gains in the intermediate grades.

The administrators brought the teachers in, showed them the growth results of their students, and congratulated them on their spectacular success with their students.

The teachers said, "Of course, we had special students to work with. It was easy, and they learned so fast."

The administrators and researcher said, "We'd like to tell you the truth. The so-called special children were picked at random. We made no selections based on IQ or aptitude."

"Then it must have been us," said the teachers, "because you said we were special teachers selected to be part of a special experiment."

"We need to tell you something else, too," replied the researcher. "All the teachers were involved in this experiment. None of you were designated special over any other teacher."

The Good Ones Are Not at Home

Ready or not, here they are! In September, 3.6 million youngsters entered school; 25 percent of these children live in poverty; for blacks the figure is 50 percent, and for Hispanics, 40 percent.

Today, out of 80 million households in the nation, 9.5 million are headed by a single female parent, 16 percent of whom are under age 25, 50 percent unemployed, 42 percent living in central cities. In fact, every day in America, 40 teenage girls give birth to their *third* child.

In 1955, 60 percent of the households matched the traditional family image of one mother, one father, and two children; today it's 4 percent.

The 1950s family is gone. The family today is different, maybe no better or no worse, but different. As Larry Lezotte said, "The parents are sending us the best kids they have. They are not keeping the good ones at home."

Larry A. Strong
"The Best Kids They Have."
Educational Leadership,
February 1989, p. 2.

This was a perfectly designed experiment. There was only one experimental variable—**EXPECTATION**.

1. The expectations of the administrators toward the teachers were stated explicitly. "You are special teachers and these 20 percent of your students are special students who show potential for intellectual growth. Thus we expect and know that you will do extremely well with these special students."

2. The expectations of the teachers toward the students were conveyed implicitly and unspoken. Because they believed that they had some very special students in the school, their body language, personality, and attitude influenced their teaching and expectations of their students.

As the researchers stated, "The results suggest rather strongly that children who are expected by their teachers to gain intellectually, in fact do show greater intellectual gains after one year than do children of whom such gains are not expected."

> **Students tend to learn as little or as much as their teachers expect. Teachers who set and communicate high expectations to all their students obtain greater academic performance from these students than teachers who set low expectations.**[2]

---

[2]U.S. Department of Education. *What Works: Research About Teaching and Learning.* Washington, D.C.: Government Printing Office, 1986, p. 7.

The Two Most Important Groups of People

A Tribute to My Parents

Before I was five years old and in kindergarten, my parents said something to me over and over again. They even got my relatives to say it to me, as well as my neighbors and the local merchants.

Several times a day, I would hear, "Little Harry Wong, when you grow up, what kind of a doctor are you going to be?" This was accompanied by their pointing out to me, as positive role models, that my uncles were all doctors and that my cousins were studying to be doctors.

They told me that it was a foregone conclusion that I would be admitted to medical school, even though the competition was tough in those days. What they wanted to know was what I planned to specialize in.

Not being in kindergarten yet, I said, "I don't know."

And then came their reply: "You're going to be a brain surgeon, aren't you?" In other words, they believed that I had the intelligence to be the ultimate of all doctors, so brilliant that I could even operate on other people's brains.

My parents conveyed a message of high or positive expectations to me. For this I will be forever grateful to them, and I send them my love.

Harry K. Wong

The two worst things a parent can give a young person are money and wheels.

The two most important things a parent can give a child are roots and wings.

After Hodding Carter

A Tribute to My Teachers

The other reason I achieved success in school and life was because of my teachers. When I was in elementary school in the early 1940s, I remember distinctly that my teachers had a saying that they would repeat often, year after year, new teacher after new teacher. This saying became ingrained in me as a driving force or expectation in my life.

They would say, "You can be anything you want to be. You can even be President of the United States."

It is sad that the young people of today are not sent a message of becoming a leader or hero. Rather, at the time of this writing, the heroes of today's children are a potato that sits on a couch, so lazy that a remote control is needed to change the channels on the television; a dog who drinks and parties; and a brat who is proud that he is an underachiever. All can be purchased as objects or dolls to serve as role models to young people.

My teachers conveyed to me a message of high or positive expectations, a powerful message that told me that I was smart and good enough to be anything I wanted to be, even to hold the highest office in the nation.

I thank my teachers for having that expectation of me.

Harry K. Wong

The two most important groups of people, as far as young people are concerned, are:

★ PARENTS
and
★ TEACHERS

Things My Parents and Teachers Never Said to Me

You are dumb.
You are stupid.
You are no good.
You will never amount to anything.
I didn't want you; you were an accident.
You don't belong in this class; they put you
    here against my wishes.
Look at it this way, summer vacation is
    only 10 months away.

W̅hat parents and teachers convey to young people in their formative years as expectations will influence young people to achieve accordingly.

> ... from conception to age 4, the individual develops 50% of his mature intelligence, from ages 4 to 8 he develops another 30%, and from ages 8 to 17 the remaining 20%.
>
> ... as much of the development takes place in the first 4 years of life as in the next 13 years.
>
> We are inclined to believe that this is the most important growing period for academic achievement and that all subsequent learning in the school is affected and in large part determined by what the child has learned by the age of 9 or by the end of grade 3.
>
> It is evident that when the school and home environments are mutually reinforcing, learning is likely to be greatest. The nature of the learning environment is most critical during the periods of most rapid change in learning—the early years of school.
>
> Benjamin S. Bloom[3]

Who you are and what you do and say will greatly influence the young people who will be the productive citizens of tomorrow's world. **Your expectations of your students will greatly influence their achievement in your class and ultimately their lives.**

[3]Bloom, Benjamin. *Stability and Change in Human Characteristics.* New York: Wiley, 1964, pp. 68, 88, 110, 128.

The Effective Teacher

1. **Has a statement of positive expectation ready for the first day of school.**

2. **Creates a classroom climate that communicates positive expectations.**

3. **Has a personal goal of high expectations.**

Key Idea: The more the school and the family are joined as partners in the cause of educating young people, the greater the child's chances for success.

Celebrate the First Day of School

> **The most important day of a person's education is the First Day of School, not Graduation Day.**

I f school does not begin with the proper, positive expectations, there may not be a Graduation Day for a student. Each year 700,000 students drop out of school, a number equal to the entire school population of Minnesota.

For some students, graduation is not a day to celebrate a joyful sense of accomplishment. Rather it is a day to mock respect, act stupid, make fun of the educational system, show disrespect to parents and teachers, and engage in wild parties that make you wonder if an education ever took place.

Effective schools celebrate the First Day of School.

FLOWING WELLS
JUNIOR HIGH SCHOOL
WELCOME BACK
MUSTANGS

> **The proper day to celebrate in all the schools of a country is the First Day of School.**

Celebrating the **First Day of School** must become a tradition of all educational systems. This day of celebration must include everyone associated with and interested in the education of the

45

future citizens of the world. In addition to everyone at the school site, this should include parents, the business community, and the neighborhood. It is important that students see that everyone is interested in helping them all succeed.

The more the school, the family, and the community are joined as partners in the cause of educating young people, the greater each child's chance for success.

The Biggest Family Holiday of the Year

In June, at the height of one of those rainstorms here that never seem to end, a quarter of the Filipino population went looking for a way out of poverty.

They went to the only place they know that holds a ray of hope—the schools.

Filipinos are among the most literate people in the world. They revere education and the promise it holds. The First Day of School is probably the biggest family holiday of the year after Christmas.

A record 15.3 million students took part in that holiday last week. Given the fact that the population is 58 million and the average family has six members, there was hardly a family that was not affected.

"Schooling Free but No Room for Students."
San Jose Mercury News,
July 3, 1988.

Welcome Them to School

Just as you go on a vacation with high expectations, students come to school with high expectations also. They come to get an education, meet friends, participate, have fun, study, and learn. Their entire day revolves around school and their friends. It is an exciting time in their life.

Therefore, the personnel of the school should extend greetings to the students before they come to school and upon their arrival. Everyone should be involved in planning the students' welcome to the school. Everyone means administrators, teachers, classified staff, district personnel, parents, and the business community. **The successful education of young people is an interrelated, community team effort.**

Everyone needs to be welcomed on the First Day of School.

Welcome Them to School

✓ Organize a **First Day of School** celebration.

✓ Stand at the bus stop and welcome them on the **First Day of School**. Wave and smile like it's Aunt Mabel who you have not seen in 14 years and her plane has just pulled up to the Jetway.

✓ Stand at the front entrances of the school. Have all entrances covered so that no one will fail to receive a warm, friendly welcome.

✓ Bring out the school band to play at the curb or entry. If you don't have a band, have a group of students and teachers assembled to bring a welcome smile on the **First Day of School**.

✓ Hang up a computer-generated banner welcoming students to school. (What did schools ever do before software like Print Shop?)

✓ Distribute a school newspaper extolling the virtues of the school and the wonderful school spirit of the teachers and the students.

✓ Have guides in the hall. Hang up directional signs to help students get to their correct classrooms.

✓ Have your name and room number clearly visible on the classroom door along with your personal greeting of welcome. (See page 107.)

✓ Let the first message spoken over the public address system be one of welcome and positive expectations for the school year.

> **School is not a place;**
> **school is a concept.**

School is not a place, a place where students come to listen to lectures, fill in worksheets, and endure boredom. Nor is it a place reserved for those who can tolerate the drab and dirty looks of many schools.

School is a concept, a concept wherein students are welcome to learn and enhance the quality of their lives without fear of intimidation or safety for their lives, guided by hospitable and caring people in a clean and orderly environment.

WE MUST TEACH AND SHOW OUR STUDENTS THAT:
- *We can be responsible for one another.*
- *School is a place to gain knowledge.*
- *School is a place to give and receive love.*
- *School is a place to become successful.*

You Will All Succeed

You will think that I'm in love with Japanese education. I'm not, but here is an anecdote that illustrates my point.

When our daughter took our granddaughter to her first day of kindergarten in Japan, she walked in casually dressed, as we might do in the United States, thinking she would drop the child off and go home. Well, not at all.

First, she discovered that all of the other parents were dressed up in their finest for a full day of ceremonies in celebration of the first day of school.

They were in the room with the children, and there were speakers on the platform with a big banner that said, "Welcome to Kindergarten. **You Will All Succeed.**"

Ernest L. Boyer
"On Parents, School and the Workplace."
Kappa Delta Pi Record, Fall 1988, p. 8.

The school, the community, and the family must all work together for student success.

Family Day

Family Day . . . We began the day by joining hands and encircling the school—parents, students, and staff—to recite our Family Day rap and sing our school song. Even the drizzling rain could not diminish the strong sense of pride and family spirit we felt that morning.

It was a glorious day. . . . Parents learned more about parenting; children learned they could say "no" to drug use and "yes" to their parents' authority. Parents and children danced together, the children mimicking the dances of yesterday and the parents struggling to do the dances of today.

Nothing else has been half as rewarding as to see more than 200 parents involved in a full day of activities with their children. On future Family Days we can continue to make positive changes toward strengthening the fiber of our society. No more lost generations at this school; **we count Family Day as an investment in our future.**

Vernon Smith
"Family Day: An Investment in Our Future."
Educational Leadership,
May 1988, p. 56.

The students must sense that the schools are the nuturing grounds for their intellectual development in a safe, caring, positive atmosphere.

The Effective Teacher

1. Helps organize a First Day of School celebration.
2. Plans a classroom welcome for the First Day.
3. Ensures the mental and physical safety of all students.
4. Creates an environment for all students to succeed.

Key Idea: The effective teacher dresses appropriately as a professional educator to model success.

CHAPTER 8

You Are Treated as You Are Dressed

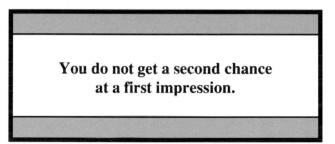

You do not get a second chance at a first impression.

Make no mistake, we judge others by their dress, and they judge us too. It may not be fair. It may not be right. But people tend to treat other people as they are dressed.

It's common sense. You will be treated as you are dressed. A salesperson sees two shoppers approaching, one appropriately dressed and the other inappropriately dressed. You know very well who will get the immediate and better service.

How much credibility would a bank have if the teller who processes your paycheck were dressed in jeans and wore a T-shirt emblazoned with the slogan "Poverty Sucks"? Would you buy life insurance from a salesperson who called on the family wearing a bowling jacket with the inscription "Ma's Donuts" on the back?

In an ideal world, viewed through rose-colored glasses, it would be wonderful to be accepted for ourselves alone, not for our appearance. In the real world, however, our all-too-visible selves are under constant scrutiny.

The fact is, most people think that the cover is the book, the box front is the cereal, and the leather jacket is the person. We all make judgments. We look at someone and judge status, income, even occupation.

> **It is not what is
> but what is perceived.**

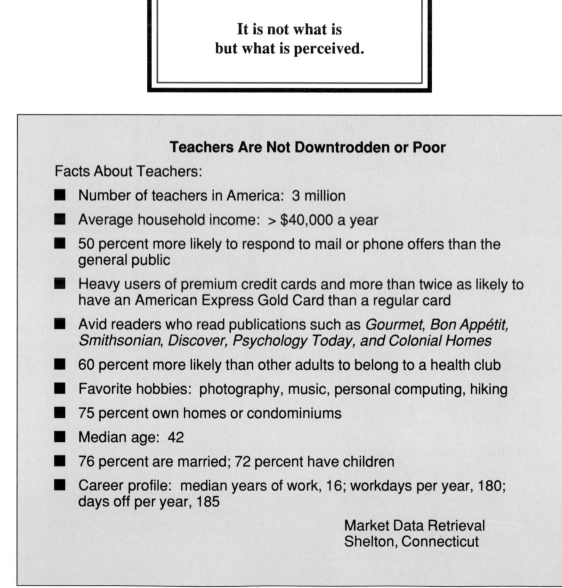

Teachers Are Not Downtrodden or Poor

Facts About Teachers:

- Number of teachers in America: 3 million
- Average household income: > $40,000 a year
- 50 percent more likely to respond to mail or phone offers than the general public
- Heavy users of premium credit cards and more than twice as likely to have an American Express Gold Card than a regular card
- Avid readers who read publications such as *Gourmet, Bon Appétit, Smithsonian, Discover, Psychology Today, and Colonial Homes*
- 60 percent more likely than other adults to belong to a health club
- Favorite hobbies: photography, music, personal computing, hiking
- 75 percent own homes or condominiums
- Median age: 42
- 76 percent are married; 72 percent have children
- Career profile: median years of work, 16; workdays per year, 180; days off per year, 185

Market Data Retrieval
Shelton, Connecticut

You Are a Walking, Talking Advertisement

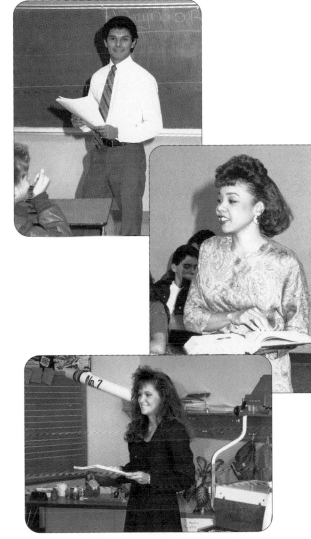

This may be a superficial world, but it is the way the world works, so saying that something is superficial will not make it go away. **You are much better off making your dress work for you than to allow it to work against you.**

The key is looking professional, not just looking good. **The advantage of looking professional is that it keeps you from self-destructing in the first few seconds, before the students make any hasty judgments about you.**

The effective teacher dresses appropriately as a professional educator to model success. The important word is *appropriately*. We often see signs like this one:

Successful teachers dress for success.

One of the reasons we have schools is for students to learn what is appropriate. Young people learn what is appropriate in society by looking at their adult role models. Your dress and your behavior are what young people will take to be appropriate.

*You give an elementary student three days
and the student will mirror you.
You give a high school student ten days
and the student will mirror you.*

Charles Galloway
Ohio State University

By the end of the first or second week, the entire class will have taken signals from you as to how they should behave for the rest of the school year.

✓ We are walking, talking advertisements for who we are.

✓ We are walking, talking advertisements for who we believe we are as professional educators.

When you walk into class late, you have just made a statement. When you walk into class late with a soda can or a cup of coffee in your hand, barely making it on time and with a growl on your face, you are making a statement.

What Is Appropriate Dress?

You expect your students to
use appropriate English,
write papers using an appropriate form, and
display appropriate behavior and manners.

Right?

Then you understand about appropriate dress.

When you walk into class early, the room and materials are ready, there is a positive classroom climate, you are standing at the door with a smile and an extended hand of welcome, and the assignments are on the chalkboard, you are making a statement.

When you allow teasing in class, you are making a statement. When you refuse to tolerate teasing in class, you are making a statement.

**Every time you act,
you validate who you are.**

The statement that you make influences how the students will behave and achieve in class. And how students behave and achieve in class will determine your success as a teacher.

Dress for Respect

Clothing may not make a person, but it can be a contributing factor in unmaking a person. Whether we want to admit it, our appearance affects how we are perceived and received in definite ways. Clothing has nothing to do with students liking a teacher. But clothing definitely has an affect on students' respect for a teacher, and respect is what a teacher must have if learning is to take place.

Research reveals that the clothing worn by teachers affects the work, attitude, and discipline of students. You dress for four main effects:

1. Respect
2. Credibility
3. Acceptance
4. Authority

The effective teacher uses these four traits as assets in relating to students, peers, administrators, parents, and the community. If you have these four traits, you have a much greater chance of influencing young people to learn than someone who lacks these four traits.

I Could Not Believe What I Saw

After Christmas vacation, one of my students left some pictures of the class holiday party on my desk. I took a look at myself and I could not believe how I looked. I looked like I didn't care about myself.

The next day I came to school more appropriately dressed, and they all noticed and commented on how nice I looked. I was so happy and they made me feel so good.

I now spend more time caring about who I am. The students care about me. I am proud of who I am. And they are also so much better behaved now as a result of who I represent.

Fifth-grade teacher
Iowa

You can be sure that students notice how their teachers are dressed, in the same way that they notice the appropriateness of their own and each other's dress. Furthermore, **students see how their parents go to their jobs each day and make comparisons between their parents and their teachers.**

They see their parents go to work each day, dressed in business attire or institutional uniforms (nurses, police officers, fast-food workers . . .). Then they come to school and observe the attire of teachers—professionals who are considered middle-class, intellectuals with college degrees, competent people with teaching credentials. You can see why the teaching profession has a difficult time gaining respect and credibility.

You can also see why some teachers have great difficulty reaching and influencing students—and if teachers cannot reach students, no teaching will take place. Not only are these teachers unable to reach students, but they also leave school at the end of the day frustrated over their own inadequacies. These inadequacies are evident in how they dress. For when you dress, you are making a statement about yourself to the world.

California Highway Patrol officer Phil Grant.

What I Wear for My Interviews

Bright colors convey positive, happy feelings. Children like bright colors, and when teachers wear them, they convey happiness and "aliveness." My staff likes my bright clothes; my father does too. Women must no longer try to dress like men—yea! The same rules for the business community do not always apply to the world of the school. I've worn green and black to every interview where I've been hired. When I interview teachers for job openings, I like to see some color. Conservative dressers aren't often willing to take a risk and try new approaches in the classroom. Color conveys confidence, confidence to take risks.

I think a more conservative dress is more appropriate at the high school. But remember, at the elementary level, especially K–1, teachers get down on the floor with their kids.

I would use a bright-colored pen to write a positive note to a student, but not to my principal, parents, or teachers.

At parent conferences, open houses, and the like, more conservative dress is appropriate.

Cheryl Ralston
Redlands (Calif.) Unified School District

What's Out

Running shoes are for jogging or mall-walking.

Sweatshirts are best left for aerobics.

T-shirts are for the beach.

Polyester died years ago and is considered low-class.

Polyester stretch slacks are unbecoming.

Bold plaids and loud colors are no-no's.

Trendy clothes do not establish authority and should be left to students.

Anything in blue denim should be worn only on Saturdays.

What's In

Bright colors are enjoyed by elementary students.

Soft muted tones are recommended for secondary school.

Men can't miss with suits and ties or a sweater or coat and a dress shirt.

A career dress or suit is appropriate for women.

Clean clothes are a sign of good hygiene.

Pressed clothes tell people you care.

Neat, cleanly-tailored career clothes establish authority.

Career clothes prepare students for a future in the competitive global world economy.

Make no mistake about reality. Teachers have a responsibility to encourage learning, and learning begins by gaining and keeping the respect of students. Your respect begins with your appearance.

If you are appropriately dressed, you will receive comments from students when you look nice, and if something is out of place, they will tell you because they know that you are a person who cares about yourself. But if you consistently come to school inappropriately dressed, they will not say a word because they surmise that if you do not care about yourself, why should they care about you. **Dress appropriately because it is very important that you know that people care about you.**

When people care about you, they will respect you, learn from you, and buy from you. And as a professional educator, you are selling your students knowledge and success for the future.

Preparing Students for the World

What does it mean to dress appropriately? It is universally agreed that one major function of schools is to prepare young people for tomorrow's world. Yes, the world, not a particular city, state, or country. **We live in a competitive, global world economy where people work for companies that are international in scope.** It is likely that many of your students will work for a company that will have offices all over the world.

Luisa Velasco, the school secretary at San Andreas High School, Hollister, California.

> **If you want to succeed in the world, you must think globally.**

If we are to prepare students for tomorrow's world, we need to know the world. If you do not know the world, ask your principal for a day off and go look at the world. Stand at a major airport and watch passengers disembark from United, Lufthansa, and Japan Air Lines.

Then go downtown in the business district of a city and watch the successful people walk by—the executives, shopkeepers, salespeople, and secretaries. And speaking of secretaries, how come the school secretary invariably comes to school more appropriately dressed than a whole lot of teachers?

After you return from observing the world and after you have dressed in the morning, look at yourself in the mirror before you go to school to face your students, who will see you as a model of success in tomorrow's competitive global world economy. Ask yourself the following three questions:

1. Would a life insurance company hire you dressed the way you are?

2. Would McDonald's allow you to hand food to a customer dressed the way you are?

3. Would you allow your loving child, grandchild, godchild, niece, or nephew to go to school and be taught by a teacher dressed the way you are?

Psychological research has shown us who is more likely to be mugged on the streets. Muggers were shown videotapes of people walking along the streets. Overwhelmingly, muggers picked people who walked slowly, with stooped shoulders, and looked helpless and downtrodden. They rejected people who walked erect, purposefully, and confidently. These latter people conveyed the message that they were in control of their lives.

Your dress announces to the world that you care or do not care about yourself. The entire public can read this message, which is a statement that we make about ourselves. As a teacher, which of the two statements do you make?

1. We are a group of poor, underpaid, slovenly, dour, and unappreciated people.

2. We are a group of professional, proud, devoted, dedicated, responsible, and appreciated people.

This message is also conveyed to the students at your school, as well as to the administration and your colleagues, many of whom find the sloppy dress of many educators totally unacceptable.

People in sales, management, and leadership training will all tell you the same thing. By how you behave, you convey to the world a message of who you are and what you expect of life.

You have every right to expect the most from your life and from the lives of your students. That expectation can begin with how you dress.

You Dress Where You Want to Be

Frances Campbell, a San Francisco high school teacher, was having image problems. "I am a competent person who was coming across as kind of flaky," says Campbell. "People weren't taking me seriously." After gazing into her soul, and her mirror, she decided that her polyester baggy pants and Olympics T-shirts were to blame.

So Campbell turned to a department store shopping service for help. She spent one afternoon, and several hundred dollars, selecting a couple of outfits; she emerged with a sophisticated new look—and something more.

"Left alone in the dressing room, I saw myself for the very first time, as a person who could do anything she wanted to," says Campbell. "If I had $1000 of therapy, I wouldn't have felt anywhere near as good. It was like a religious experience."

"A professional woman should dress at least two steps above her current position," she says. "You do not dress where you are; you dress where you want to be."

Newsweek,
June 25, 1984, p. 64.

The Effective Teacher

1. Comes to work appropriately dressed.
2. Comes to teach dressed for success.
3. Is a role model for students.
4. Thinks and behaves globally.

Key Idea: People, places, policies, procedures, and programs must work together to invite people to realize their fullest potential.

Invitational and Disinvitational

> **Effective teachers have the power and the ability to invite students and colleagues each day and in every class to learn together.**

This Is Where You Are So Far

✓ You have positive expectations for each of your students (Chapter 6).

✓ You welcome the students to your classroom with a happy smile when they appear at your door (Chapter 7).

✓ You are dressed for success and have a look of professionalism (Chapter 8).

Now what are you going to do?

You were five years old and so depressed on this day. Lucille, who wasn't all that popular, had received an invitation to Beth Middleman's birthday party. You didn't, and you thought you were Beth's friend.

Jose was asked to be in the school play; you were not.
Sara was asked to take the note to Ms. Tynan, not you.
Armand was asked to go camping, not you.
Ernie was asked to join Junior Achievement; you were not.
Dad took Peg to the game. Why not you?
Mom asked Larry to pick the cereal off the shelf, not you.

Oh, you are such a nice boy.
You really like it when Daddy tucks you in.
You feel so good when someone tells you that you look good today.

The person who is asked or complimented is INVITED. The person who is not asked or complimented is DISINVITED. This concept was formulated by William W. Purkey in 1978 and is known as *invitational learning*.[1]

Invitational learning is centered on the following propositions:

✓ People possess untapped potential in all areas of human development.

✓ People are able, valuable, and responsible and should be treated accordingly.

✓ People, places, policies, procedures, and programs all invite people to realize their fullest potential.

To fulfill these propositions, invitational learning employs the following assumptions:

✓ Opportunities are everywhere, but little happens until invitations are sent, received, and acted on.

✓ A positive self-concept is the product of inviting acts.

✓ One inviting act can make a positive difference even if everything else is disinviting.

✓ We will always be invited if we are giving the party.

✓ Human potential is always there, waiting to be discovered and invited forth.

✓ To maintain a consistently inviting stance is the essence of an effective teacher.

Why Was I Not Invited?

It upsets me to this day. When I was in junior high school, I had straight A's and was in the honor class. One day the teacher went around the class and gave invitations to several students, but not me. They were asked to join the National Honor Society. To this day, I am still puzzled, confused, and disappointed that I was not invited.

Rosemary Tripi Wong

---

[1] Purkey, William W., and John Novak. *Inviting School Success: A Self-concept Approach to Teaching.* Belmont, Calif.: Wadsworth, 1984; Purkey, William W., and John Novak. *Education: By Invitation Only.* Bloomington, Ind.: Phi Delta Kappa, 1988; Purkey, William W., and John J. Schmidt. *The Inviting Relationship: An Expanded Perspective for Professional Counseling.* Englewood Cliffs, N.J.: Prentice Hall, 1987; Purkey, William W., and John J. Schmidt. *Invitational Learning for Counseling and Development.* Ann Arbor: University of Michigan, 1990.

Are You Invitational or Disinvitational?

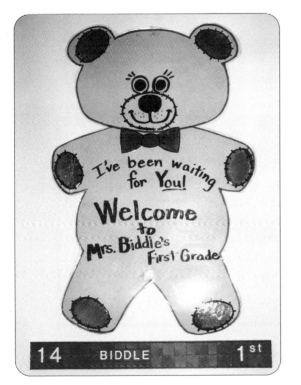

The outside of the classroom door creates a welcoming, invitational atmosphere.

Inviting Verbal Comments
"Good morning."
"Congratulations."
"I appreciate your help."
"Tell me about it."
"How can I help you?"
"Yes."

Disinviting Verbal Comments
"Keep out."
"It won't work."
"Not bad for a girl."
"I don't care what you do."
"You can't do that."
"Because I said so, that's why."

Inviting Personal Behaviors
Smiling
Listening
Holding a door
Thumbs up or high five
Sending a Valentine
Waiting your turn

Disinviting Personal Behaviors
Looking at your watch
Yawning
Letting a door swing behind
Sneering
Forgetting an important date
Shoving

Inviting Physical Environment
Fresh paint
Living plants
Clean walls
Comfortable furniture
Attractively set table
Fresh air

Disinviting Physical Environment
Dark corridors
No plants
Spray-painted graffiti
Donated, old furniture
Leftover food
Bad smells

Inviting Thoughts (Self-talk)
"Sometimes I have to think
    what to say."
"Making mistakes is all right."
"I've misplaced my keys."
"I could learn to do that."

Disinviting Thoughts (Self-talk)
"I never know what to say;
    I'm so slow to catch on."
"Why am I so stupid?"
"I've lost my keys again."
"I never could do that."

63

You Are a Significant Person

An invitation is a message that states that the person being invited is **responsible, able, and valuable.** Conversely, a disinvitation is intended to tell people that they are irresponsible, incapable, and worthless. The critical ingredient needed for people to realize their fullest potential lies in the kinds of invitations extended to individuals by the significant people in their lives.

All individuals have significant people in their lives. These include teachers, leaders, mentors, bosses, parents, relatives, coaches, administrators, spouses, and close friends.

*I have come to a frightening conclusion.
I am the decisive element in the
classroom.
It is my personal approach that creates
the climate.
It is my daily mood that makes the
weather.
As a teacher I possess tremendous power
to make a child's life miserable or
joyous.
I can be a tool of torture or an
instrument of inspiration.
I can humiliate or humor, hurt or heal.
In all situations it is my response that
decides whether a crisis will be
escalated or de-escalated, and a child
humanized or dehumanized.*

Haim Ginott
Teacher and Child,
Avon Books, 1976.

> **The invitational messages
> that are extended to learn in
> school are the products of
> the expectancies that exist
> in the minds of the significant
> people who influence the
> lives of other people.**

We all like to be invited to go shopping, to go to a party, or to join a group. And we all have the common courtesy to greet people at the door, to exchange courtesies when introduced to others, and to offer food or drink to a visitor. These are all obvious, expected, and practiced. These same concepts should be practiced in the classroom.

Effective teachers have the power and the ability to invite students and colleagues each day and in every class to learn together. Attentiveness, expectancy, encouragement, enthusiasm, attitude, and evaluation are the primary forces behind a teacher being inviting or disinviting. These are the characteristics that significantly influence a student's self-concept and increase or decrease the probability of student learning.

> **All of us need to convey to our students and our colleagues every day that "you are important to me as a person."**

Every teacher, every professor, every educator ought to spend time in a kindergarten or first-grade class each year, just to look at and feel the excitement there. Children get excited about everything in the world. All the world is their stage, and there is nothing that they cannot do, even though they cannot read, write, or spell. Yet they are ready to do anything you want them to do.

If Only the Finest Birds in the Forest Dared Sing How Quiet the Forest Would Be

If only the best readers dared read,
   how ignorant our country would be.
If only the best singers dared sing,
   how sad our country would be.
If only the best athletes engaged in sports,
   how weak our country would be.
If only the best lovers made love,
   where would you and I be?

I would be tired!

William W. Purkey

Then look at their teachers. They know that their charges cannot read, write, spell, or even speak correctly. Some of these students do not even know how to eat, use the bathroom, or hang up their jackets without help. Yet these teachers do not complain that they have a bunch of slow learners. Instead, their classrooms and their demeanor sparkle with an invitational attitude toward learning.

The Four Levels of Invitational Learning

There are four levels of invitations that are issued to students. These levels can determine your effectiveness as a teacher.

Intentionally Disinviting. This is the bottom level at which a few curmudgeonly teachers operate. They deliberately demean, discourage, defeat, and dissuade students. They use expressions like these:

> "You never do your homework."
> "Why do you bother to come to school?"
> "I failed 12 students last term."
> "I've only given one A in the 16 years that I've been teaching."
> "You will never amount to anything."

And they never smile.

Unintentionally Disinviting. Some teachers are oblivious to the fact that they are negative people. They feel that they are well-meaning, but are seen by others as chauvinistic, condescending, racist, sexist, patronizing, or thoughtless. They make comments like these:

> "I teach only students who want to learn."
> "If you don't want to learn, that's your problem."
> "What do you want me to do? I did my job, didn't I?"
> "What are they all angry at me for?"
> "These people, they just don't have the capacity to do any better."
> "I want to teach only college-bound students."
> "I was hired to teach history, not do these other things."
> "I believe that only students who want to come to school should be
>   allowed to come to school."

And they keep their arms folded when interacting with students.

THE FOUR LEVELS OF
INVITATIONAL LEARNING
□ Intentionally Disinviting
□ Unintentionally
   Disinviting
□ Unintentionally Inviting
□ Intentionally
   Inviting

Unintentionally Inviting. This is the level of the "natural-born teacher." These teachers are generally well liked and effective but are unaware of why they are effective; they do not have a consistent philosophy of education. When something does not work in the classroom, they are unable to analyze what went wrong. They are usually affable, and this characteristic often hides the fact that their students may not be learning to their fullest potential. These teachers are sincere and try very hard, and we generally like to have them on the staff and as friends. They offer remarks like these:

"Aren't you sweet!"
"Charge! Let's go team!"
"That's neat."
"Just try harder."
"I enjoy teaching."

And they bubble with excitement.

Intentionally Inviting. Intentionally inviting teachers have a professional attitude, work diligently and consistently, and strive to be more effective teachers. They have a sound philosophy of education and can analyze the process of student learning. Most important, they are purposively and explicitly invitational. They know what it means to be invitational, and they work at it. They say things like this:

Eric Abrams, principal at Douglas Elementary School in Tucson, Arizona, intentionally invites his students to communicate with him.

"Good morning. Have a great day."
"Let me show you how to improve."
"If you try this, you'll be sensational."
"Please tell me about it."
"I know that someday you will be the best at . . ."
"Would you like to help me?"
"Thank you for your help."
"No, I do not believe it will be good for you."
"Yes, I believe it is in your best interest."
"You can do better than this; let me show you how."

They also use the proper emotion at the appropriate time.

Invitational learning states that all people have limitless human potential. Expectation theory states that humans have a success instinct to reach their fullest potential.

When you apply the power of POSITIVE EXPECTATIONS and INVITATIONAL LEARNING, you become a very powerful and effective teacher.

The Effective Teacher

1. **Has an inviting personality.**
2. **Has an inviting classroom environment.**
3. **Works at being intentionally inviting.**
4. **Maintains an inviting stance.**

Key Idea: Significant people use significant words and actions to increase positive behaviors.

Five Significant Concepts

> **When you look at the truly effective teachers,**
> **you will also find caring, warm, lovable people.**

The FIVE Significant Concepts That Enhance Positive Expectations:

1. *NAME*
2. *PLEASE*
3. *THANK YOU*
4. *SMILE*
5. *LOVE* ♡

High expectation has nothing to do with getting A's in class, finishing college, making a lot of money, or having a great marriage. These are products or end results of life. High expectation has to do with attitude or behavior, and it is this behavior that gets us the A's in class, helps us finish college, or gets whatever else we want in life.

> *Life is not a destination.*
> *Life is a journey.*
> *As long as you continue the journey,*
> *you will always be a success.*

Albert Camus

How a person behaves in the journey of life is directly related to what a person expects to happen in life. There are five significant concepts that will help you achieve whatever it is you want in life.

Address a Student by Name

Effective salespeople know how to use a very simple but valuable technique. They have learned to find out your name, introduce themselves to you, and then use your name every 7 to 10 sentences when they talk with you. Why?

Your name is very important to you. It identifies and dignifies you. Other people in the world may have the same words as your name, but as far as you are concerned, you are the only person in the world with your name. It is a name that you can easily hear called above the din of a crowd. And when you hear your name, you pay attention. Salespeople know this when they use your name. You pay attention. You pay attention because you are important!

Effective teachers use names, especially when they want a student to do something or behave in a certain way.

✓ When you address a student, use the student's name.

✓ Use a student's name in a friendly, respectful manner. Never address a student in an angry or condescending tone. This is a put-down of a person's identity and dignity.

✓ Pronounce the student's name correctly. A person's name is precious and personal. It is that person's property. It is imperative that students hear the correct pronunciation of names. Failure to do so will tell the students that they do not have to respect each other's name and as a result can tease, mock, and make fun of each other's name.

✓ When you use a person's name, you are saying to that person, "You are important. You are important enough for me to identify you by name."

Say "Please," Please

Cultured, polite people can be identified by their manners. Of course, we all like well-mannered people because we know that they will treat us politely. We like it when service-oriented people treat us kindly at the shopping center, amusement park, office, or restaurant or on public transportation.

KIRBY • **RUSSELL** • *CHET*
HEATHER•**CARLOS**•NEIL
JAMES • **WENDY** • GAREN
VERONICA • YASUKO • *ELISA*
LIZ • *ANTHONY* • LESLIE

At the same time, business people know that continued customer business and satisfaction is based on how the customers are treated. The customer who is treated politely will return. Just how do people learn to treat others with politeness and courtesy? From how they were treated by others primarily during their formative years, such as at school and at home.

A child's behavior is learned and modeled after the expectations of the significant people in that child's life—and the most significant people in a child's life are parents and teachers. (See Chapter 6.)

If you abuse a child, the child will grow up with the expectation to abuse others. If you treat a child with kindness, the child will grow up with the expectation to treat others with kindness.

For a child to learn something new, you need to repeat it on the average eight times.

For a child to unlearn an old behavior and replace it with a new behavior, you need to repeat the new behavior on the average 28 times.

Twenty of those times are used to eliminate the old behavior and eight of the times are used to learn the new behavior.

✓ Kindness begins with the word *please*.

✓ Cultured, polite, and well-mannered people know and automatically use the word *please*. It has become a learned behavior.

✓ Repetitive use of the word *please* is important if a child is to learn to use the word *please* in his or her life.

✓ *Please* is usually used when you ask someone to do something for you. Thus the most effective way to use *please* is to precede the word with the person's name to whom you are addressing the request, as in "Trevor, please . . . ."

✓ Strongly consider adding the word *please* to your worksheets, assignments, and other papers that you distribute in class.

I Really Appreciate What You Did; Thank You

Y ou really cannot use *please* without using *thank you*. The two just go together. Not using the two together would be like having a knife without a fork, a belt without a buckle, a yin without a yang.

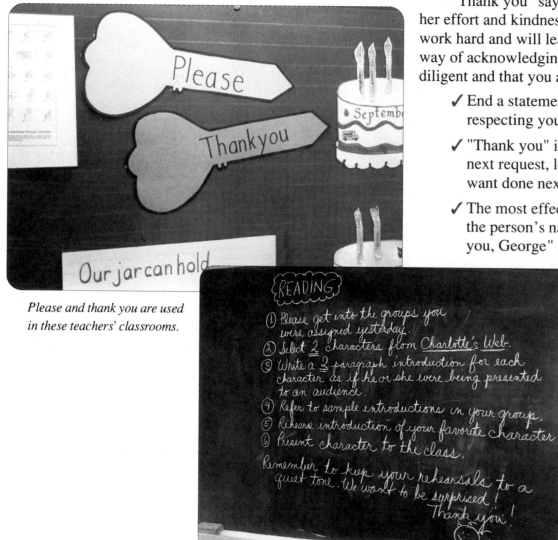

Please and thank you are used in these teachers' classrooms.

"Thank you" says to the other person that you appreciate his or her effort and kindness. If you have expectations that students will work hard and will learn to be kind, then saying "thank you" is your way of acknowledging that you know they have been kind and diligent and that you appreciate what they have done for you.

✓ End a statement of gratitude and appreciation for someone respecting your wishes with *thank you*.

✓ "Thank you" is the perfect transition; it paves the way to the next request, lesson, or task in class. It makes whatever you want done next so much easier.

✓ The most effective way to use *thank you* is to follow it with the person's name ("I truly appreciate what you did. Thank you, George" or "George, I truly appreciate what you did. Thank you.")

✓ Strongly consider adding the words *thank you* to your worksheets, assignments, and other papers that you distribute in class.

A Smile, the Frosting on the Cake

If you truly want to achieve maximum effectiveness when you use a person's name and say "please" and "thank you," **you smile**. It requires no effort and is easier than frowning, as almost everyone knows. Smiling uses far fewer muscles than frowning; thus is less tiring to do. But like using *please* and *thank you*, smiling is a behavioral trait that is learned.

A smile is like that extra garnish on the dinner plate, the extra pat on the back when a job has been done well, or the extra hug that says "I really love you." It's the frosting on the cake or, as they say in the South, the little lagniappe (pronounced "lan-yap") that sets you apart. It communicates three things:

1. You are a person who knows the ultimate of hospitality and graciousness.

2. You have that little extra bit of polish or panache that marks you as a cultured person.

3. You feel good about yourself and you want others to feel good about themselves, too.

A smile is the universal language of understanding, peace, and harmony. If, indeed, we want the next generation to have a world of peace and understanding, we need to teach its sign, a smile.

A smile is the most effective way to create a positive climate, to disarm an angry person, and to convey the message "Do not be afraid of me; I am here to help you."

✓ There is no need for a great big smile; a controlled, slight, disarming smile is all you need.

✓ Accompany the smile with the name of the person at whom you are smiling.

✓ As you smile and speak, use momentary pauses. This is called timing. Every performer knows that the key to delivering a speech, telling a joke, or giving a performance is timing. This is the pregnant pause before speaking an important or emotional line or the punch line.

Technique for Smiling, Speaking, and Pausing

Step 1. <u>SMILE</u>. Smile as you approach the student, even if you want to kill the kid.

Step 2. <u>FEEDBACK</u>. Observe the reaction to your smile. Are you receiving a smile in return or at least a signal that the student is relaxing and receptive to your approach?

Step 3. <u>PAUSE</u>.

Step 4. <u>NAME</u>. Say, "Nathan" with a slight smile.

Step 5. <u>PAUSE</u>.

Step 6. <u>PLEASE</u>. Add *please*, followed by your request. Do this with a calm, firm voice, accompanied by a slight, nonthreatening smile.

Step 7. <u>PAUSE</u>.

Step 8. <u>THANK YOU</u>. End with "Thank you, Nathan" and a slight smile.

Example

Nathan, please stop talking to Joey and get to work on your assignment. Thank you, Nathan.

Practice this in a mirror, over and over again.

It All Adds Up to Love

There are only two things needed for a happy and successful life: being lovable and being capable. The effective teacher never stops looking for ways of being more and more capable.

The two things needed for a happy and successful life are being lovable and being capable.

When you look at the truly effective teachers, you will also find caring, warm, lovable people. Years later, when the students remember their most significant teachers, the ones that they will remember the most are the ones who really cared about them. Effective teachers know that they cannot get a student to learn unless that student knows that the teacher cares about him or her.

Respect at Graduation

At our baccalaureate service, just prior to graduation, we show a videotape we make of any student who would like to say "thank you" to anyone.

Messages to parents, siblings, and teachers are <u>touching</u>. It could also be part of graduation.

David A. Mac Raild, Principal
Woodridge High School
Peninsula, Ohio

> **The effective person offers both
> a product and a service.**

Ineffective teachers think that all they have to do is offer a product, as in, "I was hired to teach history" or "I was hired to teach third grade."

Effective teachers offer more than a product; they offer a service too. **Effective teachers can help students learn as well as enhance the quality of their lives. They offer this service consistently** because they are practicing this same belief on themselves as they increase their own effectiveness in life.

The sincerest form of service requires no money, no training, no special clothes, and no college degrees. **The sincerest form of service comes from listening, caring, and loving.**

Beliefs of Effective Persons

I am not in the restaurant business;
I am in the hospitality business.

I do not serve food;
I nourish customers.

I do not sell clothes;
I dress successful people.

I do not sell insurance;
I help people solve problems.

I do not teach history;
I teach students.

I do not teach third grade;
I enhance the quality of lives.

People in our culture are starved for attention:

✓ The average child receives 12 minutes of attention each day from his or her parents.

✓ The average parent watches five to six hours of television each day.

✓ The number one problem reported by high school students is loneliness.

✓ Loneliness is the number one problem of the elderly, many of whom are afraid to venture out of their homes or apartments.

The Carnegie Foundation surveyed 22,000 teachers:

✓ 90 percent said that a lack of parental support was a problem at their schools.

✓ 89 percent reported that there were abused or neglected children at their schools.

✓ 69 percent stated that poor health was a problem for their students.

✓ 68 percent said that some children were undernourished.

✓ 100 percent described their students as "emotionally needy and starved for attention and affection."

> *There is no remedy to love,*
> *but to love more.*
>
> Henry David Thoreau

You don't need to tell a class that you love them, but you certainly can show it. If you choose to be a significant and effective person in a student's life, you must demonstrate your care and love both implicitly through your body language and explicitly through what you say.

> **When teaching the love of truth,**
> **never lose the truth of love.**

When significant people use significant words and actions, they increase the likelihood of receiving positive behaviors from other people.

Thank you.

The Effective Teacher

1. **Addresses people by their name.**
2. **Says "Please" and "Thank you."**
3. **Has a controlled, disarming smile.**
4. **Is lovable and capable.**

Love is life...
And if you miss love,
you miss life.

Leo Buscaglia

Why?

Why not?

George Bernard Shaw

UNIT C

Second Characteristic – Classroom Management

The effective teacher is an extremely good classroom manager.

◆◆◆

UNIT C

Second Characteristic — Classroom Management

The effective teacher is an extremely
good classroom manager.

◆ ◆

The classroom as seen by a fifth-grade student.

CHAPTER 11

Key Idea: The teacher is responsible for organizing a well-managed classroom where students can learn in a task-oriented environment.

The First Thing You Need to Know

> **You were hired to take a group of possibly disinterested, howling, and unruly people and turn them into interested, disciplined, and productive learners in a well-managed environment.**

Alice Waters, who introduced California cuisine to the world, is noted not only for her skill in the kitchen but also for her skill in running her restaurant Chez Panisse in Berkeley, California.

Just because you know how to cook a steak does not make you a successful restaurant owner. You need to know about accounting procedures; federal, state, and local regulations; sanitary laws; union agreements; worker relationships; and customer relationships. Cooking a steak is the last thing you need to know. The first thing you need to know is how to manage the restaurant.

Just because you have a college degree in English does not make you a teacher, much less an English teacher. You need to know about academic learning time, formative and summative testing, criterion-referenced testing, discipline plans, procedures and routines, learning styles, motivation theory, record-keeping procedures, identification of learning disabilities, higher-order thinking skills, due process, privacy rights, grouping, community services, mastery learning, remediation and correction, prescriptive learning, credibility, and a whole host of other things.

Having a degree in English is the last thing you need. The first thing you need to know is how to manage a classroom full of students. You were not hired to teach third grade, coach football, or teach English. You were hired to take a group of possibly disinterested, howling, and unruly people and turn them into interested, disciplined, and productive learners in a well-managed environment.

To do this you need to know the art of classroom management.

What Is Classroom Management?

Classroom management refers to all of the things that a teacher does to organize students, space, time, and materials so that instruction in content and student learning can take place.

The research indicates that the amount of time that students spend actively engaged in learning activities is directly linked to their academic achievement. It also shows that teachers who are good classroom managers are able to maximize student engaged time or academic learning time. (See Chapter 21.) Thus good classroom management practices maximize the amount of time that students are engaged in learning activities, such as receiving instruction, completing written assignments, reading, and working on activities.[1]

Teachers who develop skills in effective classroom management have classes in which students are on task and deeply involved with their academic work and misbehavior is rare.

---

[1]Rosenshine, Borak, and David Berliner. "Academic Engaged Time." *British Journal of Teacher Education* 15 (1978): 555-566.

Unit C will help you to accomplish these two goals, student involvement and a productive working atmosphere, so that you can be a very effective teacher.

Classroom management includes all of the things a teacher must do toward two ends:

1. To foster student involvement and cooperation in all classroom activities

2. To establish a productive working environment

To foster student involvement and cooperation in all classroom activities, the effective teacher plans a variety of activities that are appropriate for learning. These activities may include reading, taking notes, participating in group work, taking part in class discussions, participating in games, and producing materials. An effective teacher has every student involved and cooperating in all of these activities.

For all students to work on their activities, the environment must be conducive to learning. Students must pay attention, be cooperative and respectful of each other, exhibit self-discipline, and remain on task. In addition, the room must have a positive climate, all materials must be ready and organized, and the furniture must be arranged for productive work.

Characteristics of a Well-managed Classroom

You expect a department store to be well managed. When asked what that means, you would probably list some of these characteristics:

✓ **The store:** Its layout, organization, and cleanliness.

✓ **The merchandise:** Its display, accessibility, and availability.

✓ **The help:** Their management, efficiency, knowledge, and friendliness.

You could probably do the same for a restaurant, airline, or doctor's office. In fact, you have probably said more than once, "If I ran this place, this is what I would do."

Well, if you ran a school or a classroom, which is what you do, how would you run the place? That is called classroom management, and the characteristics of a well-managed classroom are well known.

The Characteristics of a Well-managed Classroom[2]

1. Students are deeply involved with their work, especially with academic, teacher-led instruction.
2. Students know what is expected of them and are generally successful.
3. There is relatively little wasted time, confusion, or disruption.
4. The climate of the classroom is work-oriented, but relaxed and pleasant.

The Effective Teacher
Has a Well-managed Classroom

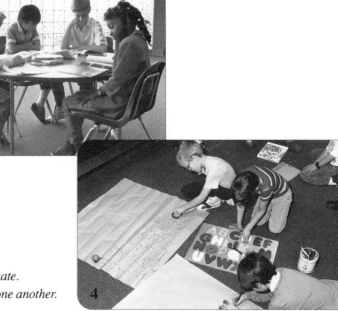

(1) This room is arranged for productive work. (2) This room has a positive climate.
(3) The students are on task. (4) The students are cooperative and respectful of one another.

[2]Sanford, Julie, Edmund Emmer, and Barbara Clements. "Improving Classroom Management." *Educational Leadership,* April 1983, pp. 56-60.

Techniques to Help You Implement the Four Characteristics of a Well-managed Classroom

Characteristics	Effective Teacher	Ineffective Teacher
1. High level of student involvement with work	Students are working. (See page 200.)	Teacher is working.
2. Clear student expectations	Students know that assignments are based on objectives. (See page 221.) Students know that tests are based on objectives. (See page 229.)	Teacher says, "Read Chapter 3 and know the material." "I'll give you a test covering everything in Chapter 3."
3. Relatively little wasted time, confusion, or disruption	Teacher has a discipline plan. (See page 143.) Teacher starts class immediately. (See page 121.) Teacher has assignments posted. (See page 121.)	Teacher makes up rules and punishes according to his or her mood. Teacher takes roll and dallies. Students ask for assignments repeatedly.
4. Work-oriented but relaxed and pleasant climate	Teacher has invested time in practicing procedures until they become routines. (See page 176.) Teacher knows how to bring class to attention. (See page 183.) Teacher knows how to praise the deed and encourage the student. (See page 185.)	Teacher tells but does not rehearse procedures. Teacher yells and flicks light switch. Teacher uses generalized praise or none at all.

We Even Have a Nordstrom

"We even have a Nordstrom at Tyson's Corner!" she said, with a pixieish smile of delight, as if the Queen of England had just moved in next door.

Surveying my puzzled look, she said, "You mean you don't know about Nordstrom or even been in one?" Her eyes say, "You poor soul. Where have you been all your life?"

"Let me tell you about Nordstrom," she continued. "The other day, my mother came to visit me, and had never been to Nordstrom. As we passed the men's clothing department, the salesman said, 'May I help you?'"

"My mother said that she was looking for some shoes. Graciously, he said, 'Please, let me show you the shoe department,' and proceeded to escort my mother and me across the store to the shoe department. He introduced my mother to one of the salesladies, then smiled and dashed back to his department."

"She bought shoes that day but never showed her purchases to anyone. All she could talk about was how she had been treated at Nordstrom."

Task-oriented and Predictable

> A well-managed classroom is task-oriented and has a predictable environment.

Awell-managed classroom has a task-oriented environment** where students know what is expected of them and how to succeed. According to the research, most of the students will make better achievement gains in a class such as this.

A well-managed classroom also has a predictable environment. The teacher knows what to do and what is supposed to happen in the classroom. You should be able to close your eyes and not only envision learning taking place but also know why it is taking place because of how you have chosen to manage the classroom environment.

It is the responsibility of the teacher to manage a class to see that a task-oriented and predictable environment has been established.

Aaron Rosander manages his classroom for student success.

More than Singing, More than Words

Brief morning meetings at which everyone sings have made the Townsend (Vt.) Elementary School a happy and productive place.

The entire school population is gathered in the entry hall and on the stairways that lead to the second floor classrooms. The joyful sound of children and adults singing together fills the hall. On the edge of the village common, Townsend Elementary School invites parents, neighbors, shopkeepers, special teachers, and aides to join the 85–100 students in singing to start the day.

During the past three years noticeable and notable changes have occurred at our school. Both the academic and social climate are different, and these changes seem to be related to our singing and meeting together every morning.

The academic changes include better work habits, more self-motivation, and a greater sense of personal responsibility among the students. Also, we have seen new interest in appreciation for all the language arts. Reading and writing have become favored free-time activities. After all, singing, reading, and writing have strong connections. Also, since the songs generate interest in the contexts they came from, social studies has been enhanced and enriched through our emphasis on music.

The social changes have been even more obvious. There have been no fist fights, unacceptable language is not heard, and graffiti has not been found anywhere in or on the school. Once common, these behaviors had been accepted as inevitable.

If we could define the new climate of the Townsend School in one word, that word would be respect.

Esther La Moria
"More than Singing, More than Words."
Educational Leadership,
December 1987–January 1988, pp. 60-62.

1. Works on having a well-managed classroom.

2. Trains students to know what they are to do.

3. Has students working on task.

4. Has a classroom with little confusion or wasted time.

Key Idea: Teachers who are ready maximize student learning and minimize student misbehavior.

Why Effective Teachers Have a Minimum of Problems

> The effective teacher has a minimum of student's misbehavior problems to handle.
>
> The ineffective teacher is constantly fighting student's misbehavior problems.
>
> And the reason why is easy to remedy.

Here is some good news for those of you who become frustrated when you cannot change the behavior of an unruly student.** It is unlikely that anyone else will be able to do any better than you with this student either!

In a 1970 study, Kounin discovered that effective teachers were no different from ineffective teachers in responding to or dealing with students' misbehavior after the misbehavior had occurred.[1] However, there was a significant difference in the behavior of effective and ineffective teachers PRIOR to the students' misbehavior. This prior behavior determines whether teachers are effective or ineffective.

---

[1]Kounin, J. *Discipline and Group Management in the Classroom.* New York: Holt, Rinehart and Winston, 1970.

Kounin's study showed that ineffective teachers were not ready. Confusion led to problems; problems led to misbehavior; and misbehavior led to constant tangling between teacher and students. The ineffective teachers, each day, became more and more stressful, burned out, negative, cynical, and angry. They quickly learned to blame everyone and everything else for their problems.

Kounin showed that effective teachers had the classroom ready. Because they had the classroom ready, they where able to prevent many misbehaviors from occurring. The reason effective teachers are effective is that they have far fewer student problems and hence are able to get their students to work and to achieve. As such, effective teachers incur far less stress in having to deal with behavior problems and are able to leave each day feeling happy, accomplished, and proud.

Kounin's work was validated by further studies in 1976 and 1980 by Brophy and Evertson.[2]

The effective teacher plans and is ready, rather than manages by crisis.

Effective Teachers Are Ready

Effective Teachers Have the Room Ready.
Unit C: Classroom Management

Effective Teachers Have the Work Ready.
Unit D: Lesson Design

Effective Teachers Have Themselves Ready.
Unit A: Basic Understandings
Unit B: Positive Expectations

---

[2]Brophy, Jere, and Carolyn Evertson. *Learning from Teaching: A Developmental Perspective.* Boston: Allyn and Bacon, 1976; Evertson, Carolyn. "Effective Classroom Management at the Beginning of the School Year." *Elementary School Journal,* May 1980, pp. 219-231.

> *All battles are won*
> *before they are fought.*
>
> Sun Tzu

A Successful Restaurant Is Ready

The Table Is Ready: The table is set and waiting when you arrive at your reservation time.

The Dining Room Is Ready: The atmosphere or ambiance is conducive to a pleasant dining experience.

The Staff Is Ready: You can expect fine service because the staff has high expectations that you will enjoy your dinner.

A Successful Teacher Is Ready

The Work Is Ready: The desks, books, papers, assignments, and materials are ready when the bell rings.

The Room Is Ready: The classroom has a positive climate that is work-oriented.

The Teacher Is Ready: The teacher has a warm, positive attitude and has positive expectations that all students will succeed.

Have your classroom ready, every single day, especially the first days of school. This is obvious. When you walk into a restaurant, an office, or a store, you expect it to be ready—for YOU. You become upset if things aren't ready.

When people come to your home for a dinner party, you increase the possibility of having a successful dinner if your table is ready. When your team or group goes out to compete or perform, you increase the chances of winning if your team or group is ready. When the students come to the student council meeting, you will probably have a successful meeting if the agenda has been well thought out.

The Perfect Tribute, The Imperfect Film

This is a true story.

In haste, a teacher whipped out her film library catalog and ordered the perfect film for her U.S. history class lesson on the Civil War. The film was **The Perfect Tribute (Abraham Lincoln)**.

She told the clerk the name of the film and the catalog number, inadvertently giving the clerk the catalog number of the next film, also called **The Perfect Tribute**.

Without previewing the film, she ran it for the class. It was a film made for morticians on how to sell caskets—**The Perfect Tribute**.

You know very well that if a client calls and you are not ready, you will lose the sale. If you are not prepared for your interview, you may not have another one. If you are not ready when the teacher calls on you, you may receive a poor grade.

In the real world, you would be fired if you were not ready. In the competitive world economy, our students must be ready. We teach readiness by modeling readiness: in our work, in our class environment, in ourselves. **People who are not organized and not ready suffer the consequences.**

> **Readiness is the primary determinant of teacher effectiveness.**

Before You Move a Single Desk

Before You Move Any Furniture or Put Anything Up, Here Are Some Truisms

1. A climate of work is what you want to establish during the first week of school.
2. The first week of school should stress large group organization and procedures.
3. Spend your time on classroom management of student behavior, rather than making your classroom look like a showcase.
4. Do not overarrange or overdecorate your room for the opening of school.
5. Your room should be neat and pleasant, but don't spend time making it the ultimate room you want by Back-to-School night.
6. A few bare bulletin boards, shelves, and flowerpots won't bother anyone.
7. And don't bother having the learning center, library, or resource center complete.

You don't need a learning center on the first day of school. Don't waste time trying to finalize one now. Wait a week or so after the students have the classroom rules and procedures and routines down pat before you allow them to work at the learning center.

Prepare the Floor Space

The following examples, like most examples in this book, are generalized and conceptual. Apply and adapt the examples to your situation.

✓ Count the number of desks and chairs needed. Arrange to have damaged furniture replaced and sufficient furniture brought in. Ask for needed items well ahead of time. Do not be hostile if things are not as you want them.

✓ Administrators and custodians are truly very helpful people and want quality education for the children as much as you do. Get to know them and you'll discover that they are competent, cooperative, compassionate, concerned, and helpful. They are not the Ogres the negative teachers would want you to believe they are.

✓ Even if you plan to change your room arrangement during the school year, it is wise to begin the year with the desks in rows facing the teacher. This minimizes distractions, allows you to monitor behavior more readily, and helps you become familiar with the students in your class.

✓ Desks do not have to be in traditional rows, but all chairs should face forward so that all eyes are focused on you.

✓ Place students' desks where students can easily see the teacher during whole class or small group instruction.

✓ Keep high-traffic areas clear. Don't put desks, chairs, and tables in front of doors, water fountains, sinks, pencil sharpeners, or your desk.

✓ Have a strategic location ready for students with behavioral problems.

Strategic Locations for Students with Behavioral Problems

Behavioral problems will occur from time to time. They come with the turf, just like infractions in hockey. And when an infraction occurs in hockey, there is an area, or strategic location, set aside for the offender.

The effective teacher states to the class that behavioral problems will be handled promptly and competently. You convey a message that you are in control and ready!

An axiom of handling behavior problems is that little or no instructional time should be lost (Chapter 19). Time is wasted when you stop to find a place or move furniture around for the offender. The good students resent this waste of time just as much as you resent the troublemaker.

Some Students Who Cause Behavioral Problems

The Aggressive—the hyperactive, agitated, unruly student
The Resistant—the student who won't work
The Distractible—the student who can't concentrate
The Dependent—the student who wants help all the time

Strategic Locations for Students Causing Behavior Problems

Separate—must be separated from the class or at least from other problem students. Appropriate for aggressive and resistant students.

Close by—must be placed close to the teacher. Appropriate for distractible, dependent, and occasionally resistant students.

Prepare the Work Area

✓ Arrange work areas so that you can see and monitor all areas no matter where you are in the room.

✓ Arrange the desks so that you can easily see all the students from all areas of the room.

✓ Students should be able to see you as well as frequently used chalkboards, bulletin boards, screens, demonstration areas, and displays.

✓ Keep traffic areas clear. Allow enough clearance to move up and down and around the last seat in the row.

✓ Keep access to storage areas, bookcases, cabinets, and doors clear.

✓ Learn the regulations regarding fire, earthquakes, tornadoes, hurricanes, and other natural disasters, and have the classroom ready for such emergencies.

✓ Make sure that you have enough chairs for the work areas.

✓ Be sure that you have all necessary materials and equipment for your work areas, such as books, laboratory supplies, kits, media, activity cards, tools, and instruments.

✓ Test any audiovisual equipment to make sure that it works before you intend to use it.

✓ Use tote trays, boxes, coffee cans, dishpans, or whatever to store the materials students will need. Arrange your room for these to be readily accessible to the students.

✓ Arrange work areas where students can go for reading and math groups, science laboratory areas, project work, learning centers, and independent study. Remember, you may not need these areas on the first days of school.

Prepare the Student Area

✓ Save yourself many a headache! Plan areas for student belongings now. Provide space for their binders, backpacks, books, lunch boxes, umbrellas, shoes, show-and-tell items, lost-and-found items, skateboards, and projects.

✓ Provide a coatrack for the students to hang their coats.

Prepare the Wall Space

The most effective classes are those where the students are self-disciplined, self-motivated, and self-responsible learners. Teach your students to consult the bulletin boards for information on what to do and how to do it. You do this by teaching procedures and routines (Chapter 20). Also, consult Chapter 15 on posting your assignments.

✓ Cover one or more bulletin boards with colored paper and trim, and leave it bare. Use it to display student work. Remember, the purpose of this bulletin board is to display student work, not to be decorated by a teacher to look like a department-store show window.

✓ Display your discipline plan in a prominent place. You can move it after the first week. (See Chapter 18.)

✓ Post procedures, assigned duties, calendar, clock, emergency information, schedules, menus, charts, maps, decorations, birthdays, and student work.

✓ Have a consistent place for listing the day's or week's assignments.

✓ Post a large example of the proper heading or style for papers to be done in class.

✓ Post examples of tests students will take, assignments they will turn in, and papers they will write.

✓ Display the feature topic, theme, chapter, or skill for the day or the current unit.

Prepare the Bookcases

✓ Do not place the bookcases where they obstruct any lines of vision.

✓ Rotate materials on the shelves, and leave out only those items you are willing to allow students to handle.

✓ Do not place books or other loose materials near an exit where they can easily disappear or where they may hide emergency information.

Prepare the Teacher Area

Maximize Your Proximity to Minimize Your Problems

Maximize your proximity to students and frequently used materials and equipment. Time is lost when teachers and students waste steps to reach each other, gather materials, or use classroom equipment.

The closer you are to your students, the more you will minimize your classroom behavior problems. When the teacher is physically close to the students and can get to them quickly, their on-task behavior increases. When the teacher is far from a student and cannot get to a student quickly, the student is more likely to stop working and disrupt others.

A teacher's discipline problems are directly proportional to the distance from the students.

A teacher's problems are directly proportional to the amount of distance between the teacher and the students.

✓ Place the teacher's desk, file, and other equipment so that they do not interfere with the flow of traffic. Do not create a barrier between yourself and your students. Place your desk so that you can move quickly to a student to assist, reinforce, or discipline.

✓ Place the teacher's desk so that you can easily monitor the classroom while at your desk or working with individual students.

✓ Place the teacher's desk away from the door so that no one can take things from your desk and quickly walk out.

✓ If you choose to have everything on and in your desk treated as personal property, make this clear during your teaching of classroom procedures and routines.

Prepare the Teaching Materials

✓ Have a letter ready with the materials you want your students to bring from home. Have a place and a procedure ready for the storage of these materials.

✓ Have a weekly desk or cabinet check to be sure that these materials are being maintained properly.

✓ Have name cards ready and on the students' desks. Avoid tags with pins and needles. If you choose to use name tags, fasten them with tape or yarn.

✓ Have your basic materials ready for the first week of school. These include books, papers, pencils, rulers, glue, chalk, felt pens, stapler, tape, clipboard, crayons, construction paper, instruments, typewriters, laboratory supplies, manipulatives, playground equipment, and computer software.

✓ Find and organize containers for your materials. Use old duplicating-paper boxes, dishpans, coffee cans, milk cartons, and shoe boxes to store materials. Label each of your containers and place an inventory card in each listing everything that should be in the container.

✓ Store seldom used, long-term materials out of the way, but be sure they are inventoried and are ready for immediate use.

✓ Place your electronic media where there are electrical outlets and where the students will not trip over the wires.

✓ Have an extension cord and an adapter plug handy.

✓ Organize and file your spirit masters, mimeograph stencils, copy machine masters, and computer disks. Do likewise with your extra worksheets so that they are immediately ready for any students who were absent or who need extra help.

Finally, Prepare Yourself

✓ Keep your purse, keys, and other valuables in a safe location.

✓ Have emergency materials handy, such as tissue, rags, paper towels, soap, first-aid kit, and extra lunch money. Store these for your use, not the students'.

Half of Your Effectiveness Is Determined Before You Leave Home

The amount of work you will accomplish will be determined before you even leave for work. We know how much work a person, whether teacher, administrator, student, or business person, will accomplish in a day.

Half of what you will accomplish in a day will be determined before you even leave home.

Three-quarters of what you will accomplish in a day will be determined before you enter the school door.

You need to prepare yourself, both academically and attitudinally, before you leave home and as you travel to school.

You increase the chance of student success and decrease the chance of student disruptions if the materials, classroom climate, and teacher are ready before the students arrive.

✔ Hang up a clock and a calendar.

✔ Buy a bell or a timer if you wish to use either as a signal.

✔ Obtain a teacher's manual for all the textbooks you will use in your class.

✔ Obtain a supply of the forms that are used for daily school routines, such as attendance forms, tardy slips, hall passes, and referral forms. Since you will use these forms each day, place them where you can find them immediately.

To be an effective teacher, be prepared. For your own sanity and mental health, be prepared. **Teachers who are ready maximize student learning and minimize student misbehavior.**

The Effective Teacher

1. **Prepares, prepares, and prepares.**
2. **Prepares the classroom for effective work.**
3. **Maximizes proximity to the students.**
4. **Maximizes proximity to materials.**

Key Idea: How you introduce yourself on the first day may determine how much respect and success you will have for the rest of the school year.

Your Reputation Precedes You

Right or wrong, accurate or not, your reputation will precede you.

People have reputations. You know of people who are sweet, kind, honest, industrious, and dependable and others who are sleazy, curmudgeonly, arrogant, lazy, and undependable.

Businesses have reputations. Some have terrible service, sell shoddy merchandise, and do not guarantee their products. Other businesses you can trust implicitly.

Companies with good images, such as IBM, Coca-Cola, McDonald's, Hallmark, Nordstrom, and Hewlett-Packard, enhance their sales. Companies with poor images, try as they may to change them, suffer in their sales. This is why companies spend billions to create a corporate image, because they know that people buy from those they trust. Their image precedes a sale.

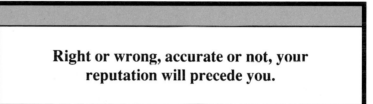

Your Image Enhances Sales

"Fly the friendly skies of **UNITED**"

HALLMARK: "When you care enough to send the very best"

UPS: "We run the tightest ship in the shipping business"

KODAK: "Depend on us"

SAAB: "The most intelligent cars built"

Even before you first see your students, your success at winning your students' respect and attention may have already been predetermined by your reputation. **Right or wrong, accurate or not, your reputation will precede you.**

✓ If you have a good reputation, the students will enter your classroom with high expectations, and this will be to your benefit.

✓ If you have a poor reputation, the students will enter with low expectations, and this will be to your detriment.

Whether you like it or not, the students will talk about you, the parents will talk about you, the administration will talk about you, and even your fellow colleagues will talk about you.

She Got Those Who Were Left

I am sure that many of your readers after reading your article would feel that Mrs. T was treated unfairly when relieved of her teaching duties. I taught in the same school for 25 years so I'm aware of what was happening in the years that she taught.

Many parents and teachers would agree that junior high students in the last 10 or 15 years have become more difficult to handle and that discipline of the age group is more and more of a problem. Mrs. T's inability to handle her class was common knowledge.

It took real courage for the school board and administration to say, "For the good of the children this teacher has to go."

As to the claim that her classes were packed with problem children: The policy in our school at the time was that parents could request a certain teacher or ask that a child be reassigned. Many parents, knowing of the problems, asked that their children not be in Mrs. T's room.

Those who were left were often the most difficult discipline problems and Mrs. T got them.

Letter to the Editor
San Jose Mercury News,
November 13, 1988.

Everyone likes and supports a winner. Parents want their children in the classes of the outstanding teachers, by reputation. No one likes or supports a loser. These teachers often get what's left after all the shuffling of students has been done.

You will attract better students, have a minimum of problems on the first day of school, and generally be much happier with your job if you have students who want to be in your class. It makes no sense to be a teacher that no one wants to have as a teacher.

Protect your reputation and create a positive image. You have nothing to lose and everything to gain.

Preschool Invitation or Visit

Here are some welcoming techniques used by effective teachers. Apply and adapt the examples to your situation.

The Importance of Parents

Parents are their children's first and most influential teachers. What parents do to help their children is more important to academic success than how well off the family is.[1]

---

1. **Send a letter home to the parents BEFORE school begins.**
   - ✓ Tell the parents that you are looking forward to having their child in your class.
   - ✓ Ask them to put the dates of the school's open house on their calendar, and explain why it is important for them to attend. You will be explaining homework, grading, discipline, and classroom procedures.
   - ✓ Include information on what materials you want the students to have ready for school.

2. **Send a letter home to each student BEFORE school begins.**
   - ✓ Include a message of welcome.
   - ✓ Tell the students who you are.
   - ✓ Invite them to call you if they have questions.
   - ✓ Give them pertinent information on dates, times, and room location.
   - ✓ Help them to be ready by listing the materials they should have with them. They will be ready if you are ready. Do not surprise your students.
   - ✓ Tell them your, not their, expectations.

3. **Visit the home of each student BEFORE school begins (check to be sure that this is an appropriate thing to do).**
   - ✓ Introduce yourself.
   - ✓ Bring the letters just described with you.
   - ✓ Share with the parents how they can help.

---

[1]U.S. Department of Education. *What Works: Research About Teaching and Learning*. Washington, D.C.: Government Printing Office, 1986, p. 7.

In Awe and Admiration of Her

Dear Mr. Mundy,

My daughter, Angela, attended Longfellow School last year. Her teacher's name was Miss Sather. The reason for this letter is to officially give a parent's commendation of the performance of Miss Sather.

First of all, we moved to Minot just weeks before the school year was to begin. After I registered my daughter for school, I did not expect any communication from the teacher until after the first day of school. However, Miss Sather came to our house a few days before school began to welcome Angela to her class. That may seem like a small factor, but it made a big impression on me and it helped my daughter in adjusting to a new school.

Never, in my life, have I known any other teacher who cared so much as to do this for a student. Later I learned that this is a common practice for Miss Sather.

Additionally, her classroom was always orderly, well organized and disciplined. She involved the parents in the student's learning by sending home parent-child homework assignments and notes of problems or progress frequently. She used positive methods of discipline and gained the respect and love of her pupils.

Other parents, my husband and myself included, were in awe and admiration of her. She is an extremely talented and outstanding teacher. I would like to ask that she be recognized for her efforts.

Sincerely yours,

Mrs. JKM

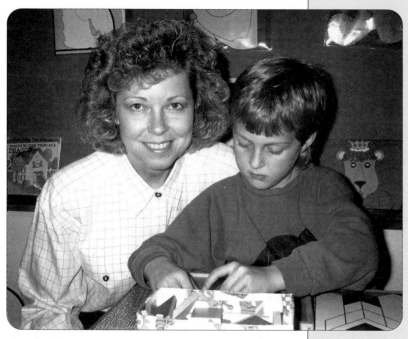

Sherry Sather Braaten

Am I in the Right Room?

Douglas Brooks discovered that the very first thing a student wants to know on the first day of school is, "Am I in the right room?"[2] **Finding the correct room on the first day of school can be one of the most frightening experiences for a student.** There is nothing more embarrassing than to discover that you are in the wrong room—15 minutes after class has begun.

The Seven Things Students Want to Know
on the First Day of School

Dear Dr. Wong,

Your credibility has increased. When I came home from your in-service meeting, I asked my 13-year-old son the following question: "What's the most frightening thing about the first day of school?"

After thinking for a moment, he said, "Having the teacher mispronounce your name, and walking into the wrong classroom."

Classroom teacher
Garland, Texas

How to Greet Them on Day 1

Stand at the classroom door with a big smile and a ready handshake. You do this when company comes or with people you meet. Airline, restaurant, and auto dealership personnel do it. Effective teachers do what is obvious—not what everyone else is failing to do at school. Just because no one else is standing at the door with a smile does not make it right.

---

[2]Brooks, Douglas M. "The First Day Of School." *Educational Leadership,* May 1985, pp. 76-78.

This is a successful technique used by many effective teachers for greeting students on the first day of school.

Step 1. Post the following information next to the classroom door:

✓ Your name

✓ Room number

✓ Section or period, if appropriate

✓ Grade level or subject

✓ An appropriate welcome or greeting

The students can see the information on the wall and can compare it to the correct information on their registration form.

This is no different from finding flight information posted at each gate at an airport, a doctor's name on the office door, or movie information, times, and prices at a theater box office.

Step 2. Stand at the door on the first day of school. Have a smile on your face, hands ready to shake the students' hands, and a look that says you can't wait to meet them.

Step 3. As they stand there, wondering if you are the right teacher and this is the correct room, welcome them to a new school year and tell them the following information:

✓ Your name

✓ Room number

✓ Section or period, if appropriate

✓ Grade level or subject

✓ Anything else appropriate, such as seating assignment

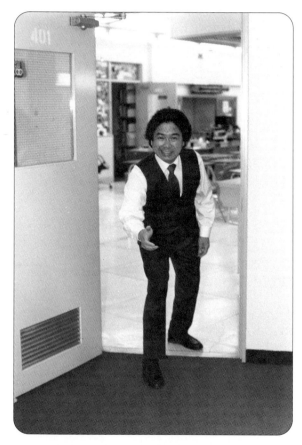

I love to stand at the door on the first day with a giant smile on my face, hand stuck out in an invitational pose, waiting for those "little darlings" to come down the hall.

Step 4. Check each student's registration card, and if the student is in the incorrect place or is lost, help the student or find a guide who will.

Step 5. After you greet a student, the student should be able to enter the classroom and see the same information written or posted in the room:

✓ Your name

✓ Room number

✓ Section or period, if appropriate

✓ Grade level or subject

✓ Any other appropriate information

Because the students are exposed to the same information three times, it is highly unlikely that any students will be in the wrong place on the first day of school. Their anxiety level and their tendency to be confrontational are reduced, and they will feel welcome and at ease.

What has just been suggested as an effective and cordial way to start a new year should be obvious. Have you ever gone somewhere on an errand or for an appointment and cannot find the right address, building, or office? You know how frustrating that can be.

Perhaps you have driven to a strange place and wished the streets were better marked. Or you were in an unfamiliar store and wished there was someone around to help you find what you were looking for.

Everything possible should be done to welcome the student and to make sure that they know where to go and how to get there on time.

Help your students find your room by posting information at the door as well as inside the classroom.

Seating Chart and First Assignment

If you choose to have assigned seats, tell each student this fact upon entering the door. Do not rearrange the seating after the class is all seated. The students will moan and groan over why they have to move and why they can't sit near someone.

How NOT to Start the First Day of School

The ineffective teacher suddenly appears through the door just as the bell rings. The teacher's name or the room number are nowhere to be found. Rather the teacher starts with an icy stare. The first day of school goes like this:

1. It begins with an icy stare as the teacher stands behind the desk, inspecting, over eyeglasses, everyone walking in with a look that says, "Who are you and what are you doing here infringing on my space?"

2. The teacher never mentions a name, the room number, the class, the grade level, or the period.

3. The teacher announces that he or she will call the roll.

4. The teacher also announces that as the roll is called the seating assignments will be changed so that everyone is seated in alphabetical order. A collective groan ensues. (See "Succeeding With Your First Request," page 114.)

5. The teacher calls the first student and points to the student sitting in the first chair and demands, "Up." That student rolls his eyes and goes and leans against the wall.

6. The teacher then points to the first student and says, "You, there."

7. As each student is dislodged from his or her chair, a motley crew of students assembles along the wall.

8. The students are all looking at each other and shaking their collective heads, "Who is this disorganized person? Our teacher? It's going to be a long year!"

How to Help Students Find Their Assigned Seats

✓ Have their names on place cards on the desks.

✓ Have their names written on a seating chart transparency that is projected on to a screen.

✓ Give them an index card with a letter and a number on it, such as B5, A8, C3, and ask them to find their seats based on the seating chart that is projected. Do not use this method if you feel it will be too difficult for your students to figure out two coordinates. You want them in their seats when the bell rings, not running around confused.

As the students go to their assigned seats, inform them that they will find their first assignment at their seat. **Tell them to start to work on it immediately!**

The first assignment should be short, maybe fun, easy to complete, and successful for all students. It may simply be an alphabet or number sheet or an information form that will not be graded.

You greatly increase the probability that school will start successfully for both you and your students when these four points are true:

1. You have your room ready.
2. You are at the door.
3. You have assigned seats.
4. You have the first assignment ready.

The important thing is to make a statement to your students about your efficiency and competence as a classroom manager and teacher. **What you do on the first day may determine how much respect and success you will have for the rest of the school year.**

How Students Are to Enter the Room

Observe how your students enter the classroom. You need to begin teaching procedures and routines (Chapter 20) the moment you meet them at the door on the first day of school.

✓ Ask any student who enters the room inappropriately to return to the door and enter appropriately. You do not send the student out of the room but rather to the door. You do not want to send anyone "out of the room" in the very first minute, as "out of the room" has a negative connotation.

✓ Do not make dubious remarks like these:

> Try coming in again correctly.
> We walk into this room like ladies and gentlemen.
> You walk in properly, understand?

✓ Rather, calmly but firmly, do the following:

1. Ask the student to return to the door or go to the door.
2. Tell the student why.
3. Give specific directions.
4. Check for understanding.
5. Acknowledge the understanding.

Example

Todd, please come back to the door.

I am sorry, but that is not the way you enter our classroom everyday. You were noisy, you did not go to your seat, and you pushed Ann.

When you enter this classroom, you walk in quietly, go directly to your seat, and get to work immediately on the assignment that is posted.

Are there any questions?

Thank you, Todd. Now show me that you can go to your seat properly.

Don't forget the importance of using the student's name, *please*, and *thank you*. (See Chapter 11.)

Your manner and voice should be gentle and calm, even with a smile, but firm. Your voice should communicate that you are not the least bit flustered or angry. You are simply in control and know what you expect from your students, and you are communicating this expectation.

It is a mistake to let any misbehavior go, such as entering a room inappropriately, with the attitude that you will have time to deal with this later. Effective teachers know that it will be much more difficult to correct misbehavior at a later date.

Ineffective teachers bark and yell, have no guidelines or expectations, and assume that misbehavior will correct itself even after it is far too late to correct. Avoiding the issue is also unfair to the students because they will not know that you care about the way they enter the room unless you communicate that concern and expectation to them. Asking students to enter the classroom according to a set of procedures indicates that there are definite boundaries to what they can and cannot do in your room.

It is important that you state the correct procedure for entering the room, whether at the beginning of the day, the beginning of the period, after recess, after lunch, or whenever. Rehearse this procedure until it becomes a routine. Praise the students when it is done properly, and encourage them to make it a routine every day. It is best to save what has been explained in this paragraph until after you have introduced yourself as suggested in the next section.

Your Important First Words

There are two major things you want to state at the outset on the first day of school: your name and your expectations. It behooves you not only to tell the class your name but to pronounce it so that they will call you by the name you want.

Students want to know who you are as a person and if you will treat them as a person ("Seven Things Students Want to Know," page 105). It is important that you allay any fears they may have about being in your class. **The best way to do this is to smile, exude care, and communicate positive expectations.**

Example

Welcome. Welcome to another school year.

My name is Mr. Wong. There it is on the chalkboard. It is spelled W-O-N-G and is pronounced "wong." I would like to be addressed as Mr. Wong, please. Thank you.

I am looking forward to being your teacher this year. Relax. I have over 30 years' experience as a teacher. I am what is called an experienced, veteran teacher.

In addition, I go to workshops, conferences, in-service meetings, college classes, and seminars. I also read the professional journals and work together with my fellow teachers. I am a competent, knowledgeable, experienced, and professional teacher.

Also, I love to teach, I enjoy teaching, and I am proud that I am a teacher. So relax. You are in good hands this year with me, Mr. Wong.

You are going to have the greatest educational experience of your life. We will not only study (subject), but I will also share with you some life-skill traits that will help you to be successful in tomorrow's world.

I can assure you that if you should run into me at the shopping mall 25 years from now, you will say, "You were right, Mr. Wong. That was the most memorable, exciting, and fascinating class I ever had."

So welcome!

The Effective Teacher

1. Cultivates a positive reputation.

2. Communicates with parents and students before school starts.

3. Greets the students with positive expectations.

4. Has the seating assignment and first assignment ready.

CHAPTER 14

 Key Idea: The students must sit in such a way as to accomplish what you want them to accomplish.

Your Very First Set of Directions to Your Class

The Success of Your First Request

How the class reacts to your first directions will be an indication of how they will react to your directions for the remainder of the year.

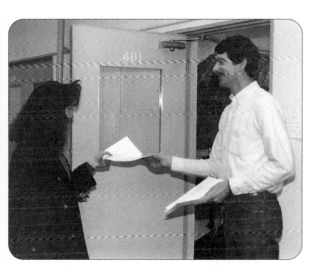

"Hi, here's your seating assignment."

You can tell right away how successful you will be in giving directions by the success of your first request. Your very first request of your students will probably be to tell each one of them where to sit.

They will react in one of two ways:

1. Follow your orders promptly and courteously

2. Grumble and argue over everything you want them to do for the rest of the year

Yes, the rest of the year!

Here's why.

Succeeding with Your First Request

The Effective Teacher

✓ Is present in the room or at the door when the students arrive.

✓ Assigns seating to everyone as they enter the room.

✓ Has an assignment ready for the students on each desk.

By what you do the instant the student enters the school, the library, the office, or the classroom, the student knows immediately if he or she is wanted.

The teacher is standing at the door with a smile and an extended hand to shake. The teacher bids everyone to enter, and each student gets a safe, nonthreatening smile. The welcome mat or red carpet is at the door for the class. This conveys a positive message to the students.

People welcome people. Textbooks, chalkboards, lectures, worksheets, and examinations do not welcome students to school. Teachers, bus drivers, administrators, secretaries, aides, and counselors invite students to have a successful experience at school.

Upon entering the classroom, the students find a pleasant environment. Your name, the room number, the period, and the class are on the chalkboard. Directions for seating (whether assigned or open) are reiterated. Information about the first assignment, which is on their desks, is clearly stated and tells them to get to work even before the bell rings. The message you are relating to these students is the classroom is a safe, work-oriented, positive environment where each second will be devoted to learning.

If students are invited to have successful experiences in the classroom, they will know that they are welcome, appreciated, cared for, and wanted. **And if the students feel wanted, they will be more likely to accede to your directions and requests.**

How to Make Your First Request Effective

Step 1. Check each registration at the door.

Step 2. Put a firm but friendly smile on your face.

Step 3. Look the student in the face and communicate understanding and acknowledgment.

Step 4. Verbally welcome and acknowledge each student.

Step 5. Then lower your voice to a firm but soft tone. Speak slowly and communicate understanding and acknowledgment.

Step 6. Then tell the student if seating is open or assigned. (See page 119.)

Step 7. Follow this with "And when you sit down, you will find an activity on your desk. I think you will enjoy doing it. Please begin working on it right away. Thank you." (See page 108.)

Failing with Your First Request

The Ineffective Teacher

✓ Is nowhere in sight when the students arrive.

✓ Reshuffles the whole class after everyone has found a seat.

✓ Grumbles about all the administrative details that must be done before class can begin.

The students walk into the classroom and no teacher is in sight. Some students find a chair; others wander around. But they all ask, "Who's the teacher? What grade is this? Is this the right room? Is this history? What period is this?" And they all respond, "I don't know."

The bell rings, and suddenly a teacher appears from an office or from around a corner, like a monster from a dungeon. It is Cold Start Charlie, the perennial ineffective teacher.

He can always be found in the faculty lounge, gulping coffee and puffing away on his cigarettes. On this day, the first day of school hasn't even begun yet, and he's already griping about the same thing he's been griping about for years.

Hurrying down to his classroom, he arrives just as the bell rings. The students immediately read the growl and the menacing look that dares anyone to breathe out of unison.

He never introduces himself and may or may not identify the class or period. Standing in front of the class with the posture of a drill sergeant, he says, "When I call your name, come up and bring your registration card for me to sign."

When seemingly everyone has been registered, he looks up and asks if everyone has been called. One hand goes up.

Discovering that the student is in the wrong classroom, Cold Start Charlie tells him where he should be. As the student leaves the room, all eyes are focused on him, with two

messages behind the stares: "Dummy. How can you be so stupid as to be the wrong room?" and "Isn't he lucky not having to put up with this jerk of a teacher for the rest of the year!"

A student has just been humiliated because a teacher was not prepared and acted in an noninvitational manner. And the students have made a judgment about Charlie's first impression that will be reflected in their work for the rest of the year.

Your First Request Will Be Ineffective . . .

1. If you are not in the room when the students enter.

2. If you do not check any of the registration cards before the students enter the room.

3. If you do not tell the students your name, the room number, the period or grade level, and the class.

4. If you do not welcome the students.

5. If you reshuffle the class after they have all found a seat.

6. If you grumble that you have to do administrative work, which is really classroom management.

7. If you have provided no assignment, and the students have nothing to do while you register the class.

Seating Arrangements or Seating Assignments?

**Should I assign seats or allow students
to sit wherever they choose?**

That question is germane only after you decide what you want the students to do. Seating assignments is not the issue. Seating assignments come after seating arrangements are determined. **Seating arrangements is the priority.**

**The purpose of arranging seats is to
accomplish classroom tasks.**

The teacher must know what the students are to accomplish. Then the desks are arranged to maximize the accomplishment of the tasks and to minimize behavior problems. After the seats are arranged, students may be assigned seating in whatever order is desired.

Seating Arrangements:

Arranged to coincide with the task you have designed.

Examples

First-day registration and procedures
Cooperative learning
Listening to a lecture
Sitting to hear a story
Class discussion and interaction
Small group activity
Taking a test
Individual research or desk work

Seating Assignments:

Assigned to maximize learning and classroom management and minimize behavioral problems.

Examples

By height or age
In alphabetical order
For peer-group tutoring
For paired problem solving
Placing low-ability students at the
     front of the room

Seating Arrangements

To determine seating arrangements for accomplishment of classroom tasks, you need to ask, in order, the following questions:

1. What do I want to do?

Do I want to read a story, do small group activities, teach discipline, procedures and routines, lecture, show a movie, conduct a chorus, lead exercises, have individual study?

2. What kind of seating arrangements are possible?

These photos show some possible seating arrangements.

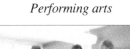

Performing arts

Test, movie, or lecture

Group activity

Discussion or demonstration

Story time

3. Which seating arrangement will I use?

Different seating arrangements need to be used to accomplish tasks efficiently. The students must sit in such a way as to accomplish what you want them to accomplish.

There is no one form of seating that should be permanently used the entire school year. Change may be as frequent as furniture is moved in the living room, changed in the ballroom of a hotel, or rearranged in a store window display.

The only way for the students to learn discipline and procedures and routines is to have the seats arranged so that every pair of eyes will be looking at you. Assuming that you want to teach discipline and procedures and routines, do not arrange your room in a series of centers or circles in which half the students have their backs to you. Discipline and procedures and routines are explained in Chapters 18 to 20. To teach these is best done with the chairs arranged in columns and rows.

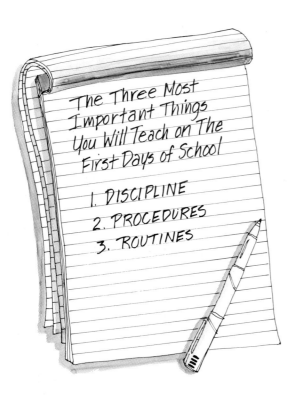

The Three Most Important Things You Will Teach on The First Days of School

1. DISCIPLINE
2. PROCEDURES
3. ROUTINES

Problems When Students Have Their Backs to You

1. You explain a rule of discipline, and the students sitting in a small group look at each other and roll their eyes toward the sky. They have just invalidated the rule by their actions.

2. You explain a procedure, and half the students must turn around and write it down, then turn around again. You have invalidated the procedure for teaching procedures.

3. You explain another procedure, and you cannot tell if half the students understand because you cannot see them practicing the procedure with their backs to you.

Seating Assignments

The effective teacher assigns students to their seats on the first day of school. Don't make finding a seating assignment on the first day of school a frustrating treasure hunt. This task should be over within a matter of seconds. It is not a topic for class discussion. It should then be a dead issue because you are the teacher in charge of the instructional program. When you wish to rearrange the room or the seating, deal with the change in the same expedient way.

You will have a much more effective class, most of the time, if you assign students to their seats. For group work, you should assign students to their groups and then assign the groups to their workstations or seating arrangements. For instance, you are hosting a dinner party with guests at three separate tables. You don't ask your guests to get their own utensils out of the drawer and sit wherever they please. If you are a gracious host, you tell your guests where you'd like them to sit.

Whatever the classroom arrangement, do not seat students with their backs to either the teacher or to the front of the room on the first day of school.

Airlines, theaters, and restaurants—the good ones—will designate a seat or seat you in the chair of mutual choice. Do likewise in the classroom. You are the teacher, the conductor, the facilitator.

Seating assignments are sometimes made for social and behavioral reasons. When you do not want certain students to sit together, separate them. At an assembly, you say, "And you can sit anywhere you want, but you may not sit next to Lon."

There are times when seating assignments are not important—for instance, when a primary class sings, you read a story, or there is individual research.

Seating assignments should not become an issue in the classroom. Student success and the instructional program are your major focus.

The Effective Teacher

1. **Assigns seating as the students are greeted.**

2. **Has all the seats facing the teacher for the activities of the first day of school.**

3. **Arranges the seats to expedite the task.**

What If the Chairs Are All Bolted to the Floor and Cannot Be Moved?

Then you are restricted to that arrangement and must adapt your activities to that kind of a seating plan.

For instance, you would not play football in the bathroom, cook in the bedroom, or take a shower in the kitchen sink. Similarly, you just cannot effectively have small group activities or have eye-to-eye class interaction and discussion if you have to teach a class in the school auditorium.

For your own sanity, adjust your classroom instruction and teaching techniques. This is life. You have been in situations before where the circumstances and the budget dictated the terms—for example, that you could invite only 75 guests to a wedding reception and it had to be held in your home and not the ballroom of The Ritz.

Accept that all things are not the way you want them, so stop beating yourself over your head.

Learn to nourish your body and go on with improving the quality of your life.

Key Idea: Post your assignments if you want your students to do them.

CHAPTER 15

Your First Priority When Class Starts

Assignments should be posted daily, always in the same place.

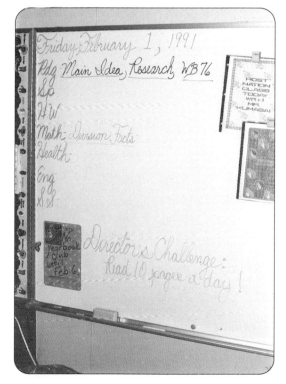

> **Your very first priority when the class starts is to get the students to work.**

Your first priority is not to take roll; it is to get the students to work immediately. It is no different in the private sector. When your students go to work, as in a part-time job, they are expected to begin working at the appointed hour.

At the appointed hour, the part-time workers also know what to do. They do not stand around waiting for directions or ask questions like "What do you want me to do today?"

When class begins, you can easily get students to work if three criteria have been met:

1. The students have an assignment.
2. They know where to find the assignment.
3. They know why they are to do the assignment.

Daily and in the Same Place

Common sense and research on the effective classroom emphatically tell you to POST YOUR ASSIGNMENTS EVERY DAY!

Post the assignments in the same place every day. Even if it is the same assignment, post it. There is no need for students to ask "What is the assignment?" or "What am I supposed to do?" if they know that the assignment is in the same place every day.

Assignments can be posted anywhere—on the chalkboard, on a bulletin board, handed out at the door, or displayed from a transparency. Just make sure that the assignment is posted in the same place so that the students know exactly and consistently where to look.

Assignments Must Be Posted Daily and Consistently

✓ Post the assignments DAILY.

✓ Use a CONSISTENT location.

This Helps Them Take More Responsibility

Diane Boyd, a high school teacher in Texas, has her daily assignment written on the right side of the board each day. When the students enter, they are to copy this assignment and keep it in their pocket folder. She says, "While they are busy copying their assignment, I can quickly get roll."

Diane says, "Then when they get their graded papers back, they record the grade by each item. This helps them take more responsibility for their grades, and they can keep their parents informed."

She also says jokingly, "They expect a grade for keeping their folder, though."

What Diane Boyd has done is not unique with effective teachers. What's important is that she has her assignments posted. And she gets results with her class.

This is an example of how she writes her assignments.

Assignment

June 2	Go over the points about haiku
	Do worksheet p. 4
	Study poem on p. 713
	Write own haiku (finish for homework)
June 3	Collect haiku
	Discuss fig. lang. in several poems on pp. 714–718
	Write examples

Are We Doing Anything Today?

The ineffective teacher keeps the assignment a mystery until it is announced, and it may be announced in different ways and posted in different places each day. Sometimes there may be no assignment, even though the students ask for one. This may be because the teacher does not know what should be done, what the student is to learn, or how to teach it.

You can always tell classes where no assignments are posted. Ineffective teachers say things like this:

"Where did we leave off yesterday?" (I have no control.)
"Open your books so that we can take turns reading." (For what reason?)
"Sit quietly and do the worksheet." (To master what?)
"Let's watch this movie." (To learn what?)
"You can have a free study period." (To do what? I do not have an assignment for you. I am unprepared.)

The textbook is not the curriculum. Having students fill in worksheets to keep them busy and quiet is not the curriculum. Teachers who have no curriculum follow the textbook, page by page, cover to cover, and look for busywork for the students. When this happens, you have students who walk into the classroom and say things like this:

"Are you going to show us a movie?"
"Are you going to read to us?"
"Are you going to let us play games?"
"Are you going to lecture to us?"
"Are you going to let us have a study period?"

Or worse yet,

"Are we going to do anything today?"
"Are we going to do anything important today?"
"Did I miss anything important while I was absent?"

In classes where students make comments like these, they take no responsibility for their work. The teacher is the only responsible person in the classroom. That's why they ask the teacher what is going to happen. They look to the teacher for direction, for entertainment, and for work.

Responsible Students Have Assignments

The student must be responsible for classwork. The direction and responsibility for a student's classwork, however, are based on the teacher's having an assignment ready.

> **Post your assignments if you want the students to do them.**

Post your assignments if you want your students to do them.

The effective teacher teaches RESPONSIBILITY. This is because effective teachers have their assignments posted. It is a joy to watch such teachers and such classes in action. The students in these classes know where to look for their assignments and how to go about doing the work on their own. You cannot teach students to be responsible unless they know what to do.

You Start the Class, Not the Bell

Shirley Bert Lee is a California mentor teacher. This means that she has been recognized for her excellence in the classroom. In addition, students want to be in her class and parents pressure administrators to have their children in her class.

You can understand why Shirley's fifth- and sixth-grade classes are so effective when you see how efficiently she opens each day of her class.

- She has a posted morning routine, which is followed.

- She posts her assignments every day.

- She knows how to develop routines with her students.

On the first day of school, this is what she tells her students:

"Mrs. Lee does not start the class. The bell does not start the class. YOU start the class.

"This is what will happen when you come to class, each day. There is a morning routine you are to follow. You immediately go to your seat, you get out your materials for work, and you get to work on the assignment.

"The assignment will be posted on the chalkboard in the same place every day. For instance, you may be given the following seven questions and these new vocabulary words.

"Please get to work on these new vocabulary words when you come in. Do not wait for the bell to ring or for the teacher to tell you to get to work.

"You will have ten minutes after the bell rings to get the assignment done." (See Chapter 20 for how routines like these are implemented.)

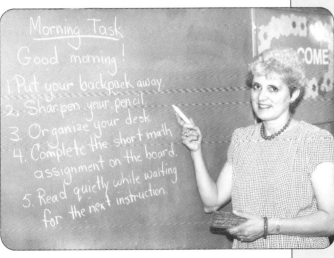

Shirley Bert Lee

Shirley Lee's class is a joy to behold. She doesn't even have to open her mouth when the bell rings. She may say, "Good Morning" or compliment the class on their appropriate behavior, but while the students are quickly and quietly at work, she completes her chores, which typically must be done by all teachers, like taking roll.

Yes, she takes roll <u>after</u> the students are at work. The first priority of a teacher is to get the students to work, not to take roll.

The Effective Teacher

1. Has a posted morning or class-opening routine.
2. Has the assignment posted daily.
3. Posts the assignment in a consistent location.
4. Teaches the class where to find the assignment.

Key Idea: Do not involve the class in the roll-taking process.

CHAPTER 16

The Results of Ineffective Roll Taking

> **The effective teacher starts the class
> immediately with an assignment,
> not roll taking.**

Y ou can't imagine how many teachers with 10, 20, even 30 years experience are still taking roll at the beginning of each day or period, wasting five or more minutes of student learning time, and arguing with the class as to who is absent.

Please do not take roll at the very beginning of the class.

The Drill Sergeant or Camp Counselor

These people ask the class to answer by signifying "present" when their names are called. This is what actually happens.

"Justin." "Present."
"Kimberley." "Present."
"Mario." "Present."
"Hank." "Here." Several students look at Hank for his cute, unauthorized answer.
    The teacher blithely continues, despite the inappropriate answer.

"Maria." "Present."
"Irwin." "Present."

"Tanya." "Yep." More students now look at Tanya, some giving her positive signals for her inappropriate answer. But the teacher just goes on. And the class noise level is now higher.

"Tran." "Present."
"Susan." "Present."
"Marion." "Yo." The whole class breaks up. But the teacher, glancing up for a second, goes right on.

The students quickly learn that the teacher does not mean what is said. Worse yet, the teacher does nothing whenever inappropriate behavior occurs.

During the prep period you can find this teacher in the lounge, one of the lounge lizards, complaining about the noise level in his class. The problem is not the students. The problem is the teacher who wants his class to bark out responses like they were at reserve camp or summer camp.

The Grade-Book Mumbler

This is the teacher who says, "All right, everyone, I want it quiet while I take roll." Translated, this means, "I want you hyperactive, psychosexual, pubescent, junior high school students to sit still, without talking or doing anything for the next four to five minutes (that'll be the day!) while I take roll."

This ineffective teacher stands in front of the room and reads the roll, just as she has been doing for decades. She is totally oblivious to the fact that the class couldn't care less about the procedure, not to mention that the noise level is slowly increasing.

The problem begins because students have a weird sense of attendance. They believe that if they are anywhere on campus, or even within a mile of the campus, they are present. Whereas most teachers consider a student absent if a warm body is not residing in an appropriate seat.

When this teacher comes to a name in the roll book that gets no response or sees that a seat is empty, the teacher says, "Ah, Ernie is absent," and is about to mark Ernie absent. Then a voice, maybe more than one, shouts out—without permission—"Ernie is not absent. He's coming down the hall. He'll be here" or "I saw him in the library. There's a long line. He'll be here."

Now what is this teacher going to do? It's the teacher against the class. The class says that Ernie is present on the campus, but the teacher does not see Ernie in his seat. She marks Ernie absent nonetheless.

And with four absences in the class, the scene repeats itself four times. Each time, the noise level rises and more on-task time is wasted.

Since roll taking does not concern the class, do not involve them in the process.

The Outcomes of Ineffective Roll Taking

✓ Each time the class yells out a response, the noise level gets higher and higher.

✓ Confrontation builds up between the class and the teacher as to whether or not a student is absent.

✓ Valuable minutes are wasted.

✓ Many students sit there bored while precious study time is wasted with a bookkeeping chore that really does not concern the class.

They Know You Are Taking Roll

Even when you do not involve the class in the roll-taking process, some of the students are so astute in the teaching process that they will volunteer attendance information without your even asking for it.

For instance, you are quietly taking roll. They see you with the grade book in your hand. And as you scan the class, someone says, "Miss Hirsch, Joey is not absent. He's at the counselor's office. I saw him."

Isn't it wonderful that the students know how to run a class? Many of them could possibly run a more effective classroom than many of the teachers—unless the teachers themselves constantly work at excellence.

Excellence is the process of constantly working at making a process operate better and better.

The old way of taking roll that you saw your teachers use 10 to 15 years ago is really quite inefficient. **The effective teacher is constantly evaluating how the teaching process can be improved.**

Effective Roll Taking in an Effective Class

The effective teacher starts the class immediately with an assignment, not roll taking. The effective teacher not only starts the class but has trained the class to start class on their own. (See Chapter 20 on procedures and routines.)

The Class That Has Been Effectively Taught Knows . . .

✓ How to enter the room quickly and courteously.

✓ How to go to their seats and get out their materials.

✓ Where to look for their assignment.

✓ To begin their work immediately.

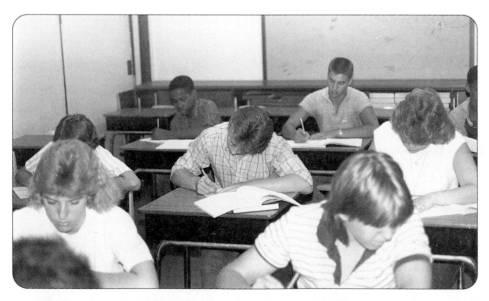

WHEN should you take roll? After the students are on task.
HOW should you take roll? Without involving the students.

There are many ways to take roll; however, your first priority is to get the students on task.

✓ As soon as the tardy bell rings, your first task is to scan the room, not to take roll, looking for students who are not at work.

✓ You quietly signal these students to get to work immediately—with a firm smile and a hand gesture that clearly indicates that you want them to work.

✓ They know where the assignment is located, and they know what to do. You are maximizing academic learning time. (See Chapter 21.)

✓ As soon as the class is at work, proceed to do whatever administrative chores are necessary. Taking roll is usually one of these.

Three Ways to Take Roll Efficiently and Effectively

1. Look at your class and refer to your seating chart. Mark whoever is absent.

2. Have folders or something personal in a box at the door. When the students come in, they are to take their folders, go to their seats, and get to work on the posted assignment. After the students are at work, you look in the box. You see three folders left, note the names, and mark these students absent.

3. Have each student's name on a bulletin board, perhaps on a cutout of that student that the student has made. At the bottom of the cutout, have a paper loop that holds a pencil.

   When the students come in, they are to take their pencil and go to their seats to work. After the students are at work, you note the pencils remaining on the bulletin board and mark these students absent.

There are many other ways to take roll. **Regardless of which method you use to take roll, you are to take roll quickly and quietly without disturbing the class.** There is no need to involve the class in the roll-taking process.

Loops still holding pencils indicate that the students are absent.

The Effective Teacher

1. Has a posted assignment ready for the students.
2. Takes roll after the students are on task.
3. Does not disturb the class during roll taking.
4. Takes roll quickly and quietly.

Key Idea: A grade record book must show the results and progress of each student at all times.

CHAPTER 17

It's Prime Time

> **Prime time in school is the first few moments in a class.**
> If you blow these moments, you blow the impression,
> the sale, and the success of a class.

Prime time is a term invented by the television industry to denote the time when the audience is potentially at its largest. It is the most important time during the broadcast day; thus shows and sponsors jockey for position. That is why it is called *prime* time.

> **Student on-task work is the major activity during prime time. The students must immediately get to work when they enter the room.**

Thus an assignment must be available, and the students must know the procedure for getting to work immediately. (See Chapter 20.) Do not destroy prime time with non-prime-time activities such as taking roll, announcements, or paper shuffling.

An organized grade record book keeps time spent on roll taking and other record-keeping activities to a minimum. This is another practice of the efficient and effective teacher.

It's Really a Grade Record Book

From Day 1, if not beforehand, you will need to have a book to keep student records. You need to have this ready before you see a single class. This book is typically called a "grade book," and it comes in all different sizes, shapes, and configurations, depending on which one the district buys for you.

A grade book should more correctly be called a student record book or a grade record book. A grade record book contains far more than grades. It is used to keep various records about each student.

Typically, schools buy one kind of grade book and give it to all of their teachers. This, of course, assumes that if you are an elementary school teacher, you will keep records the same way whether you teach kindergarten or sixth grade.

Likewise, if you are a secondary school teacher, the physical education teacher, the vocational technology teacher, or the English composition teacher, you will all keep records identically. Ridiculous, yet this is what is assumed when all the teachers get the same grade record book!

The Problems with Most Grade Record Books

The problem with many grade books is that they have only one line, maybe two lines, to record information for a student. Thus you have these problems:

✓ You only have space enough to show one record, such as attendance.

✓ To record additional information, you have to turn to another page and possibly even write all the names again. You are constantly flipping pages back and forth.

✓ If the number of students in your class exceeds the number of lines on a page, you have to repeat the information, such as dates, assignments, and tests, at the top of every page.

✓ The major problem comes when you need a progress report or a summary for report card grades. Because there is only one line to record all information for each student, you must sift through attendance, homework grades, projects, tests, and anything else you may record for the student to determine the student's progress. Progress is not readily apparent at a glance.

Because of the inadequacies of most grade books, the correct title for this chapter should be "How to Prepare Your Own Grade Record Book." Or, if you are planning to buy your own grade record book, you must first determine how you will be grading and what records you will be keeping so that you will know what to look for when you shop.

It is imperative that you decide before you begin the school year just what you want to record. People in other professions do the same thing:

✓ An ACCOUNTANT sets up the categories on a ledger before entering numbers.

✓ A BUSINESS PERSON names the columns on a spreadsheet before entering the data.

✓ A RESEARCHER names the columns and rows in a table so as to know what data to look for as the research progresses.

✓ A STATISTICIAN names the columns in a baseball box score so that the results can be entered in the right places as the game progresses.

✓ A BRIDE-TO-BE designs a chart to record information about the people coming to the wedding.

You must determine what you want for each student, for example:

Attendance	Project grades
Homework assignments	Extra-credit work
Classroom work	Class participation
Test grades	Classroom behavior
Skills mastered	Cumulative progress

FIRST SEMESTER

Begins _____ 19____

Ends _____ 19____

QI

Subject CORE B		1st WEEK					2nd WEEK				
Indicate Calendar Date ➔		8/27	28	29	30	31	9/3	4	5	6	7
Grade ATTENDANCE		M	T	W	T	F	M	T	W	T	F
The Blank Columns at the Right May Be Used to Indicate Assignments	Text Book No.						Holiday				
ANDRIANO, LEO	1				A						
AQUINO, JODY	2										
CASTRO, RHONDA	3				A		T				
COLLINS, JOEL	4			A			A				
DOAN, DUC	5										
ELDER, SCOTT	6										
FLYNN, SANDI	7										
GILBERTSON, ERIC	8				A						
HUNG, VINCENT	9										
JAEHNICHEN, TONY	10										
KIM, PETER	11						A	A	A		
KWONG, MAY	12										
LEVINE, SALLY	13						T				
McBIRNEY, NANCY	14										
POLOMSKI, ROBYN	15										
SAKAI, AKIO	16										
	17										

Grade books with one or two lines may not have enough space for all the information you wish to record.

> **Designed properly, a grade book should let you see each student's RESULTS and PROGRESS immediately.**

Keeping the Three Basic Records

To keep good student records, you probably need three, maybe even four lines after each student's name. Because most commercial grade books have one or two lines after each name, you may have record-keeping problems if you are given an inadequate grade book.

Neat Shelves Were More Important than School Effectiveness

Mr. Fussy was the most appropriate name for the registrar at our school. His dress, his office, and his record keeping were immaculate, to the point where Felix Unger of *The Odd Couple* would have been Oscar Madison in his office.

For nearly two decades at this high school, he was the sole determiner as to what grade book we were to use. He ordered the grade books, distributed them during preschool orientation, and collected them on the last day of school and checked them to be sure that the grades were recorded properly. You did not get signed out until you got his seal of approval.

Why did he use the same grade book for decades? Because all the grade books were the same size and they all fit on the same kinds of shelves in his record-keeping room!

After all, he would tell us, he needed to be able to find and interpret a student's records, if needed, years after you may be gone. No argument there.

However, the fact that the grade books were outdated in their design was immaterial. What mattered to Mr. Fussy was that they all fit neatly on his shelves.

The Three Basic Records in a Grade Record Book Each Require a Separate Line

1. Attendance
2. Scores
3. Running Total

First Line: Attendance

An attendance record is probably mandated by the administration, if not by the school board. Attendance is a fact of life in most of our everyday endeavors. Schools are paid, people are paid, and students are graded by their presence on a job or in school. So make the recording of attendance as efficient and painless as possible. (See Chapter 16.)

The four common attendance records you need to keep are *present*, *absent*, *unexcused absence*, **and** *tardy*.

1. **Present:** Typically, nothing is noted in the space. This tells you that the student was in class on this day.

2. **Absent:** Typically, an *A* is noted in the space, telling you that the student was absent on this date. If the student brings a note that excuses the absence, you may want to draw a diagonal line through the *A*. This tells you that you have asked to see a note or authorization from the office, excusing the absence. If you do not see a diagonal line, it means that you are still waiting to see the excuse.

3. **Unexcused Absence:** If no note is presented explaining the absence, place a check or a breve (ˇ), the mark used to indicate a short vowel sound, above the *A*.

   An unexcused absence is simply one for which the student does not have a note of explanation, typically from a parent, a doctor, or another teacher. In some schools, you will determine if the absence is excused or not. In other schools, an attendance office will process this beforehand.

   How you treat an unexcused absence may be determined by school policy. Ask. A school may allow only so many unexcused absences before administrative action is taken. A good school will notify the home at once if an unexcused absence or cut has been determined. You should make it your responsibility to work with the administration and the home to nip the cutting of school or classes as quickly as possible. The principal beneficiary of this action will be your sanity and the lessening of stress in the classroom.

   Also, ask other teachers how they treat unexcused absences. **In most cases, an unexcused absence does not release a student from responsibility for the missed work or assignment.** The student must still make up the work.

   What an unexcused absence may mean is that the teacher may not be obligated to help the student make up the work; for instance:

   > *You cut the class, so you must accept the responsibility*
   > *for having missed the lecture, movie, or activity. You must*
   > *find the material you missed on your own. That is the price*
   > *you must pay when you do not show up for class.*

4. **Tardy:** This is typically denoted with a *T*. If the student has a pass excusing the tardiness, erase the *A*. If the student does not have a pass, the student is tardy. Erase the *A* and write a *T*, or just write a *T* over the *A*. Find out what the school policy is concerning tardiness. You may be asked to refer the student to the office after a certain number of tardies.

Computerized Grade Record Keeping for $3

Educational software is available for grade record keeping for no more than $3. This software is known as freeware or shareware and is public-domain material. There is software, such as **Grade Book Plus** or **Classroom Deluxe**, that will allow you to keep attendance, homework, and test scores. It will also calculate grades, generate and print progress reports, print class lists, make seating charts, and give a complete status on any student at the touch of a few keys.

Ask the computer teacher or look in the back of most computer magazines and you will see advertisements from companies offering public-domain software for sale, usually for less than $5. Send or call for a free catalog.

Second Line: Scores

You really need a second line to record the results of individual assignments, such as tests, projects, papers, worksheets, and homework. You can show results using whatever system you choose, in letter grade or numerical form. However, a numerical system is much better if you want to weight each score differently or if you want a running progress report.

Third Line: Running Total

Teachers are bombarded with requests for results on students' progress. You will get calls from parents, requests from the counseling department or the main office, forms to complete for determining extracurricular activity eligibility, and students' questions about their own progress. **An up-to-date overview of the progress of each student must be available at all times.**

With a three-line grade record book, as each score is entered on line 2, add it to the previous score on line 3. The progress report or running total allows immediate access to any student's cumulative grade. A student's progress is then available at any time.

You will appreciate having a three-line grade record book when it is time to turn in grades at the end of the grading period. Because you have a running progress report, you will not need to ask someone to summarize weeks of grades, wait in line to share a calculator or a computer, or waste valuable time determining a cumulative record.

While all others are gnashing their teeth, "trying to get their grades in," you can have time to go shopping, visit a health club, have a candlelight dinner, or rest with a good book because you planned the records you wanted to keep for each student and then constructed a grade record book to keep them.

You now have a grade record book that shows the results and progress of each student at all times.

The Three-Line Attendance and Grade Record Book

Merle Whaley is a teacher who was frustrated with the one-line grade book supplied by his district. So he told his wife, "I want to make a grade book anyone could understand that would also show each student's progress immediately." After two years and many changes, his *Three-Line Attendance and Grade Record Book* became more than a dream.

He says, "I finally had a book and a method of doing grades that easily displayed a student's records and progress in seconds. With three lines per student, I could now have attendance and-or essential skills on the first line. The second line could be used for all of the student's scores, such as daily work, quizzes, and test scores. Last, the very important third line would show a running total for each student. Now when parents call or visit the school, the progress is available in seconds."

Whaley's grade record book also has a tear-off top to each page. You only need to record the date or assignment ONCE, at the top of one of the pages, for all the

students having the same activity. All unused tops are torn off and index tabs are applied so that you can have fast access to any class. For instance, in a large class such as a band with 100 students, the band teacher writes the student's name once and the dates, activities, and scores just once for all 100 students. The tops of the five unused pages are torn off, saving a tremendous amount of time on grade record book work.

Whaley has also developed a continuous-form version of his grade record book for teachers who like to enter names and data on a computer before placing it in a loose-leaf binder.

What's admirable about Merle Whaley is that he epitomizes the professional teacher. He strives for excellence, constantly seeking and working on ways to make teaching more effective.

Information about the three-line grade record book is available from:

Merle J. Whaley
2941 B 1/2 Road
Grand Junction, CO 81503
(303) 241-7777

With a three-line grade book, you can show each student's attendance, score, and running total.

The Effective Teacher

1. Knows what results should be recorded.

2. Designs or modifies a grade record book to record these results.

3. Keeps a running progress of student work.

Key Idea: Effective teachers present their rules clearly and provide reasonable explanations of the need for them.

Investing Time in Teaching Discipline

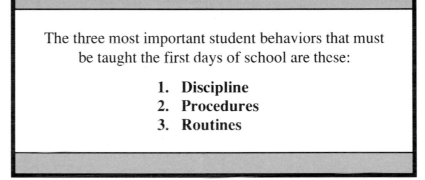

The three most important student behaviors that must be taught the first days of school are these:

1. **Discipline**
2. **Procedures**
3. **Routines**

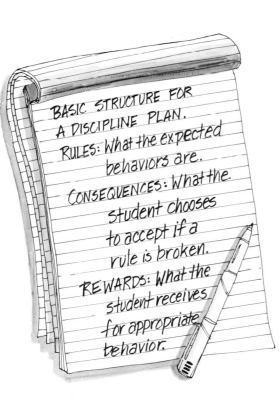

BASIC STRUCTURE FOR
A DISCIPLINE PLAN.
RULES: What the expected
behaviors are.
CONSEQUENCES: What the
student chooses
to accept if a
rule is broken.
REWARDS: What the
student receives
for appropriate
behavior.

The ineffective teacher is anxious to start the textbook, whereas the effective teacher invests time in teaching discipline and procedures, knowing that this will be repaid manifold in the effective use of class time. The key word is *invests*.

The Effective Teacher Invests Time in Teaching

Discipline Plan: Rules—Chapter 18

Discipline Plan:
    Consequences and Rewards—Chapter 19

Procedures and Routines—Chapter 20

Schoolwide Discipline Plan

The most effective discipline plans are applied universally, so that no matter where the students go, they encounter the same plan. **The key to a good discipline plan is schoolwide consistency.** This is why there are many schools where the students are all busily working and the teachers are all busily teaching—and everyone is happy and succeeding.

I Did Not Even Have a System

Dear Dr. Wong,

Thank you very much for the tapes you sent to me. The tape on <u>discipline</u> literally saved my sanity!

I did not have a fair system or even any system that worked until I heard and applied your advice.

My students, after we had the plan in effect, commented on how quiet the room was and how easily they could do their work. The principal commented about the plan and said how pleased he was to see quiet, working, behaved students!

As for me, I was really thinking of quitting the job, because I was so uptight, before you sent me those tapes. Thanks a million!

Sheila
Lethbridge, Alberta

The best discipline plan is a schoolwide discipline plan. In a schoolwide discipline plan, all persons in authority are trained in an agreed upon discipline plan, support the discipline plan, and continuously work together to refine the discipline plan. As a result, the students recognize and are familiar with the discipline plan. **The key to an effective schoolwide discipline plan is that everyone uses it with consistency!**

An analogy of a schoolwide discipline plan is the speed limit law. We know that there are speed limits, however, the limits differ for each neighborhood, community, and state. The acceptable speed is posted for all to see and abide by.

Likewise, in a schoolwide discipline plan, everyone does not necessarily have the same set of rules. The bus drivers may have different rules from the teachers, food-service personnel, nurses, librarians, paraprofessionals, and counselors. Each person in authority can have a separate set of rules.

- A schoolwide discipline plan is posted in every room, bus (yes, bus), office, gymnasium, cafeteria, library, hall, and everywhere else where there is an employee responsible for the safety and education of the students.

- The plan has the same basic design so that when a student goes from room to room or to the office, cafeteria, bus, library, or out to recess, it is the same basic plan.

- Since everyone at the school uses the same plan with consistency, the students know what is expected of them and the staff support each other. This also makes life much easier for each new employee, because a plan is already in effect.

- Introducing a discipline plan to each new class of students is made easy because a prevailing plan and culture already exists at the school.

Why You Should Have Rules

> **In a classroom, you want a discipline plan that will minimize classroom disturbances and maximize learning.**

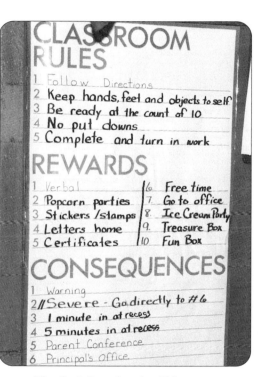

The discipline plan should be posted for the first day of school, with a copy ready for distribution to each student.

You, not the administration or the counselors, are primarily responsible for communicating and maintaining behavior. The others will help, but you, first and foremost, must know what you expect from your students.

The most successful classes are those where the teacher has a clear idea of what is expected from the students and the students know what the teacher expects from them. Expectations can be stated as rules.

✓ Rules are expectations of appropriate student behavior.

✓ After thorough deliberation, decide on your rules and write them down or post them **before the first day of school**.

✓ Communicate clearly to your students what you expect as appropriate behavior.

✓ It is easier to maintain good behavior than to change inappropriate behavior that has become established.

✓ You will have firm confidence in your ability to manage a class if you have a clear idea of what you expect from your students and they know that that is what you expect from them.

✓ Rules immediately create a work-oriented atmosphere.

✓ Rules create a strong expectation about the things that are important to you.

> **The research shows that the most effective schools are those with a well-ordered environment and high academic expectations.**

Continuum of Discipline Plans

There are many discipline plans. They all have their good and bad points, but they are all plans. Plans are not charters, laws, or theorems.

If you are looking for a foolproof discipline system that works automatically, you will never find one. What you need to do is to develop a plan of your own, based on what you want to accomplish. You have plans for vacations, parties, and weddings. **If you do not have a plan, you are planning to fail.**

Discipline plans range from those where the student is in charge to those where the teacher is in charge. These form a continuum. The method suggested in this book falls more toward the teacher-in-charge end of the spectrum.

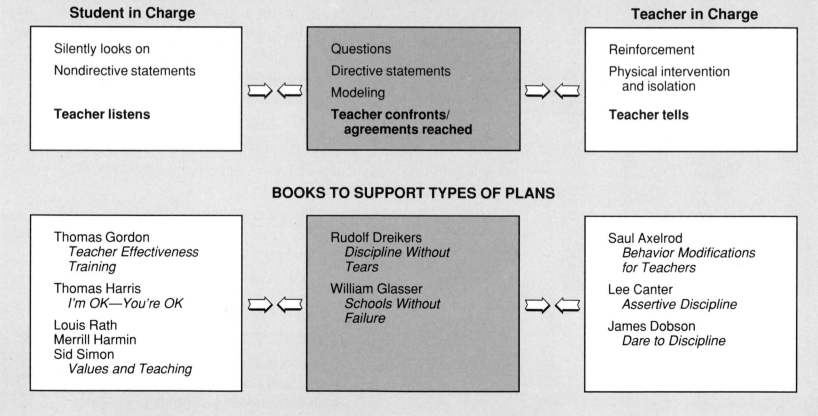

TEACHER BEHAVIORS

Student in Charge

Silently looks on

Nondirective statements

Teacher listens

Questions

Directive statements

Modeling

Teacher confronts/ agreements reached

Teacher in Charge

Reinforcement

Physical intervention and isolation

Teacher tells

BOOKS TO SUPPORT TYPES OF PLANS

Thomas Gordon
Teacher Effectiveness Training

Thomas Harris
I'm OK—You're OK

Louis Rath
Merrill Harmin
Sid Simon
Values and Teaching

Rudolf Dreikers
Discipline Without Tears

William Glasser
Schools Without Failure

Saul Axelrod
Behavior Modifications for Teachers

Lee Canter
Assertive Discipline

James Dobson
Dare to Discipline

The Two Kinds of Rules

The function of a rule is to prevent or encourage behavior by clearly stating student expectations.

The Two Kinds of Rules

✓ General

✓ Specific

General Rules. General rules are more encompassing and may cover a plethora of behaviors. Here are some examples:

> Respect others.
> Take care of your school.
> Be polite and helpful.
> Keep the room (or cafeteria) clean.
> Behave in the library.

The advantage of general rules is that they offer more flexibility in that a great deal of behavior can be covered by a few general rules.

The disadvantage of general rules is that they must be explained, otherwise students will not know exactly what behaviors are acceptable and not acceptable in the classroom. For instance, students must be told that respecting others includes no hitting, no stealing, no tattling, no name-calling, and so on.

Specific Rules. Specific rules are to the point and clearly cover one behavior. Here are examples:

> Be in class on time.
> Keep your hands, feet, and other objects to yourself.
> Listen to instructions the first time they are given.
> Do not curse or use profanity.
> Have all materials ready to use when the bell rings.

The advantage of specific rules is that they clearly state the expected student behavior.

The disadvantage of specific rules is that you are limited to no more than five rules. (See page 148.) Therefore, you must (1) have good classroom management skills and (2) know exactly what behaviors are important to you.

General rules are more successfully used by effective, veteran teachers who have learned how to develop good classroom behaviors over the years. Go and watch these teachers, as this is where you want to be someday. They never raise their voice; they seldom get angry; they don't get flustered. All they do is give the student a signal, a wave of the hand, or a stare—and the student behaves. (The stare is called the "teacher look" and is discussed on page 167.)

Specific rules are probably better for the newer teacher or the experienced teacher looking for a better discipline system. You can always move from specific to general rules during the school year as the students learn about your expectations.

✓ Academic behavior should not appear on your list of rules. Such things as doing homework, writing in ink or typing, and turning in assignments fall in the realm of procedures (Chapter 20) and academic performance (Unit D). Your discipline plan should be concerned with behavior, not academic work.

✓ If possible, state rules positively, not negatively. This is not always desirable, as the following are to the point, understandable, and incontestable:

> No cursing or swearing.
> No smoking.
> No fighting on the playground.

Regardless of whether you use general or specific rules, the important thing is that you must have clear expectations. These must be ready on the first day of school so that everyone, including yourself, knows what they are.

What Should My Rules Be?

Refrain from copying and using other people's rules. You cannot expect your students to behave if you do not know how you want them to behave. **It is urgent that you state your specific behavior expectations.**

What should my rules be? Just close your eyes and say to yourself:

This is what I want to accomplish. Now, if the students will only do these three things, I'd be the happiest...

Here are some examples of specific rules that you may want to consider for your discipline plan.

Suggested Specific Rules

1. Follow directions the first time they are given.
2. Raise your hand and wait for permission to speak.
3. Stay in your seat unless you have permission to do otherwise.
4. Keep hands, feet, and other objects to yourself.
5. No cursing or teasing.

Specific Rules for Elementary Grades

1. Wait for directions with no talking.
2. Eyes front when the teacher is talking.
3. Change tasks quickly and quietly.
4. Complete the morning routine.
5. Report directly to the assigned area.

Specific Rules for High School

1. Be in your seat when the bell rings.
2. Bring all books and materials to class.
3. No personal grooming during class time.
4. Sit in your assigned seat daily.
5. Follow directions the first time they are given.

Specific Rules for the Playground

1. Swing only forward and backward on the swings.
2. Do not throw ice or snow at anyone.
3. Sliding paths must be clear before you start your slide.
4. Only two on the seesaw or teeter-totter at a time.

Read Chapter 20 before working on your discipline plan. What you think is a rule may be a procedure. Know the difference between a rule and a procedure.

Specific Rules for the Cafeteria

1. Follow correct traffic flow from serving counter to table and from table to trash to exit.
2. Make your seating choice and stay put.
3. All food is to be eaten in the cafeteria.
4. Raise your hand to be excused when finished eating.
5. Scrape food into bins with a rubber spatula and put utensils in the water.

How to Introduce Your Rules

It is important to introduce the discipline plan on the first or second day of school. Before you do so, check to see that the following things have been done:

✓ You have carefully planned for what you want to accomplish.

✓ You have written the rules to help you accomplish those goals.

✓ You have posted the rules, along with the consequences and rewards. (See Chapter 19.)

✓ You have welcomed the class (Unit B), introduced yourself (Chapter 13), and taken care of administrative duties (Chapter 16).

Why You Should Have Only Three to Five Rules

Have you ever noticed that your phone number, credit card, social security number, auto license number, and zip code are in groups of five or less? That is because people find it easier to remember numbers in groups of three to five.

■ Limit rules to a number that you and the students can readily remember—never more than five.

■ If you need more than five rules, do not post more than five at any one time.

■ The rules need not cover all aspects of behavior in the classroom.

■ You have the right to replace a rule with another.

■ As a new rule becomes necessary, replace an older one with it. The rule you replace can be retained as an "unwritten rule," which the students have learned. The students are still responsible for the one you have replaced.

Numbers in groups of three to five are easy to remember.

To introduce your discipline plan this is what you might say:

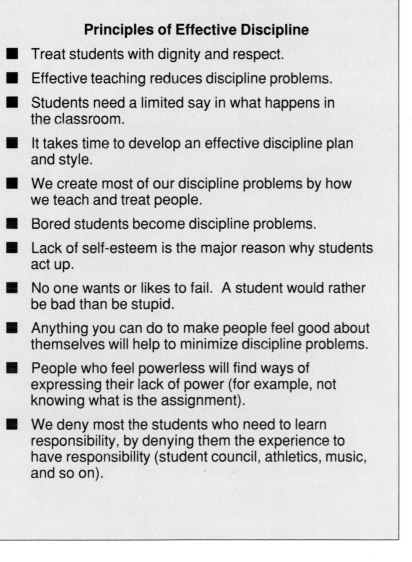

Principles of Effective Discipline

■ Treat students with dignity and respect.

■ Effective teaching reduces discipline problems.

■ Students need a limited say in what happens in the classroom.

■ It takes time to develop an effective discipline plan and style.

■ We create most of our discipline problems by how we teach and treat people.

■ Bored students become discipline problems.

■ Lack of self-esteem is the major reason why students act up.

■ No one wants or likes to fail. A student would rather be bad than be stupid.

■ Anything you can do to make people feel good about themselves will help to minimize discipline problems.

■ People who feel powerless will find ways of expressing their lack of power (for example, not knowing what is the assignment).

■ We deny most the students who need to learn responsibility, by denying them the experience to have responsibility (student council, athletics, music, and so on).

Step 1. "We are all here for **YOU**, for you to succeed and to enjoy this class. Because I care for each of you, I am here to help you. So I will not allow you to do anything that will interfere with your success in this class."

Step 2. "We will be working together this year. We need to have a class where you can come without fear of being ridiculed or threatened. Because I care for all of you, I will not allow you to do anything that will interfere with someone else who is trying to learn."

Step 3. "I am the teacher, and I am looking forward to being your teacher this year. I have an exciting year of learning planned for you, and I will not allow you to do anything to interfere with my desire to teach you. Nor will I allow you to do anything that will interfere with all of us having an enjoyable year."

Step 4. "So that **YOU** can learn, so that **WE** can all learn, so that **I** can teach, I have a set of rules to ensure that we will have an orderly classroom."

The rules should be written and permanently posted in the classroom and given to students on paper or copied by students into their notebook.

Should You Involve Students in Forming Rules?

The extent to which students can participate in the formation of rules is quite limited.

1. Schoolwide and district rules must be accepted as they are. These generally refer to such things as attendance, substance abuse, use of the facilities, and fund-raising activities. These and many more are in a policy book.

2. Classroom policies essential to managing instruction cannot be left to student discretion, for example, attentiveness, homework, attendance, hitting, profanity, smoking, and use of the facilities and equipment.

What is left is rather limited: gum chewing, eating, talking during seat work, and pencil sharpening. Most of these are not rules anyway and should be treated as procedures (Chapter 20).

The best discipline plan is an industrywide or schoolwide discipline plan.

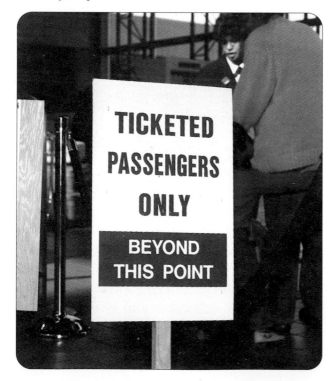

TICKETED PASSENGERS ONLY

BEYOND THIS POINT

District and School Rules

Many schools have rules prohibiting or requiring certain behaviors, and the teachers are expected to enforce these rules. It is to everyone's advantage to do so! A set of rules enforced consistently acquires greater legitimacy because the rules are everyone's rules. You must know the school rules.

■ You can be sued for negligence if you allow a behavior that is forbidden and the student is injured.

■ Find the rules in the teachers' handbook.

■ Listen carefully at orientation, faculty, and department meetings.

■ Ask your administrators, department head, another teacher, or the secretary about school and district rules.

Rather than spend too much time involved with whole class formation of rules, it may be better to discuss matters such as these:

✓ Why rules are needed

✓ Why a particular rule will help students succeed

✓ Specific examples of general rules, such as "What does it mean to 'respect others'?"

Rules or Responsibilities

Rules can be orders, or they can be responsibilities. They are orders if you autocratically impose them on the class. They are responsibilities if the class agrees that they are fair rules and are essential for the running of the class.

Effective teachers present their rules clearly and provide reasonable explanations of the need for them. After the rules have been explained to the students, there should be an understanding and agreement that these will the class rules. The rules then become the responsibility of the students.

There are rules for driving, for playing baseball, and for using a credit card. If you accept playing by these rules, you are a responsible person. In the best discipline plan, the students are responsible for their own behavior.

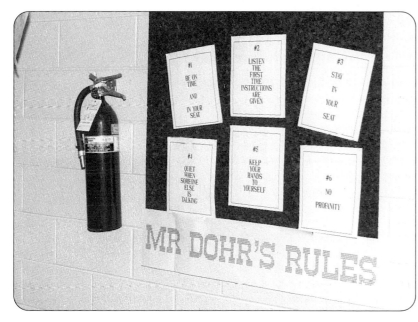

A typical set of rules posted by a teacher. An unwritten rule was reviewed at mid-year.

The Effective Teacher

1. Has the discipline plan posted when the students arrive on the first day of school.

2. Posts a maximum of three to five rules or responsibilities.

3. Explains the posted rules and is willing to make changes as the class situation requires.

CHAPTER 19

 Key Idea: Rules are most effective when there are consequences to enforce and reward them.

Why Rules Are Broken

> **When dealing with young people, especially children, many rules must have consequences to enforce them and rewards to validate them.**

The world is full of rules. There are rules at home, at school, and in the community. There are rules when you play baseball, fly on an airplane, and smoke on an elevator. Why are there rules?

Rules Are Used to Set Limits

✓ The effective teacher has fair and reasonable rules that set limits on appropriate behavior.

✓ Appropriate behavior can then foster student participation, achievement, learning, and success.

✓ The rules are posted and distributed to or copied by the students.

Teachers have rules:

Raise your hand for permission before speaking.
The teacher dismisses the class, not the bell.
Return all supplies to where you got them.
No grooming in class.
Follow directions the first time they are given.

A typical set of consequences posted by a teacher.

IF YOU CHOOSE TO BREAK A RULE

FIRST TIME: Name on board. Warning.
SECOND TIME: One check.* 15 minutes after school on Thursday.
THIRD TIME: Two checks. 30 minutes after school on Thursday.
FOURTH TIME: Three checks. 45 minutes after school on Thursday. Parents called.
FIFTH TIME: Four checks. 60 minutes after school on Thursday, referral written and student sent to the office.
SEVERE DISRUPTION: Student sent immediately to office.

Names and checks erased each Thursday afternoon

*Secondary school classroom: Erase names once a week if students meet one period a day. This is why Thursday was used in the example.

Elementary school classroom: Erase names at the end of each day if the teacher has the same students all day.

Parents have rules:

Do not leave your dirty clothes on the floor.
Come in by 10 P.M.
Do your homework.
Practice your piano lesson.
Do not hit your sister.

The community has rules:

Stop your car at the red light.
Pay your taxes.
Place garbage in the receptacles.
Do not deface public property.
Pull to the curb when you hear a fire engine.

With so many rules, why are rules broken? Rules are broken, perhaps, when consequences are not evident. **When dealing with young people, especially children, many rules must have consequences to enforce them.**

Students know that they can break certain rules because the results are consistent and predictable. That is, nothing will happen to the violator who breaks a rule. The responsible adult may find this hard to accept, but many children believe that nothing is wrong until they are caught.

Imagine this typical classroom setting. A teacher is speaking at the front of the room. The students are in their seats facing the teacher. The teacher is explaining a diagram on the chalkboard.

Student A . . . Without permission goes to the pencil sharpener.

Student B . . . Walks over to another student to ask to borrow a pencil.

Student C . . . Abruptly speaks up to ask the teacher a question not relevant to the topic.

Student D . . . Leans over to say something to student E.

Students F through Z . . . Look on.

Students are aware of a teacher's enforcement or nonenforcement of the classroom rules.

✓ Students will test the rules to find the limits of their behavior and to determine whether a rule will be enforced or not.

✓ Students will swiftly violate a rule that others are violating if the rule is not enforced.

✓ Students often observe that teachers do not mean what they say.

Therefore, do not say anything—**POST YOUR CONSEQUENCES.**

Consequences Can Be Positive or Negative

Consequences are what result when a person abides by or breaks the rules. When students break a rule, there needs to be a penalty or negative consequence. Many teachers, especially at the elementary level, prefer to use the simpler word *penalty* on their posted discipline plan. Most children understand *penalty* because it appears in many of their games. The word *consequence* is used in this book to imply a negative consequence or penalty.

> ## The Two Kinds of Consequences
>
> Positive consequences: **REWARDS** that result when people abide by the rules.
>
> Negative consequences: **PENALTIES** that result when people break the rules.

Example of Negative Consequences

Classroom Rules:

1. Follow rules the first time they are given.
2. Raise your hand for permission to speak.
3. Raise your hand for permission to leave your seat.
4. Do not touch anyone else with your hands, your feet, or any object.
5. No cursing or profanity.

Consequences or Penalties:

1. Your name on the board =
   10 minutes' detention at lunch hour
2. One check =
   20 minutes' detention at lunch hour
3. Two checks =
   30 minutes' detention at lunch hour
   and your home will be called
4. Three checks =
   Entire lunch hour detention, home called,
   and you will be sent to the office

Rules must have consequences.

The consequences shown on the previous page are examples only. They are not to be used universally. Lunch hour detention may be illegal in your district, as board policy may state that you cannot deprive anyone of lunch. Lunch hour detention is also not recommended for students in the primary grades. Having lunch in the room with the teacher may be considered a reward rather than a penalty by many children.

Reasonable and Logical Consequences

The best consequences are reasonable and logical. Students will rebel only when the consequences do not make sense.

✓ A reasonable consequence is one that follows logically from the behavior rather than one that is arbitrarily imposed.

✓ The best logical consequences teach the students to choose between acceptable and unacceptable actions.

Logical and Illogical Consequences

Student Behavior	Logical Consequence	Illogical Consequence
Chews gum	Disposes of gum; writes rule 50 times	Everyone disposes of gum
Turns in sloppy paper	Redoes the paper	Teacher refuses the paper
Walks in noisily	Walks in again	Teacher ignores
Passes paper in incorrectly	Repasses the paper 10 times	Teacher deducts 10 points
Arrives late	Misses instruction and suffers consequences	Teacher ignores
Does not bring textbook	Does without for period	Teacher supplies textbook
Does not bring pencil or pen	Teacher has a box full (why fight it) and has student sign for it	Student sits without one

---

Reasonable and Logical Consequences

A demerit or fine

Detention

Write six ways to correct the problem

Being the last to leave

Deprivation of some reward

Exclusion from class participation

✓ Avoid consequences that are related to the academic grade, such as deducting a grade or points for that day. (This may not always be possible, however.)

✓ Most students will accept reasonable consequences because they recognize the need for teachers to maintain an orderly classroom to help them learn.

✓ A consequence is reasonable when the student sees that it is reasonable and logical and in the student's best interest.

✓ When students see the logical connection between what they do and what happens to them, it helps them learn to choose what is appropriate and what is inappropriate behavior.

If a student chooses to break a rule, put the student's name or a check on the board without interrupting the lesson.

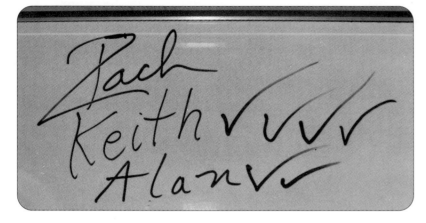

✓ Students will cooperate more readily when they understand how consequences follow logically from their behavior.

✓ Explain consequences ahead of time, when the rules they accompany are presented. The subsequent use of the penalty will be more acceptable to the students.

✓ The consequence should be suitable and proportional to the violation; that is, the penalty should fit the crime.

✓ Choose consequences that are uncomfortable for the student.

✓ Tell the student that the consequence was the result of his or her choice. (See "What Are You Picking on Me For?" on page 160.)

Do Not Stop the Lesson

Cardinal Principle

Do not stop instruction when giving out the consequence.

When you see a violation of one of the rules, immediately give out the penalty.

Give out the penalty quietly as you continue with the lesson or classwork.

When you stop the lesson to penalize a student, you disrupt a class in the middle of a lesson, interrupt an important point you are making, or disturb the class while they are working. **DO NOT STOP THE LESSON.**

Here are some suggested ways for giving out penalties.

Chalkboard: Do not stop the lecture, discussion, or movie. Just go to the designated area on the chalkboard and write the student's name or place a check after the student's name.

You may need to take a few seconds at the end of the period or day to remind those students of their penalty.

Failure to work off the penalty automatically moves the student up to the next level of the consequences or doubles it.

Lucy's smile is an indication of appropriate behavior.

Transparency: This is similar to the chalkboard method except an overhead projector is used. This method is especially useful for floating teachers, who must move from room to room. You can take the transparency with you and have a record for each of your classes.

Ticket: This is the same concept as receiving a traffic ticket. Develop a method for giving the student a ticket. There is no need for any fancy form. A piece of paper with the **student's name and the number of the rule broken** is all that is needed.

This method is ideal for circumstances where you do not have a chalkboard or transparency projector, such as physical education classes, an assembly, or a field trip.

You will need to keep a record of who has been given a ticket. This can be done in your grade record book, with a carbon, or with carbonless forms.

Pattern: If the students have made patterns or cutouts to represent themselves for the bulletin board (page 131) and you see a rule violation, go to this board and "red-flag" the student's pattern. A red flag could be the addition of a self-adhesive note, removing the pattern, or turning the pattern over. If the pattern has been laminated, a felt pen mark may suffice.

This method is effective in the primary grades where children may not be able to read their names on the chalkboard or a transparency.

Heart: Have the students make another pattern with their name on it. Place all the patterns inside a heart, your heart, on the bulletin board. If there is a violation of a rule, remove the pattern and place it outside your heart. No primary grade student wants to be outside the teacher's heart!

What Are You Picking on Me For?

What do you say to the following three major questions asked by students worldwide?

What are you picking on me for?
What did I do?
Everyone else is doing it. Why me?

Stand in front of a mirror and practice the following 100 times until you can say it calmly and automatically every time one of these questions is asked:

Because you CHOSE to break the rule.
Because you CHOSE to break rule number x.

Do not argue. Do not ask the student if he or she is questioning your authority. Do not yell, scream, or raise your voice. Just calmly say every time:

Because you CHOSE to break the rule.
Because you CHOSE to break the rule.
Because you CHOSE to break the rule.
Because you CHOSE to break the rule.

After a few days no one will ever ask, "Why are you picking on me?" because they will all know exactly what you will say.

The key word in the phrase is *CHOSE. Chose* means that you are responsible and accountable for your actions. You are teaching your students responsibility and accountability.

The teacher is not picking on you. There are five rules in the classroom. The rules were discussed, agreed on, and signed. So when you CHOOSE to break one of the rules, you must accept the consequence.

After a few weeks or months, if someone should ask you, "Why are you picking on me?" all you have to do is stand and smile at the student. The entire class will respond for you:

Because you CHOSE to break the rule!

Getting Administrative Support

You will be indeed fortunate if you are hired as a new teacher and find yourself at a school with a schoolwide discipline plan. This is like getting hired to work at Nordstrom (page 88). Successful businesses and schools have an established culture. You can fit into the culture and devote more time to student achievement.

Have high expectations that the administration wants to help. They want to help and cooperate with you, as they want a disciplined situation as much as you do, maybe even more so. You need to approach them in the same way you would approach your students, in a nonconfrontational, friendly, cooperative manner.

✓ If there is no schoolwide discipline plan, go to your administrator with your plan.

✓ It is imperative that you have thought out your plan. You need to know what you want to accomplish.

✓ Present your plan, in writing, with your rules, consequences, and rewards. Most administrators know this system, so it will not be a surprise to any of them.

✓ Check that your plan does not violate any board policy and can be supported by the administration.

✓ Show the administrator what YOU plan to do if the students violate the rules.

✓ Show the administrator that you plan to refer the student to the office after a certain number of violations.

✓ Ask the administration what they plan to do when you refer the students to the office. It is only consistent and fair that the office knows what you plan to do, that you know what the office will do, and that both the students and their parents know what you and the office will do.

Getting Parental Support

Your objective is to acquire parental support to work cooperatively with you in correcting a student's misbehavior. Your purpose should not be to humiliate the student, "get the student into trouble," aggravate the parents, or have the parents "do something to the kid."

To assist in acquiring parental support, give the parents a copy of the discipline plan to use as a basis for home-school cooperation.

Parents need to see your discipline plan, discuss it with the child, and sign it. You will, of course, want the students to sign it also as an indication that they understand and accept the plan as discussed in class and at home.

The form should be simple and easy to understand. Don't forget to give the parents and the student an extra copy for their records. The form can be as simple as the one shown here.

How to Call the Home

Effective teachers communicate and work with **the homes cooperatively.** However, calling the home is not something most teachers like to do. This is because most teachers do not know how to call the home. They are as scared to call the home as the homes are as scared to hear from the school. Such a call usually brings bad news. But it need not be that way, even if it is the third violation and you need to call the home to have a misbehavior corrected.

Here is a wonderful system that not only works but also teaches the student at the same time **problem solving, responsibility, and self-discipline.**

Note on your discipline plan that you will be calling the home during one of the consequences. At this consequence, have the student complete the form shown on the following page, "My Action Plan."

Discipline Plan for Room 16
Classroom Rules

1. Have all appropriate materials and supplies at your table and be seated when the bell rings.

2. Respect the people, equipment, and furnishings of Room 16.

3. Adjust your voice level to suit the activity.

4. Follow directions the first time they are given.

5. Observe all rules in the student handbook.

If You Choose to Break a Rule

First Time: Name on board. Warning.
Second Time: One check. 15 minutes after school on Thursday.
Third Time: Two checks. 30 minutes after school on Thursday.
Fourth Time: Three checks. 45 minutes after school on Thursday and parents called.
Fifth Time: Four checks. 60 minutes after school on Thursday, referral written, and student sent to the office.

Severe disruption: Student sent immediately to the office.

Names and checks erased each Thursday afternoon.

Rewards

Praise (daily)
Positive notes home (random)
Whole-class radio time or free time (weekly)
"Raise a Grade" certificate (monthly)
"Good as Gold" raffle ticket (every 9 weeks)
Movie and popcorn party for class (every 9 weeks)
Various other positive perks throughout the school year

STUDENTS: I have read this classroom discipline plan and understand it. I will honor it while in Room 16.

_____   _____
Signature   Date

PARENTS: My child has discussed the classroom discipline plan with me. I understand it and will support it.

_____   _____
Signature   Date

****IMPORTANT****
KEEP THIS SHEET IN YOUR BINDER AT ALL TIMES.

Thank you for your help.

_____
Teacher's signature

My Action Plan

1. What's the problem?

2. What's causing the problem? (Please list the factors.)

3. What plan will you use to solve the problem?

Student's signature _____

Date _____

My Action Plan

1. What's the problem?
   I have too many tardies.

2. What's causing the problem? (Please list the factors.)
   I can't make it here in 7 minutes from PE.
   It's too far away.
   I have to shower.
   I have to return the towel.
   I have to get a drink.
   I have to see my girlfriend.
   I have to return my library book.
   I have to go to my locker.
   The lock is hard to open.
   I have to go to the bathroom.
   I have to see the counselor.
   I have to check and see if I made the team.

3. What plan will you use to solve the problem?
   I will shower.
   I will return the towel.
   I will see my girlfriend quickly.
   I will go to my locker.
   I will move faster.

Will Watson
Student's signature

October 3, 1991
Date

Step 1. Give the student a copy of "My Action Plan" and be prepared to work with the student on answering the three questions:

1. What's the problem?
2. What's causing the problem?
3. What plan will you use to solve the problem?

What's the problem? Indicate the rule or rules the student has violated.

What's causing the problem? The student is to list all the factors that are causing the problem to occur.

Work with the student in a **PROBLEM-SOLVING** mode here. Share with the student that the only way a person can solve a problem is first to isolate and identify it. You are not interested in degrading or scolding the student. You want to teach the student how to solve a problem, a technique that the student can use in future life.

What plan will you use to solve the problem?
The student is to write the action plan needed to solve the problem.

Have the student look at the factors causing the problem. Show the student that the way to solve a problem is to change, eliminate, or correct the factors causing the problem. Help the student to see this logic.

Have the student write a plan based on the causative factors listed under the second question. The student now takes **RESPONSIBILITY** for the plan. You did not tell the student what to do. The student, through problem solving, devised his or her own plan to correct the problem. You are teaching responsibility.

Now, for the student to carry through with his or her responsibility, encouragement is needed from the home and the school to get the student to achieve **SELF-DISCIPLINE**.

> **Note the three key concepts in the value of using "My Action Plan":**
>
> ✓ Problem solving
>
> ✓ Responsibility
>
> ✓ Self-discipline

Step 2. Have the student indicate responsibility by signing the action plan.

If the problem is not corrected, go back and modify the third part of the action plan. It is much better to teach problem solving, responsibility, and self-discipline than to yell, scream, and flunk.

Yelling, screaming, and flunking benefit no one. Learning to be responsible and self-disciplined benefits all of society. Through persistence, have the student work on the action plan over and over until the problem is corrected.

Commend the student when that occurs.

Step 3. Tell the student to show the action plan to a parent. Inform the student that when you call tonight, you will not call to cause trouble. You will be calling to discuss the action plan.

You will be calling to discuss the plan or the behavior, not the person. This is another one of those cardinal principles of teaching:

> **Always deal with the behavior, not the person. You leave a person's dignity intact when you deal only with the behavior or the issue.**

Step 4. Call the home in a pleasant, friendly, but businesslike manner. Explain that you are happy to have the student in your class and that the purpose of tonight's call is to discuss the action plan.

The beauty of the action plan system is that there is no argument, confrontation, or aggravation with the parents. Neither party wants that. You did not call to degrade the child, because no parent likes to hear, "You have a no good, rotten kid who can't come to class on time." Tell them this and they will say, "The schools are doing a terrible job." No one wins and the child is not helped, which is the reason for your call.

Step 5. Explain to the parent that the child has come up with a plan. Butter up the parent by explaining that this is something the student has done as a result of problem solving and the use of higher-order thinking skills.

Step 6. The reason you are calling is simple:

> *Mrs. Watson, I am calling to see if I can enlist the cooperation of the home, working together with the school, to see if we can encourage Will to follow through with what he said he would be RESPONSIBLE for doing.*

If the parent refuses, go on with your life. You tried. But most parents will not say no because the one thing that both parents and teachers want is RESPONSIBILITY.

They can't say no to responsibility.

The parents will think the world of you. So will the student. This was all possible because you operated in a responsible, problem-solving, self-disciplined way yourself.

A typical set of rewards posted by a teacher.

Rewards or Positive Consequences

Everyone likes and expects special recognition, rewards, or incentives when good work is done. Perks, rewards, honors, prizes, and awards are commonplace.

Although rewards are a fact of life, the time has come in education when the wholesale bribery system of giving out endless supplies of stickers, candies, and other tangibles has got to come to a halt. Let's stop the "what's in it for me" welfare and bribery system. The best reward is the satisfaction of a job well done. That is self-discipline, and self-discipline is what discipline is all about. You can't teach self-discipline if the students are always looking for more "goodies."

One of us has operated very successfully during our years of teaching with only one reward: **30 minutes of free time on Friday.** This was also a classwide reward. Everyone had to work together cooperatively the entire week for the reward.

The "30 minutes of free time on Friday" was effective because it was not a thing. The time was used, mostly, for schoolwork. There were no popcorn parties, pizza parties, or movies to plan for and cleanup after, just free time to work!

> **Rewards**
>
> Praise (daily)
>
> Positive notes home (random)
>
> Whole-class radio time or free time (weekly)
>
> "Raise a Grade" coupon (monthly)
>
> "Good as Gold" raffle ticket (every 9 weeks)
>
> Movie and popcorn party for class (every 9 weeks)
>
> VIP certificate from principal (every 9 weeks)
>
> Various other positive perks throughout the year

✓ Like rules and consequences, post your rewards.

✓ Indicate the time factor associated with the reward. Will the reward be given daily, weekly, when?

✓ Explain the system by which the reward is to be earned. That is, you do not give rewards; the students earn their rewards.

✓ The most common way of earning rewards, on a class basis, is to put a tally mark somewhere when you catch someone following directions or doing good. When the class has earned 50 tally marks, it can have the reward.

✓ If you don't like tally marks, use marbles in a jar, raffle tickets, or red indicators on a thermometer.

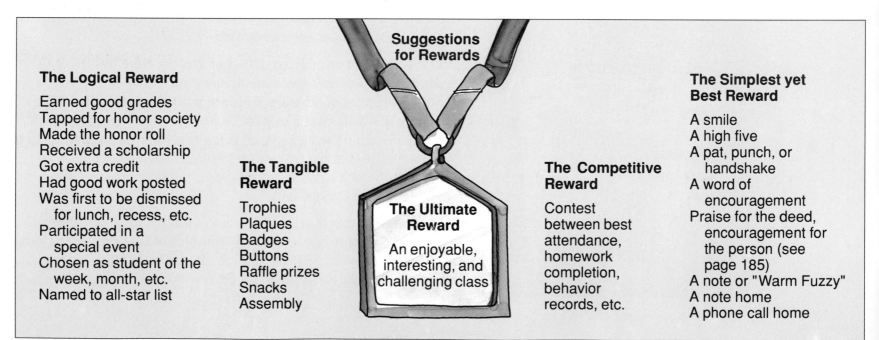

Suggestions for Rewards

The Logical Reward

Earned good grades
Tapped for honor society
Made the honor roll
Received a scholarship
Got extra credit
Had good work posted
Was first to be dismissed for lunch, recess, etc.
Participated in a special event
Chosen as student of the week, month, etc.
Named to all-star list

The Tangible Reward

Trophies
Plaques
Badges
Buttons
Raffle prizes
Snacks
Assembly

The Ultimate Reward

An enjoyable, interesting, and challenging class

The Competitive Reward

Contest between best attendance, homework completion, behavior records, etc.

The Simplest yet Best Reward

A smile
A high five
A pat, punch, or handshake
A word of encouragement
Praise for the deed, encouragement for the person (see page 185)
A note or "Warm Fuzzy"
A note home
A phone call home

Effective Communication of Your Discipline Plan

Now that you have thought out, constructed, and posted your discipline plan, all that is left is to communicate this plan to your students on the first day of school. How you communicate your plan will determine its success or failure.

The "Teacher Look" or Stare

Practice the follow technique in front of a mirror over and over. It is a recommended and effective technique.

An effective teacher's look, signal, or body language is all it takes to get students on task.

1. STARE, really stare, at the student to stop the misbehavior.
2. If the student does not stop, calmly WALK to the student.
3. LEAN over and place your hand on the desk or the student's shoulder, lightly.
4. WHISPER into the student's ear or face.
5. SAY the student's name.
6. TELL the student what you want the student to do.
7. SAY, "Thank you."
8. STARE at the student and WAIT three seconds.
9. Leave the student with an affirmative SMILE.

The Effective Teacher

✓ Communicates the plan in a firm but controlled and friendly manner,

✓ Does not wince, shrug, or otherwise convey disbelief in what is being said.

✓ Makes eye contact with each student while presenting the plan.

✓ Provides an understandable reason for the plan.

✓ Provides a copy of the plan for each student.

✓ Sends home a copy of the plan to the parents.

✓ Enforces the rules consistently.

✓ Tells the students that the administration supports the plan.

✓ Has learned how to master the stare or "teacher look."

✓ Has high expectations that all of the students will abide by the rules.

Useless, Meaningless, Phrases Used to Discipline

All phrases listed are ones solicited from teachers. They said they have actually used these words at one time or another in the classroom. This is not a recommended list for your use.

Cool it.
Knock it off.
Shape up.
Buckle down.
Keep your nose to . . .
Behave yourself.
Watch out.
Straighten up.
Act your age.
Get your tail in gear.
Would you like to see your mother again?
Listen up.
Sit on it.
Park it here.
Hang it up.
Pack it in.
Button up.
Bite your tongue.
Turn it off.
Hold it down.
Get your heels clicking.

Give it up.
Come off it.
Screw your head on.
Get the lead out.
Pipe down.
Watch it.
Zip your lips.
Are you crusin' for a brusin'?
It's either my way or the highway.
Enough.
Either you go or I go, and I don't plan to go.
Simmer down.
Get on the ball.
Shape up or ship out.
Stifle it.
Get your act together.
Blow it in the other direction.
Do you want me to fix your face?
You know how to pray, don't you?
If you want your life on this planet to continue, you had better behave.
Hit the bricks.
I've got one nerve left and you are dancing on it.
I'm going to kill you and tell God it was an accident.

The Ineffective Teacher

✓ May have no clearly defined rules.

✓ Communicates rules sporadically and as they are suddenly needed to stifle a situation.

✓ Conveys rules in a gruff, angry, and condescending manner.

✓ Winces, shrugs, or conveys with facial or body motion disbelief in what is being said.

✓ Conveys that "I'm only doing this because the administration wants me to do it."

✓ Conveys that "I don't believe in this plan, but I've got to go along with it because everyone else is using it."

✓ Implies that "I was hired to teach literature, not to maintain discipline."

✓ Tells the students, "If you don't want to learn, that's not my problem."

✓ Berates students with meaningless phrases to convey expectations of appropriate behavior, such as "Don't you know any better?" or "How many times do I have to tell you?"

✓ Uses rules (if indeed they do exist) and body language to stifle student participation, attention, learning, and success. All this teacher wants is peace and quiet in the classroom, for his or her sake, not for the students'.

Ineffective teachers stifle the behavior, creativity, and success of others because they do not want others to succeed. They stifle students in the classroom, and they stifle teachers in the lounge and at faculty meetings.

By contrast, effective teachers are confident in themselves and their capabilities. As such, they can help others to achieve and succeed, too. Effective and caring teachers have discipline plans that do not denigrate or degrade students. Rather, they teach students the concept of consequences and responsibility.

What to Do with Your Discipline Plan

Chapters 18 and 19 have been devoted to explaining the three components of a discipline plan. To **ACTIVATE** the plan, you must put it into practice daily. Do this and you will be the effective teacher you were meant to be.

To be an Effective
Teacher
1. Post your rules.
2. Post your consequences. and rewards.
3. Immediately enact the consequence when a rule is broken.
4. Give a reward when you catch a student doing good.
5. Make your behavior predictable and consistent.

The Effective Teacher

1. Thinks through a discipline plan before school begins and conveys the plan to the students when school begins.

2. Discusses the plan so that students understand the logic of it and consider it reasonable.

3. Involves the administration to help guarantee and enforce the plan.

4. Communicates the plan to parents and has it accepted by them.

5. Has high expectations and confidence in his or her capacity to teach young people self-discipline.

Key Idea: A smooth-running class is based on the teacher's ability to teach procedures.

CHAPTER 20

The Problem Is Not Discipline

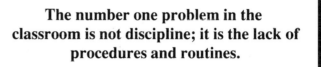

> **The number one problem in the classroom is not discipline; it is the lack of procedures and routines.**

Most teachers will tell you that their number one problem in the classroom is discipline. But that tells more about the teacher than the class.

✓ Good teachers don't worry about discipline.

✓ Behavior is rarely a problem when effective teaching is taking place.

A vast majority of the behavior problems in the classroom are caused by the failure of students to follow procedures and routines. These are the main reasons why students do not follow procedures:

1. The students do not know the procedures.

2. The students have not been trained to follow the procedures.

3. The teacher has not thought through what happens in the classroom.

Why Procedures Are Important

A procedure is not a discipline plan. Neither is a procedure a threat, a rule, or an order. **A procedure is simply a method or process for how things are to be done in the classroom.**

Since a **PROCEDURE** is how you want something done, it is the responsibility of the teacher to have procedures clearly stated. A **ROUTINE** is what the student does automatically without prompting or supervision. Thus a routine becomes a habit, practice, or custom for the student.

Procedures are necessary for an effective classroom for several reasons.

✓ Classroom procedures are statements of student expectations necessary to participate successfully in classroom activities, to learn, and to function effectively in the school environment.

✓ Classroom procedures allow many different activities to take place efficiently during the school day, often several at the same time, with a minimum of wasted time and confusion.

✓ Classroom procedures increase on-task time and reduce classroom disruptions.

✓ Classroom procedures tell a student how things operate in a classroom, thus reducing discipline problems.

Students are less likely to act up in frustration, trying to figure out what the teacher wants, if the classroom procedures are clearly stated.

PROCEDURE:
- What you want done.
ROUTINE:
- What the students do.

**The Difference
Between Discipline and Procedures**

Discipline: Has penalties and rewards.
Procedures: Have no penalties or rewards.

Discipline: Concerns how students behave.
Procedures: Concern how things are done.

Procedures Differ from a Discipline Plan

Procedures and routines are different from a discipline plan. The student is generally not penalized for not following a procedure or rewarded if a procedure is followed.

Example of a Procedure

There is a procedure for opening a lock on a locker. It's usually two turns to the right, one turn to the left, and a right turn to the number.

There is no teacher penalty if the procedure is not followed. The lock just does not open. Likewise, there is no teacher reward if the procedure is followed. The lock simply opens.

Classroom Procedures

Every time the teacher wants something done, there must be a procedure or a set of procedures. For instance, have procedures for taking roll, exchanging papers, registering the students on the first day, collecting lunch money, and moving from task to task. If not, time that should be spent on learning will be wasted getting these procedures done.

Classroom procedures answer such questions as these:

What to do when the bell rings
What to do when the pencil breaks
What to do when the fire drill bell rings
What to do when the bus does not show up
What to do when you finish your work early
What to do when you have a question
What to do when you need to go to the rest room
What to do when you want to sign up for something

A set of procedures must be followed to open a combination lock.

Tell your students that classroom procedures are for their benefit. Following procedures will help them do their work with less confusion and thus help them to succeed. Knowledge of classroom procedures tells your students such things as these:

> What they are to do when you want their attention
> Where to find the assignment
> How a paper is to be done
> Where you want the paper placed
> What they are to do when they enter the classroom
> How to respond when they hear an emergency alert
> What to do if they want to sharpen a pencil

Every class needs to have a set of procedures. Procedures allow a class to operate smoothly. A smooth-running, effective class is free of confusion and is a pleasure to teach and learn in.

> **A smooth-running class is the responsibility of the teacher, and it is based on the teacher's ability to teach procedures.**

Procedures Are a Part of Life

There are procedures in real life. As adults, we follow some of these procedures, for instance:

Telephone Book: At the front of a telephone book are procedures on how to make a long-distance call, make a foreign call, contact directory assistance, get emergency help, and contact the business office.

Airplane: After the "discipline plan" is stated at the beginning of the flight, the flight attendants explain the procedures. These procedures include how to use the seat belt, how to use the oxygen mask, where to find the life vest, and how to find the aisle in case the cabin is filled with smoke.

Traffic Light: There are procedures at an intersection with a traffic light. The light governs who will turn, who will stop, and who will go. A procedure also determines whether a right turn is permissible after stopping at a red light.

Wedding: At the conclusion of a wedding, a procedure is followed. The parents in the first row leave first, followed by each row from the front of the seating area.

The reason we have procedures in life is so that people can function in society knowing the acceptable and efficient ways other people do things. When we say that someone is ill-mannered, it is because that person doesn't know or doesn't care what the local customs or procedures are. To function successfully with other people, the best guideline is generally "When in Rome, do as the Romans do."

Procedures Are a Part of School Life

As in real life, there are procedures in the classroom. Here are some that nearly every teacher must teach.

TYPICAL CLASSROOM PROCEDURES THAT MUST BECOME STUDENT ROUTINES

PROCEDURE FOR:
1. Beginning of period or day.
2. Quieting a class.
3. Students seeking help.
4. Movement of students and papers.
5. End of the period or day.

Procedure for Dismissal at the End of the Period or Day: When the dismissal bell rings, are the students already standing at the door waiting to leave, or do they just get up and leave, while you are in the middle of a sentence? You can always tell who is running the class, the students or the teacher, by how the students behave at the end of the period or day. (See page 179.)

Procedure for Quieting a Class: Do you know how to quiet a class in 15 seconds or less? It can be done easily! Do you yell, scream, and flick the lights—all to no avail? Or if you do succeed, does it take untold time to get the students' attention, not to mention untold years on your life span from stress? (See page 183.)

Procedure for at the Beginning of the Period or Day: When the students enter, do they know what to do, where to sit, and what materials to have ready? Or do they sit and wait for the teacher to tell them what to do? (See page 187.)

Procedure for Students Seeking Help: Do your students raise their hands when they want your help, wigwagging their hands to attract your attention, calling your name at the same time, stopping work in the process accompanied by muttering and complaining to their classmates because you do not respond instantly? (See page 188.)

Procedure for the Movement of Students and Papers: Do your students take forever to pass their papers in and even longer to change from group to group or task to task? And when they turn their papers in, do they throw them in a pile on your desk or punch each other in the back as the papers are passed forward? (See page 191.)

There are also procedures on the school bus and in the cafeteria, library, and attendance office. And if these are run effectively, you can be sure that the bus driver, food-service person, librarian, and secretary have taught the students the correct procedures in their area of authority.

The Three-Step Approach to Teaching Classroom Procedures

Most behavior problems in the classroom are caused by the teacher's failure to teach students how to follow procedures.

The Three Steps to Teaching Procedures

1. **Explain:** State, explain, model, and demonstrate the procedure.

2. **Rehearse:** Rehearse and practice the procedure under your supervision.

3. **Reinforce:** Reteach, rehearse, practice, and reinforce the classroom procedure until it becomes a student habit or routine.

Step 1. **Explain Classroom Procedures Clearly**

Effective teachers know what activities need to be done and have worked out the procedures for each of them. These procedures are posted or distributed to the students early in the school year or when the activity surfaces in class. Unless the students read well, primary grade teachers should teach the procedures verbally rather than post them.

It is urgent that you have the procedures for each opening of school activity ready on the first day of school. Revise and hone these procedures year after year until they become models of efficiency.

Explain

✓ Define the procedure in concrete terms.

✓ Demonstrate the procedure; don't just tell.

✓ Demonstrate a complex procedure step by step.

Step 2. **Rehearse Classroom Procedures Until They Become Routines**

Effective teachers spend a good deal of time during the first weeks of school introducing, teaching, modeling, and rehearsing procedures. Do not expect the students to learn all the procedures in one day, especially at the elementary school level. Behaviors must be taught, modeled, practiced, monitored, and retaught.

Watch a good music, athletic, or foreign-language coach. Such people are masters at the rehearsal technique. They tell and show you a technique, even have you watch a video of the technique. Then they have you do it repeatedly while they watch you. Some people call this technique "guided practice."

Rehearse

✓ Have students practice the procedure, step by step, under your supervision. After each step, make sure that the students have performed the step correctly.

✓ Have the students repeat the procedure until it becomes a routine. The students should be able to perform the procedure automatically without teacher supervision.

Step 3. **Reinforce a Correct Procedure and Reteach an Incorrect One**

Again, watch a coach because good coaches are the best teachers. As the coach guides a team, class, or student through practice, corrections are made instantly. They tell, show, demonstrate, cajole, and even yell, "Do it right!"

And when it is done right, there are words of praise, hugs, pats, and smiles. But good coaches don't stop there. They reinforce the correct technique by having the student do the acquired technique over and over again, each time exhorting the student to do it better.

Reinforce

✓ Determine whether students have learned the procedure or whether they need further explanation, demonstration, or practice.

✓ Reteach the correct procedure if rehearsal is unacceptable, and give corrective feedback.

✓ Praise the students when the rehearsal is acceptable.

Using the Three-Step Approach to Teach Procedures

The following are examples of how some procedures are taught. You may not need or want them, but note how each procedure is taught. Then substitute your own procedure, using the **explain, rehearse, reinforce** technique described.

✓ How to dismiss a class.

✓ How to quiet a class and have their attention.

✓ How to have a class working when the bell rings.

✓ How students are to ask you for help.

✓ How students are to pass in papers.

Procedure for Dismissal at the End of the Period or Day

The ineffective teacher has students standing at the door waiting to leave before the bell rings.

Explain

Students, there is a procedure at the end of the period. You are to remain in your seat (or at your desks with the chairs pushed in) until I dismiss the class. The bell does not dismiss the class. You do not dismiss the class. The teacher dismisses the class.

You will want to explain the criteria for dismissal, such as how clean you want the desk area and where you want the chairs to be positioned.

Show and demonstrate this procedure. Have several students (never one, as it makes a show-off example of one) demonstrate the procedure. Praise each so that the students know that you are validating the correct procedure.

Rehearse

Be alert a few seconds before the bell rings on the first day of school. Anticipate that you will need to make an immediate correction if the procedure is not followed. If the class starts to file out, it is too late to correct the procedure. The failure to correct a procedure will only escalate the problem until it is the students who dismiss themselves and are really the ones in control of the class.

On the first day of school, remind the class a few seconds before the bell rings at the end of the period or day of the dismissal procedure. This will reduce the hassle of correcting the class; however, if any students begin to leave at the bell, you simply say,

No, no, no. Tom, Joel, Anne, please return to your desks.

Do not scold, yell, or demean. And do not use meaningless phrases or questions like "Listen to me" or "What did I say was the dismissal procedure?" You do not want a discussion, an argument, or a response. You want everyone at their desks. Calmly, but with a voice of authority, tell the students who began to leave to return to their desks.

Reinforce

Every time a procedure needs to be corrected:

1. **REMIND** the class of the procedure.
2. Have the class **EXPERIENCE** the procedure.

Remind

Class, I would like to remind you of the procedure at the end of the period. You are to remain at your desks until I dismiss the class.

Experience

Look around the room. You are all at your desks (and your chairs are pushed in). This is the correct procedure, and I commend you.

Effective teachers have the students see, feel, and experience the procedure. The students see each other in their seats and experience the procedure correctly. Ineffective teachers only tell students what to do. The students do not experience an example of what should be done. This is why many teachers fail when they want students to follow procedures.

Well done. Please do it again tomorrow. Have a nice day!

Repeat the procedure every day until the procedure becomes a routine. By the end of the third or fourth day, the procedure will have become automatic.

Thereafter, all you need to do a few seconds after the bell rings is smile and say, "It's been nice seeing all of you. See you tomorrow. Have a nice day." This is much better than, "You're dismissed."

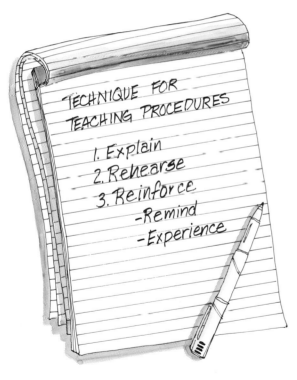

TECHNIQUE FOR TEACHING PROCEDURES

1. Explain
2. Rehearse
3. Reinforce
   - Remind
   - Experience

Why Children Never Tell Mom They Are Going Out

So many parents shake their heads in frustration when their children leave the house and never say, "I'm going out, Mom." They just leave, showing no respect or manners.

If, every day, for 180 days, when the class is seated and ready for dismissal at the end of the period or the day, the teacher says, "Have a nice day" to dismiss the class, **the teacher is modeling respect and manners.**

The students may not realize it, but they are getting a lesson in the appropriate behavior of well-mannered people. Perhaps they too will learn to say, "Have a nice day, Mom."

An adult should repeatedly model appropriate behavior so that a student may experience how to behave in society.

How to Teach a New Student All the Class Procedures

You have invested a few weeks of practice and rehearsal of the classroom procedures. Your class is now a smooth-running, well-oiled, humming learning environment.

Suddenly a new student checks into class. What do you do? No problem!

First, understand that you cannot tell a new student the classroom procedures if you haven't first told your existing class. If your class is never sure what to do, there is no way you can ever orient and teach a new student.

Second, if you have a class where the students have learned the routines, you have developed a classroom culture. A culture is the prevailing way a group behaves; for instance:

- When people stand before an elevator, they know to let people off before they get on.

- In Chicago at Wrigley Field, when an opposing player hits a home run, the fans all yell, "Throw the ball back (on to the field)."

- At a Chinese family dinner table, the prevailing culture is never to help yourself first. That would be considered selfish and uncouth. You always say, "You first, please."

You create a culture when students behave in a manner understood to be appropriate in your classroom.

- When a new student enters the class, give the student a copy of the classroom procedures.

- Explain to the student what the procedures are and why you have them.

- Tell the student that you will help with the procedures but that the student will probably be able to learn them by observing how the rest of the class behaves.

  For example, the bell rings at the end of the period and the new student begins to leave. Suddenly the student notices that no one else is leaving.

  The student says mentally, "Oh, oh, I'd better stay here like the rest of the class." The student has just learned the procedure.

Procedure for Quieting a Class

Explain

Students, I have a procedure when I want your undivided attention. You will see me stand here with my hand up. Or I may hit a bell because some of you will not be able to see my hand while you are working in a group. When you see my hand or hear a bell, the procedure is as follows:

1. Freeze.
2. Turn and face me; pay attention and keep your eyes on me.
3. Be ready for instruction. I will have something to say.

Let me repeat and demonstrate what I said.

Repeat and look for class understanding.

Byron, please tell me the procedure when you see my hand or hear a bell.

Byron does so.

Yes, yes, yes. Thank you, Byron.

Repeat this with several more students.

Is there anyone who does not understand or know what to do if you see my hand or hear a bell?

Rehearse

Good, let's rehearse the procedure.

We will be working together this year, so let's get to know one another. Please look at the people to the right of you. You may have two minutes to introduce yourself and get acquainted.

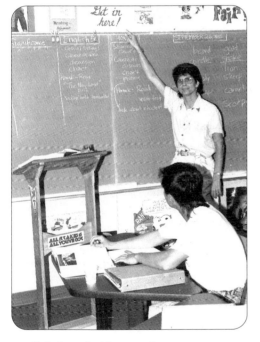

Calmly and without saying anything, raise your hand when you want the class quiet.

At two minutes hold up your hand or hit the bell, perhaps doing both this first time. Do not say a word when you raise your hand. Do the demonstration exactly as you will be doing it for the rest of the year. Be patient and wait until the class does the three steps and pays attention.

Do not give up as you wait for the students to give you their undivided attention. Compliment them when you have their attention.

Thank you. You practiced the procedure correctly.

Now, please look at the people to the left of you. You may have two minutes to introduce yourself and get acquainted.

At two minutes hold up your hand or hit the bell. Compliment them.

Thank you. You followed the procedure correctly.

We are not finished with the rehearsal. You will often find yourself out of your seat working in groups or alone somewhere in the room away from your seat. So let's try a different scenario.

I would like two of you to stand by the pencil sharpener, two of you at the sink, two of you at the bookcase, and one of you at the computer.

You then hold up your hand and watch for the seven students to pay attention.

Reinforce

Thank you. That was the correct procedure when you see my hand or hear a bell. Please do the same thing each time you see my hand or hear a bell.

You keep using the same language because you must use the same procedure if you want the students to exhibit the same student routine. You also use a technique called "Praise the deed, encourage the student," described on the next page.

Praise the Deed, Encourage the Student

An effective way to praise is to praise what the person did, rather than the person, and then encourage the person to do the achievement or deed again. The technique is called specific praise, or "praise the deed, encourage the student."

Praise is nice, but not tangible or meaningful; for instance:

Charlene, you are a bright kid.

For a more effective kind of praise, point to something the student did well. Then encourage the student to do it again; for instance:

Charlene, please get your last spelling test out. What did you get? Right, 19 out of 20 correct. Great! Pat yourself on the back. Shake your own hand. Congratulate yourself. DO IT AGAIN ON THE NEXT TEST.

Here are some other examples:

Thank you. That was the correct procedure when you see my hand or hear a bell. Please do the same thing each time you see my hand or hear a bell.

Melissa, thank you for the excellent report at the faculty meeting. The next time I need assistance, I would truly appreciate your help again.

Wayne, thanks for helping with the dishes tonight. Mom had a meeting to go to, and you helped out. The next time Mom needs help, I would appreciate your helping again.

The reason people are more likely to do well again is because they know that you saw them do something specific. They believe, "You were paying attention to me. You noticed me! And you thanked me for doing something I did personally."

Pep talks are nice but hollow. They become meaningless quickly because no one is sure whom the message is directed to. When you praise the deed and encourage the student, you help the student do two things:

1. The student accepts responsibility for having done the task.
2. The student accepts ownership of the accomplishment.

The two key words are *responsibility* and *ownership*, what all successful people must develop in order to be successful.

She Quieted 100 People in Five Seconds

We were invited to our daughter-in-law's class to attend their International Day celebration. Three sixth grades were gathered in a large room to show the culmination of their studies in the country of their ancestry or choice. The students were dressed in native attire and had information and food samples typical of the country.

There were over 100 people in a room for a sixth-grade activity, and Mrs. Cindy Wong quieted the room in five seconds.

The three classes and an assortment of guests—parents, teachers, administrators, and friends—numbered about 100 people. As we were walking from display to display, talking with the students and tasting food, we suddenly heard the students call out, "... 3, 4, 5."

Then there was silence in the room. Everyone faced the teacher, Mrs. Cindy Wong, and she spoke. Then everyone went back to what they were doing.

Later I asked Cindy what she did to quiet the room so quickly.

She said, "Dad, it's a variation on your three-step technique. I have a five-step procedure because I teach younger students than you do, so I wanted to be more specific as to what I wanted.

"My five steps are these:

1. *Eyes on speaker*
2. *Quiet*
3. *Be still*
4. *Hands free (put things down)*
5. *Listen*

"The way it works is, I say, 'Give me five.' They go through each of the five steps in their mind.

"I have rehearsed them in this procedure, so when I say, 'Give me five,' it takes them no more than five seconds before I have their attention."

I asked, "Do all three sixth-grade classes know this routine?"

"No, only mine," she said.

I replied, "Wow. Your class did it and everyone else in the room quickly caught on to the procedure—the culture of the room."

GIVE ME FIVE!
1. Eyes on speaker
2. Mouth quiet
3. Being still
4. Hands free
5. Listening

The Give Me Five plan as posted in Cindy Wong's classroom.

Procedure for at the Beginning of the Period or Day

Three more examples of classroom procedures will be presented; however, the technique of explain, rehearse, and reinforce will not be illustrated. Refer to the two previous procedures for the technique.

An effective teacher always has the procedure or schedule posted or ready for distribution when the students arrive. For previous examples of how efficiently this is done, see pages 122 and 125.

Here is another example of a procedure for the beginning of the school day.

Routines are the hallmark of an effective classroom.

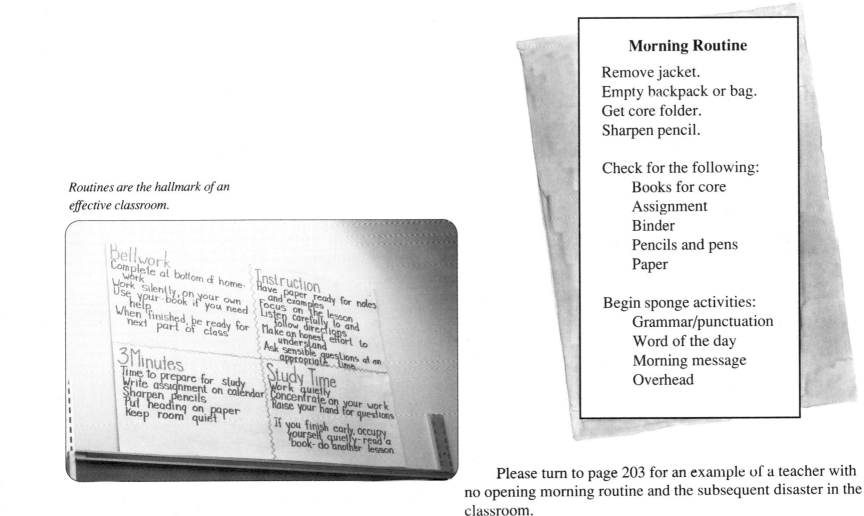

Morning Routine

Remove jacket.
Empty backpack or bag.
Get core folder.
Sharpen pencil.

Check for the following:
    Books for core
    Assignment
    Binder
    Pencils and pens
    Paper

Begin sponge activities:
    Grammar/punctuation
    Word of the day
    Morning message
    Overhead

Please turn to page 203 for an example of a teacher with no opening morning routine and the subsequent disaster in the classroom.

Procedure for Students Seeking Help

Hand raising is not effective when students want your attention. There are better methods for students to use to get your attention.

The class is at work and you are walking around the room helping. You see a hand up and say, "Pam." The whole class stops—to look at you and Pam.

Pam says, "May I sharpen my pencil?"—a reasonable request.

You say yes or no, and the class goes back to work.

A few seconds later, you see another hand up. You say, "Carlos," and the whole class stops—to look at you and Carlos.

Carlos says, "I need your help"—an appropriate request.

You say, "Wait a minute," and the class goes back to work.

Every time you speak, you interrupt the class. These interruptions occur frequently, often two or three times a minute.

You would be distracted if the principal came over the loudspeaker two or three times a day, no less two or three times a minute. Before you complain that the principal makes a few announcements during the day over the intercom system, consider how many times a teacher interrupts a class when the students are concentrating on their work.

**Student Methods for Getting Teacher's Attention
Without Interrupting the Class**

Hand signal: The student signals with different number of fingers.
Toilet tissue tube: The student signals with a colored tube.
Styrofoam cup: The student signals with the position of a cup.
Index card: The student signals with a message on an index card.
Textbook: The student signals with an upright textbook.

Hand Signal

In this system the students signal the teacher with a predetermined number of fingers. The number of fingers raised corresponds to a predetermined request established by the teacher.

Post a sign on the wall with your hand signal chart. Then train your students to use the system.

✓ If they wish to speak, they are to raise the index finger.

✓ If they wish to leave their seat, they are to raise two fingers.

✓ If they need your help, they are to raise three fingers.

✓ When you see a signal, silently respond to the signal with a nod of the head or a gesture of the hand.

The important thing is that the class is not disturbed.

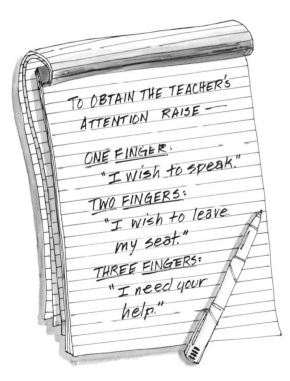

TO OBTAIN THE TEACHER'S
ATTENTION RAISE —

ONE FINGER:
"I wish to speak."

TWO FINGERS:
"I wish to leave
my seat."

THREE FINGERS:
"I need your
help."

A Difference in the Noise Level Alone

Dear Rosemary,

If I were to try and tell you all the ways in which you (and Harry) have inspired and encouraged us in both our personal and professional lives, it would take many pages. I'm sure you're aware of the benefits you bring to the many lives you touch.

We really enjoyed seeing you again at our symposia. The wonderfully creative and practical ideas you gave us will be put to good use. My husband is already using your 1,2, and 3-finger hand signals in his grade 5/6 classroom, and can't believe the difference it has made in the noise level alone.

Thanks again for all of the above, and so much more.

Debbie Fraser
Kinburn, Ontario

Toilet Tissue Tube

Take an empty toilet tissue tube and wrap one end with red construction paper and the other end with green construction paper. The tube is placed with the green end up on the student's desk.

The procedure when the student wants the teacher's attention is to turn the tube so that the red end is up and to <u>continue to work</u>. When the teacher comes to help the student, the green end is turned back up.

Styrofoam Cup

Tape a short length of string to the bottom of a Styrofoam cup. Styrofoam cups are suggested because they are noiseless. Tape the other end of the string near the edge of the desktop, and leave the cup dangling off the table.

The procedure when the student wants the teacher's attention is to place the cup on the desk and to <u>continue to work</u>.

Index Card

Fold and tape an index card into a three-sided pyramid. On one side write, "Please help me." On another side write, "Please keep working." Leave the third side blank. Place the card on the table so that the blank side is facing the student.

(faces student)

(faces teacher)

The procedure when the student wants the teacher's attention is to turn the card so that "Please help me" is facing forward. The student sees "Please keep working" and is reminded to <u>continue to work</u>.

Textbook

High school teachers may appreciate this simple system. The procedure when the student wants the teacher's attention is to take a textbook and place it in an upright position and to <u>continue to work</u>.

Procedure for the Movement of Paper

> **Students should pass their papers across the
> rows, not up the rows.**

Assuming that the students are sitting in columns and rows, it is more effective to have your students pass their papers across the rows to the side of the room rather than up the row to the front of the room.

Why? Here are the problems with passing papers up to the front of the room.

1. If papers are passed up the row, you cannot see what is happening behind each student's back as you stand at the front of the room waiting for the papers.

2. Some students tap, poke, shove, and hit the back of the student in front to get their attention to receive the papers coming up the row. Others wave the papers in the face of the student in front. No matter what is done, the student in front is irritated, words are spoken, and the disturbance in the class increases.

3. When papers are passed from hand to hand, some papers may fall to the floor.

4. There are frequently more students up a row than across rows.

5. Thus passing papers up a row takes longer to accomplish and is frequently accompanied by student agitation.

There are advantages for passing papers across the rows to the side of the room. The procedure is as follows:

Step 1. Have the students place their papers on the desk next to theirs starting with the student at one end of the row.

Step 2. The next student is to add his or her paper to the stack and place the papers on the next desk. Do not have the students pass the papers from hand to hand. This will eliminate flicking of papers as papers are passed.

Step 3. As the students pass the papers from desk to desk, monitor the procedure, making corrections when necessary and praising when appropriate.

Step 4. Walk to the side of the room and look across all the rows to monitor the procedure. This tactic allows you to see across the rows, whereas you cannot see behind the backs of students when you stand in front of the room and they are passing papers forward.

Step 5. Pick up the papers or ask a student to pick up all the papers.

If the students are sitting at tables instead of chairs in a row:

1. Have the students place their paper at the head of the table (point to the designated spot).

2. Have one or more students or an aide pick up the papers, or do so yourself.

It is not a good procedure to have the students place their papers in a basket on the teacher's desk. This procedure involves too much movement and too much of a mess left behind.

Whatever procedure you choose to use for collecting papers, rehearse the procedure the first time you collect papers.

1. Has well-thought-out and structured procedures for every activity.

2. Teaches the procedures for each activity early in the year.

3. Rehearses the class so that procedures become class routines.

4. Reteaches a procedure when necessary and praises to reinforce when appropriate.

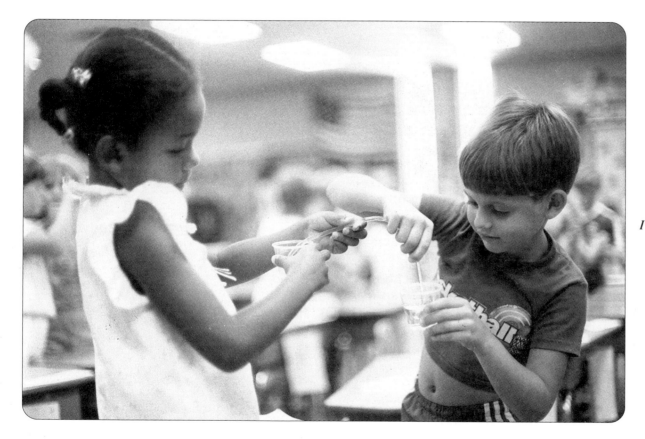

I am not a teacher,
  but an awakener.

Robert Frost

UNIT D

Third Characteristic–
Lesson Mastery

*The effective teacher knows how to design
lessons to help students reach mastery.*

◆◆◆

UNIT D

Third Characteristic — Lesson Mastery

*The effective teacher knows how to design lessons
to help students reach mastery.*

◆ ◆

Key Idea: To increase student learning and achievement, increase the amount of time the student is working.

The Students Must Learn

> **If the student cannot demonstrate learning or achievement, then WE have failed the student; the student has not failed.**

The student must learn or comprehend. The student must master the subject or skill. The student must show achievement. **If the student cannot demonstrate learning or achievement, then WE have failed the student; the student has not failed.**

Schools exist and teachers are hired for one reason only: to help students achieve.

> *The highest stake of all is our ability to help children realize their full potential.*

> Samuel J. Meisels
> *Educational Leadership*,
> April 1989, p. 21.

CHAPTER 21

Three Major Characteristics of Effective Teachers

1. They have high expectations that all of their students will succeed (Unit B).

2. They are extremely good classroom managers (Unit C).

3. They know how to design lessons to help students reach mastery (Unit D).

Many Students Have Never Really Tried the Educational System

As a teacher, I don't need studies to tell me the true state of things. About five or six years ago, I began to do my own informal survey of student attendance. The pattern has been consistent. On the average, my "good" students, that is, those who are "sort of" functioning, are absent 10 days each term (or 20 days per academic year), a rate of more than 10 percent. I doubt if many employers could run their business with that kind of liability.

I never include in my calculations the records of the three, four, or five chronic truants in each class whose 30 to 60 absences would send the overall average through the ceiling.

In 1985 a national study reported that the "typical" student cut 100 classes annually.

Unfortunately, our youngsters don't seem to get any more serious about education after they leave high school and enter college. "The American Freshman: National Norms for Fall 1986," a study of more than 200,000 students at 372 colleges, recently reported on how students spend their time each week while attending school:

- More than 50 percent admit to spending on average less than 45 minutes a day studying or doing homework.

- Nearly 20 percent put in less than three hours of schoolwork a week.

- Fewer than 10 percent claim to spend 16 or more hours on their studies.

- Nearly 20 percent of college freshmen spend 11 or more hours a week "partying," which is not to be confused with the more popular "socializing with friends."

- Fifty-eight percent of those polled spend 11 or more hours socializing with friends.

- More than 1 out of 10 spends a whopping 30 or more hours "hanging out."

The evidence shows that large numbers of youngsters have never seriously tried the educational system. The success of recent Asian immigrants in our schools reveals the astonishing truth that highly motivated **students who attend school regularly and work conscientiously suddenly make our schools and teachers look good.**

We perpetually rediscover the wheel.

Edward Janko
Education Week,
April 22, 1987, p. 32.

The Learner Must Work at Learning

There is only one way for a student to learn anything. The student must put in effort; the student must work to learn. Learning does not come from the teacher doing the work, such as lecturing, leading a discussion, or showing a film. An effective teacher knows how to manage the time allocated to maximize student time and effort.

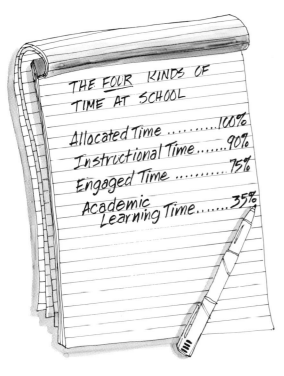

THE FOUR KINDS OF
TIME AT SCHOOL

Allocated Time 100%
Instructional Time 90%
Engaged Time 75%
Academic
    Learning Time 35%

Allocated Time. Allocated time is the amount of time given to a student for learning. First, there is the time a school board adopts as the school calendar. The time may be negotiated with the teacher's organization and other interested parties, but once the time is adopted, it becomes the allocated time. Typically this is about 180 days, some 6 to 7 hours each day.

Another kind of allocated time is the time given to an activity. Usually this is determined by board policy, the administration, or a curriculum committee. So many hours a day or a week may be mandated for spelling, language arts, physical education, math, and science.

Thus allocated time is the total time within which teacher instruction and student learning can take place. It is 100 percent of the available time.

Instructional Time. Instructional time is the time you can observe a teacher instructing. Instructional time is easy to ascertain because the teacher is the focus in the room. All eyes are on the teacher because the teacher is talking, orchestrating, WORKING.

Research has shown that the typical teacher consumes 90 percent of the allocated time. Yes, the teacher is center stage or in the limelight almost every minute of the school year.

Engaged Time. Engaged time is the time you can observe a student involved or engaged in a task. The students are now the focus in the room, and the teacher is walking around helping those who are in need. It is easy to identify engaged time. This is the time the students are on task, WORKING.

Research has shown that engaged time is about 75 percent of the allocated time. If this appears to be in conflict with the 90 percent devoted to instructional time (90 and 75 percent exceed 100 percent), it is because the teacher and the students may be working at the same time.

Academic Learning Time. **Academic learning time is the amount of time that the teacher can prove or demonstrate that the student comprehended or learned the content or mastered the skill.** According to the research, this provable or demonstrable time is only 35 percent of the allocated time.

Academic learning time has nothing to do with worksheets, boardwork, storytelling, lecturing, films, or discussions. The ineffective teacher spends time covering materials.

The effective teacher has the students spend time working and earning their own achievement and success. Academic learning time has to do with answering two questions:

1. Did the student learn what you wanted the student to learn?

2. Can you prove or show that the student learned what you wanted the student to learn?

Allocated, instructional, and engaged time are all factors in a classroom, but none answers the question "Has the student learned anything?" More days or hours do not guarantee more learning. Just because a teacher is teaching and a student is engaged does not guarantee learning either.

The bottom line in education is ultimately student learning or student achievement. Achievement is the result of academic learning time.

Academic Learning Time
(35 percent)

The time students spend demonstrating comprehension of a skill or content.

Why Some Students Are at the Head of the Class

Harold Stevenson, University of Michigan psychology professor, studied 240 students in kindergarten, first grade, and fifth grade in cities in the United States (Minneapolis), Taiwan (Taipei), and Japan (Sendai).

In his six-year study, using carefully devised standardized tests, he concluded, "We didn't find any difference in IQ levels, but we found significant differences in performance." Asian students are no smarter than American students, so . . . why are Asian students so successful in school? He found:

- An American first grader spends an average of 14 minutes a night on homework and hates it.

- A Japanese first grader (in Japan) spends an average of 37 minutes a night on homework and likes it.

- A Chinese first grader (in China) spends an average of 77 minutes a night on homework and likes it.

- Japanese and Chinese students also go to school on Saturday mornings, have fewer holidays, and attend school for 240 days a year, in contrast to American elementary school children, who generally go only 178 days a year.

In a survey of 7,836 San Francisco–area high school students, Sanford M. Dornbusch, professor of sociology and education at Stanford University, found that Asian-American boys spend an average of 11.7 hours a week doing homework, compared to 8 hours for whites and 6.3 hours for blacks.

Among girls, the figures were 12.3 hours a week for Asian-Americans, 8.6 for whites, and 9.2 for blacks. Asian-Americans also registered the best figures on other measures of work: attendance, cutting classes, paying attention to the teacher, and daydreaming.

Professor Dornbusch said that these numbers, taken together, represent what he termed a "powerhouse statistic in EFFORT." A nationwide study by the U.S. Department of Education, "School Experiences and Performance of Asian-Pacific American High School Students," found:

- Nearly half of Asian-American sophomores spend five or more hours per week on homework, compared to less than a third of whites and a quarter of blacks.

- Half of the Asian-American high school students were never absent from school, compared with only a quarter for whites.

Fox Butterfield
"Why Asians Are Going to the Head of the Class."
New York Times, August 3, 1986.

Research has shown that Asian students spend more time on task than non-Asian students.

The Teacher's Function is Not to Get Students to Settle Down

"I can't get them to settle down and get to work," so many teachers complain.

It is not the function of the teacher to get the students to settle down every morning. Can you imagine what kind of a world we would have if every morning no one would start to work until:

■ The principal came to every class and told the teachers to settle down and start teaching?

■ The boss came to every desk to tell all the secretaries to settle down and start typing?

■ The foreman asked every worker to settle down and start working?

■ The coach hollered at every ball player to settle down and start practicing?

The effective teacher has a posted assignment. When the students enter class, they go right to work. It is a routine that has been learned in class.

BELLWORK:

"Last night as I was sleeping, a light beamed in through the window. Then ..."

Please write the rest of the story.

Thank you!

The next time you go to a baseball game early, notice the pregame practice sessions. The manager is probably nowhere in sight, yet everyone is practicing or warming up. There is a pregame procedure, and everyone performs his part in the procedure without anyone's telling him what to do.

Effective teachers have opening-of-class procedures. The students know the procedure (Chapter 20) and go about their job without anyone's telling them what to do.

In stark contrast, the next page shows the actual scenario of an ineffective teacher.

I Left Them at Home

8:00	Students enter classroom, walk around, and talk.
8:12	One side of front panel on ventilator unit falls to floor (student has been sitting on it, banging it with heels).
8:14	Student continues to "beat it."
8:14:10	Student makes eye contact with principal, who is seated on other side of room.
8:14:11	Student stops "beating it."
8:22	Teacher asks students to be seated and be quiet.
8:24	Students find desks (two in closet area, three in front of room with backs to the board, one in the back corner between wall and filing cabinet).
8:25	Students are told schedule for day.
8:29	Students share news (Michael Jackson tour, fight last night, etc.).
8:35	Students are instructed to get books out for silent reading.
8:37	Five students hang on bookshelf trying to find books.
8:40	Two students are still discussing a fan magazine.
8:47	One student returns from very long visit to rest room.
8:48	Two students return carrying 5-inch jar of a mysterious substance.
8:49	Two students hang on bookshelves; principal notices good muscle coordination.
8:50	Teacher asks students to put away reading books; 70 percent are able to do so.
8:51	Teacher starts discussion of worksheet.
9:00	Teacher breaks students into groups for another subject.
9:01	As students group, principal asks teacher for lesson plans or objectives.
9:02	Teacher tells principal, "They are at home."

This is an actual observation of a sixth-grade teacher's class. In addition to wasted academic learning time, the teacher is modeling that young people do not have to be ready to get to work when they come to work.

Successful people prepare themselves daily for their work. That is why they are successful.

You Can Increase Student Learning

Allocated time, instructional time, engaged time, and academic learning time all have one variable—**TIME**.

> **Increase the amount of time the student is working, and you increase learning.**

Why do parents berate their children to practice on the piano? Because every parent knows that the more the student WORKS on a piece of music, the better the student will be able to perform.

What is the one thing all coaches of teams want out of the school schedule, if they can wrangle it from the allocated time? It is practice time, because every coach knows that the more a team practices and WORKS, the better it will be at the game.

What is the one thing all teachers who are directing the spring production want from the school schedule? It is rehearsal time, because every teacher knows that the more time the cast rehearses and WORKS, the better it will be on the night of the performance.

It's common sense—the person who does the work is the one who learns. Yet look into several rooms, especially in a secondary school, and guess who you find invariably working? Yes, the teacher. And what does the research say about learning?

> **The person who does the work is the ONLY one who learns.**

$369,636 Spent to Find Out Who Does Better in School

We taxpayers recently spent $369,636 for a study by a fine organization, the National Endowment for the Humanities. The study, titled "American Memory," found that **students who do more homework, attend school regularly, and read more tend to do better in school.**

It took $369,636 to discover that? Any teacher could have told Uncle Sam that for a 25-cent telephone call. Who knows what it will cost Uncle Sam to discover that **students who appear in class with paper, pencil, and textbooks will be able to do the assignments?**

Because the teacher does most of the work at school, this explains why there is so little learning in school. According to the research, only 35 percent of the allocated time is devoted to learning. Any business that operated at 35 percent efficiency would be bankrupt shortly.

For learning to take place, it is the student, not the teacher, who must be working.

I was successful with my students because when they walked into my room, my assignment was posted. They immediately got to work because that was the routine they had learned.

Fifty minutes later, when the period was over, I said, "Have a nice day. See you tomorrow," and they went staggering out of the class huffing and puffing, moaning "Boy, the guy works us hard, and on top of that, look at all the homework he's given us."

As for me, I leave the school full of energy. Why? Because I haven't done a thing at school other than walk around the room helping students, giving individual attention and pixieishly snarling, "Stay on task!" or "Stay focused!"

At 4 o'clock I go play racquetball, drink margaritas, and teach my Italian bride how to cook Chinese food. Life and love begin for me at 4 o'clock.

You don't see me dragging out at the end of the school day groaning, "I can't take this any longer. I'm going to take early retirement at the end of this school year—and I'm only 29 years old—to sell aluminum siding!"

The reason teachers are so tired at the end of the school day is that they have been working. If I worked as hard as many teachers do, I'd be as tired, too.

But have you ever noticed what happens at 3 o'clock when the students leave? "Yea, yea, yea!" Why are they so full of energy? Because they have been sitting in school all day doing nothing while the teacher is doing all the work.

The person who does the work is the only one doing any learning!

Harry K. Wong

The next time you go into a restaurant, notice who is doing all the work. It is the cooks, busboys, waitresses, and waiters, not the owner. The owner is sitting behind a cash register counting money.

The next time you walk past a construction job, notice who is doing all the work. It's the workers, the construction crew, not the foreman. He's standing around with the blueprints in one hand and a cigar in the other.

The next time you walk into an office, notice who is doing all the work—the workers again, secretaries, clerks, and bookkeepers, not the bosses. They are all sitting around with phones to their ears.

But walk into a school and notice who is working. Not the students. No, it's the teachers who are beating their buns off. **The research says that the person who does the work is the only one doing the learning.**

To increase the amount of time the student works to learn:

1. Have an assignment posted daily to be done upon entering the classroom.

2. Teach procedures and routines to minimize interruptions and maximize uninterrupted learning time.

3. Constantly monitor students so as to keep them on task.

**The student should be the worker.
Make the student work!**

He Came to Work Two Hours Before the Game

The most valuable player came to work with the people who wire the court for television and the people who pull the hot dogs out of the freezer and mix soft-drink syrup with water. He came to work before the other players.

More than two hours before the game, Larry Bird walked onto the floor with the material possession he worships most, a basketball. The court was empty, except for the workmen going about their business.

This is where the show really started Thursday night.

Harvey Araton
New York Daily News,
June 1, 1986.

He Puts In Even More Time

Lights flicker off at the Seattle Seahawks' offices. Secretaries step into the chilly Pacific Northwest air in noisy twosomes. Football players start their cars. Maintenance workers push brooms. While others head home for dinner, somewhere in a darkened room, Steve Largent intently watches film.

The Seahawks' premier wide receiver already stayed after practice to run and rerun patterns with his quarterback. Now, Steve Largent is putting in even more time.

"He's his own motivator and preparer," said receivers' coach Steve Moore. "He wins football games through his preparation."

Denise Tom Brown
USA Today,
December 11, 1986.

The bottom line is always the same. People who work and put in effort always achieve more than those who do not.

The truism of work and effort applies not only to students but to teachers and administrators as well. The work ethic is best modeled by teachers who put great effort and work into being effective teachers.

Students who do more homework, attend school regularly, and read more tend to do better in school.

The Effective Teacher

1. Teaches students, not a subject or a grade level.
2. Maximizes academic learning time.
3. Has students earning their own achievement.
4. Keeps the students actively engaged in learning.

CHAPTER 22

Key Idea: The greater the structure of a lesson and the more precise the directions on what is to be accomplished, the higher the achievement rate.

What Teaching Strategy Fosters Student Accomplishment?

> **If students know what they are to learn, you increase the chances that the students will learn.**

Researchers Kevin Wise and James Okey wanted to know what teaching strategies were most important in helping students to achieve. They looked at these 12 possible factors:

1. Audiovisual
2. Grading
3. Inquiry-discovery
4. Focusing on objectives
5. Hands-on manipulation
6. Modifying the textbooks and instructional materials
7. Presentation mode of teacher
8. Questioning strategies
9. Testing
10. Teacher direction
11. Wait time
12. Miscellaneous

Their research showed that "the effective classroom appears to be the one in which students are kept aware of instructional objectives and receive feedback on their progress toward these objectives."[1] **Focusing on objectives made the most difference on student achievement.** In very simplistic terms, if students know what they are to learn, you increase the chances that the students will learn.

The use of objectives increases the chances that the student will learn.

The Bottom Line Is Student Achievement

The bottom line in the real world is achievement. The world rewards those who are successful.

✓ In baseball, achievement is measured by the batting average.

✓ In making cars, achievement is measured by number of defects.

✓ In knitting a sweater, achievement is measured by dropped stitches.

✓ In typing, achievement is measured by errors per page.

✓ In selling, achievement is measured in sales.

If there are no sales, you are not a salesperson. If the batting average is low, you are traded or released. If the cars have too many defects, the customers buy another brand. **The bottom line in education is student achievement.**

If the students do not do their assignments and do not show achievement, no learning has occurred.

---

[1] Wise, Kevin, and James Okey. "A Meta-analysis of the Effects of Various Science Teaching Strategies on Achievement," *Journal of Research in Science Teaching*, 1983, pp. 419-435.

The ineffective teacher is concerned with covering history, science, math, art, or language arts. These teachers spend most of the class time on the textbook and having students fill in worksheets in a mind-numbing environment. They do not teach to objectives, nor do they know how to teach for learning, comprehension, or mastery.

The effective teacher can define three key words:

✓ Learning

✓ Comprehension

✓ Mastery

They can even explain how to teach for these:

✓ Accomplishment

✓ Achievement

Learning: The student shows that information or a skill has been acquired. Learning has taken place when you see a student perform a skill or grasp (define, identify, recall) information.

Comprehension: The student shows understanding of what has been learned. Comprehension has taken place when you see a student interpret, translate, explain, or summarize the information learned.

Mastery: The student shows the ability to use what has been comprehended. Mastery has taken place when you see a student use or apply what he or she understands. The student can also break down, reorganize, and evaluate what is known and understood.

This chapter shows how to write assignments in which students demonstrate that learning, comprehension, or mastery has taken place.

Are You Teaching for Accomplishment or Just Telling the Students What to Do?

Ineffective teachers do not teach for learning; they tell the students what to do. Often the work that is assigned is used to kill time. Unfortunately, there are teachers who thumb through the teacher's manual, saying to themselves:

What am I to do?   What can I use to keep them quiet?
What can I find to keep them busy?   What can I do to kill the period?
What activity relates to the unit?

As a result, an ineffective assignment tells students what to do; for example:

Read Chapter 24.   Complete this worksheet.
Do the problems on page 34.   Sit quietly and read pages 23 to 30.
Write a paper on Brazil.   Do this activity.
Answer the questions at the end of the chapter.

These are not accomplishments. They are jobs. They tell the student what to do. They do not tell the student what is to be comprehended, learned, or achieved. When the student is told what to do, no sense of accomplishment or responsibility is associated with what the student is to achieve.

Assignments like those in the example cause students to say:

What are we doing today?   What's our assignment?
Are you going to show us a movie today?   What are you going to do today?
Are we doing anything important today?   What's our assignment for tomorrow?
I'm finished; what do I do now?

The student may be finished, but did the student learn anything? In an ineffective classroom, the students just sit around waiting for the teacher to tell them what to do.

Effective teachers teach for student accomplishment and responsibility. When an assignment tells a student what is to be accomplished, you are also teaching responsibility. Students who are responsible and are working for accomplishment or achievement will ask questions like these:

How am I doing?   Am I doing all right?
Will I be first chair?   Am I first string?
Is this good enough for an A?

Questions like these tell you that the student is constantly and responsibly working to improve.

Teach for accomplishment, using structured assignments with objectives, and not only will the students demonstrate competence, but you will be regarded as a competent teacher also.

Your Assignment Is Chapter 24

Why didn't someone tell me how to give an assignment? I thought giving an assignment was telling the students what chapters to read.

"Students, your assignment for this week is Chapter 24. And the test this Friday will cover everything in Chapter 24."

When I gave them the test a week later, I was horrified at all the poor test scores. Then I started to blame the students for their failure and poor achievement.

- *They were not studying "hard enough."*

- *They were not spending "enough time" on their homework.*

- *They were not reading "carefully."*

- *They were not "focusing."*

I had assigned, lectured on, led discussion on, and given them study time on the chapter. I even had a worksheet of questions for homework. It had to be the students' fault.

Little did I know that when the students went home to do their homework, the parents would ask, "What's your assignment?"

The students would respond, "Chapter 24."

Both the parents and the students were at a loss as to what the assignment was. What does "Chapter 24" mean? What is the student supposed to do? How is the parent to help?

It never occurred to me that the problem was me. I did not know how to give an assignment.

I now know how to give assignments that help students achieve. It was not until years later that I learned this:

The greater the structure of a lesson and the more precise the directions on what is to be accomplished, the higher the achievement.

A High School Teacher

Assignments Must Be Clear and Precise

Yes, not only can you have more of your students complete their assignments, but more can even demonstrate that they have learned the subject matter. To have this happen, the teacher needs to know how to write assignments and tests. Assignments and tests are related.

This chapter gives an example of an effective assignment and its construction. The next chapter gives instructions in how to construct a test. Read both chapters as one.

Chapter 22

How to write an assignment

How to increase student achievement

Chapter 23

How to write a test

How to demonstrate achievement

An Assignment Must Have Structure

✓ It must have a consistent and familiar format that the students can recognize as their assignment.

✓ The assignment must be posted daily and in a consistent location before the students enter the room. (See Chapter 15.)

An Assignment Must Be Precise

✓ The assignments must state clearly and simply what the students are to accomplish.

✓ The key word is *accomplish*.

An effective assignment must have STRUCTURE and BE PRECISE!

The Difference Between a Procedure and an Assignment

Procedures: Tell a student what to do.
Assignments: Tell a student what to accomplish.

A poor assignment tells the student what to do at the BEGINNING of the assignment.

A good assignment states what a student is to accomplish or achieve when the assignment is FINISHED.

You tell a student what you want accomplished. Then you give a student procedures to help accomplish the assignment.

The Optimum Length of an Assignment

The shorter the assignment, the MORE likely the student will complete it.

The longer the assignment, the LESS likely the student will complete it.

The shorter the task, the greater the rate of success; the longer the task, the greater the rate of failure. This holds true whether you are giving tasks to children at home, employees in an office, or students at school.

Except for term papers and other longer projects:

■ No high school assignment should exceed three to five days.

■ No junior or middle school assignment should exceed two to four days.

■ No intermediate school assignment should exceed one to three days.

■ No primary school assignment should exceed a day or, occasionally, two.

■ No special education assignment should exceed 15 minutes.

The Same Textbook, Yet Only One Class Succeeded

Two teachers taught the same course, used the same textbook, covered the same materials, showed the same movies, did the same activities, and had the same kinds of students. One teacher was a success, the other a failure—in the eyes of the students, the parents, and the administration. Why?

The ineffective teacher used units that were two to three weeks long. When ask why, she would say that since there were six to nine weeks in the grading period, she divided her units accordingly into two- to three-week units. And since deficiency notices had to be sent four weeks into the grading period, she structured her units to end at that time; that also suited two- to three-week units.

Her curriculum consisted of following the textbook with 12 to 15 units of two to four weeks each for the year. And her assignments consisted of telling the students that they were responsible for whatever was in the chapter.

Her first test was given on the second or third Friday and taken home to grade. Her students did not know the result of their accomplishment until the third or fourth week of school. By that time it was far too late to help those who needed help. But then, she wasn't interested in helping anyway.

**She had covered the materials, and it was
up to the students to pass the tests.**

The effective teacher taught single concepts or skills, and her lessons were one to three days long. She knew that it was the students' learning style, not the grading period, that governed the length of the assignments.

Her curriculum consisted of 70 lessons, each teaching a single concept or skill culled from the textbook, activities, media, and current issues. The students completed two assignments a week and took two tests a week. (See Chapter 23.) They experienced four successes a week, and the teacher knew within the first week what had to be done to review, adjust, and correct to help her students succeed.

**She had a curriculum that uncovered the materials and
gave assignments that helped her students to succeed.**

A teacher's job is to uncover, not cover, the subject matter. **One best way to do this is to have short lessons with assignments that are structured and precise about what the student is to accomplish.**

The Most Important Words to Use in an Assignment

To teach for accomplishment, you must have a series of sentences that clearly and precisely state what is to be accomplished. These sentences are called objectives.

Each sentence must begin with a verb that states the action to be taken to show accomplishment. The most important word to use in an assignment is a verb, because verbs show if accomplishment has taken place or not.

> **To teach for learning, use words, especially verbs, that show that learning has taken place.**

Verbs are "action words" or "thinking words." The chart on the next page lists some verbs that can be used. The verbs have been organized into levels like floors in a building. The chart is based on the work of Dr. Benjamin Bloom, of the University of Chicago, and is known as Bloom's taxonomy. His taxonomy arranges the verbs into six related groups:

✓ Knowledge

✓ Comprehension

✓ Application

✓ Analysis

✓ Synthesis

✓ Evaluation

To help you remember the six levels of Bloom's taxonomy, remember this acronym: **K**eep **C**alm **A**t **A**ll **S**ports **E**vents.

Thinking Words to Use in Assignments

Bloom divided the verbs into six categories. **All the verbs in a group indicate a kind of thinking skill needed to complete an assignment.** *The verbs denote what a student is to do.*

6 **Evaluation**	appraise, choose, compare, conclude, decide, defend, evaluate, give your opinion, judge, justify, prioritize, rank, rate, select, support, value
5 **Synthesis**	change, combine, compose, construct, create, design, find an unusual way, formulate, generate, invent, originate, plan, predict, pretend, produce, rearrange, reconstruct, reorganize, revise, suggest, suppose, visualize, write
4 **Analysis**	analyze, categorize, classify, compare, contrast, debate, deduct, determine the factors, diagnose, diagram, differentiate, dissect, distinguish, examine, infer, specify
3 **Application**	apply, compute, conclude, construct, demonstrate, determine, draw, find out, give an example, illustrate, make, operate, show, solve, state a rule or principle, use
2 **Comprehension**	convert, describe, explain, interpret, paraphrase, put in order, restate, retell in your own words, rewrite, summarize, trace, translate
1 **Knowledge**	define, fill in the blank, identify, label, list, locate, match, memorize, name, recall, spell, state, tell, underline

Levels of Student Thinking Desired in an Assignment

The level of thinking you want from a student in an assignment is based on the level from which you select the verb you use. The type of thinking required at each level becomes more complex as you go from knowledge to evaluation.

6 **Evaluation** Use these verbs to ask a student to make a judgment based on criteria.	This thinking skill tells you that a student can appraise, assess, or criticize on the basis of specific standards and criteria.
5 **Synthesis** Use these verbs to ask a student to take parts of information to create an original whole.	This thinking skill tells you that a student can originate, combine, and integrate parts of prior knowledge into a product, plan, or proposal that is new.
4 **Analysis** Use these verbs to ask a student to show that he or she can see parts and relationships.	This thinking skill tells you that a student can examine, take apart, classify, predict, and draw conclusions.
3 **Application** Use these verbs to ask a student to use learning in a new situation.	This thinking skill tells you that a student can transfer selected information to a life problem or a new task with a minimum of direction.
2 **Comprehension** Use these verbs to ask a student to show comprehension or understanding.	This thinking skill tells you that a student can grasp and interpret prior learning.
1 **Knowledge** Use these verbs to ask a student to recall information.	This thinking skill tells you that a student can recall or recognize information, concepts, and ideas in the approximate form in which they were learned.

What Are Objectives?

> **OBJECTIVES are what a student must achieve in order to accomplish what the teacher states is to be learned, comprehended, or mastered.**

O bjectives do two things: assign and assess. They should also be written as a single sentence.

1. **Assign:** Objectives give direction or tell a student what is to be comprehended or mastered in an assignment.

2. **Assess:** Objectives tell the teacher if additional study is needed to master an objective. (See Chapter 23.)

Here are examples of typical objectives:

✓ Name, in order, the parts of the digestive system.

✓ Summarize the class discussion on important study skills.

✓ Plan a pizza party.

✓ Categorize the contents of the box.

✓ Create a new ending for the story.

✓ Judge the use of Agent Orange in Vietnam.

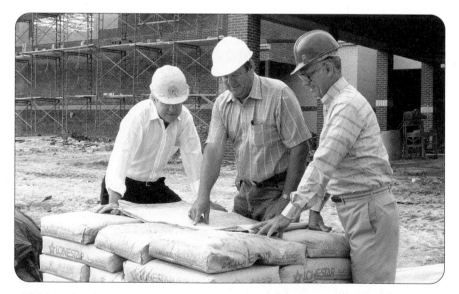

A blueprint gives a contractor directions for building a structure and the means to assess its construction. Likewise, objectives tell the students what is to be accomplished.

When and How to Write Objectives

Objectives state what you want the students to accomplish. The students must know before the lesson begins what they are responsible for learning.

✓ Objectives must be written before the lesson begins because objectives tell a teacher what is to be taught.

✓ Objectives are to be given to the students when the lesson begins so that the students know what they are responsible for.

Objectives Begin with Verbs

Verbs are action words that do two things:
1. Verbs tell a student what is to be accomplished.
2. Verbs tell a teacher what to look for to see if the student has accomplished what the teacher specified.

It is easy to write objectives. There are only two things to do.

Step 1. **Pick a verb.** Refer to the list on page 218, and use the verb you select as the first word in a sentence.

Only you know which verb to pick because you know what you want or need to teach, the readiness and level of competence of your students, and what you want to prepare your students to do next.

Refrain from choosing verbs all from one category, as this would challenge your students at only one level of thinking.

Step 2. **Complete the sentence.** The verb tells the student what action is to be taken, and the rest of the sentence tells the student what is to be performed or mastered.

Make sure that the sentence is precise and easily understood by you, the students, and their parents.

Words like the following are not good action verbs because it is difficult, if not impossible, to determine from them what the student is to do. They are also not on Bloom's list. **Do not use these verbs when you write objectives.**

appreciate	enjoy
be happy	like
beautify	love
celebrate	understand

It is important that a lay person can easily read and understand an objective. **The more understandable the sentence, the greater the chance that the student will do what is intended.**

Do not write complex objectives like the following:

Given two different molds growing on the same plate, the student will describe the inhibiting reaction at the interface of the molds.

Taken from a published elementary science program

Write precise objectives that state what you want the student to accomplish. The objective at the left could have been written in simple English:

Describe what happens when two molds grow together.

Applying Bloom's Taxonomy to the First Manned Landing on the Moon

Knowledge: Who was the first person to set foot on the moon?

Comprehension: Explain why the astronauts had to wear space suits while walking on the moon.

Application: Compute how much you would weigh on the moon.

Analysis: Compare the type of food taken on this journey to the type of food you would take if you were going mountain climbing for a week.

Synthesis: Pretend that you were the first person on the moon. What would your famous words be?

Evaluation: In your opinion, has the money that has been spent on the space program been worthwhile?

Objectives do not have to be written; they can be stated verbally, a useful approach in the primary grades and certain special education situations. You need not present all the objectives at one time, either. For elementary students, it may be more appropriate to state the objectives one or two at a time.

Most important, you must look at the objectives continually to make sure the class is on course.

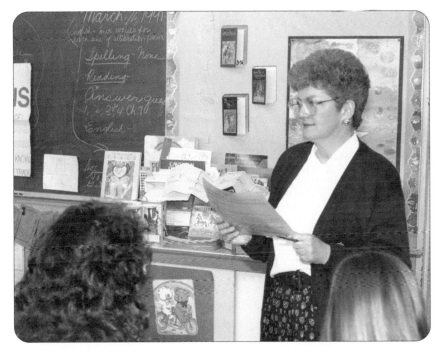

For instance, if you are driving, you refer repeatedly to your map. If you are building a house, the contractor, inspector, and you refer frequently to the blueprints. And if you are at a conference, you refer now and again to the program to determine the topic of the next session and where it will be held.

Schools typically have an open house about a month after school begins. Since the parents are going to ask you, "How do I tell what my child's assignment is?" tell the parents how you give assignments.

When you show the objectives to the parents, use the analogy of a map, blueprint, shopping list, or agenda. This will help them to understand what you are doing. The better they understand what you are doing, the better they can help their children do what they need to do.

One teacher holds a list of verbs during class discussion to keep track of the verbs that have been used.

How to Write an Assignment for Learning

The assignment on the next page, used with great success for years, is presented as an example only. Ignore the subject and focus on how the objectives for the assignment are written. Then apply the example to your own subject matter.

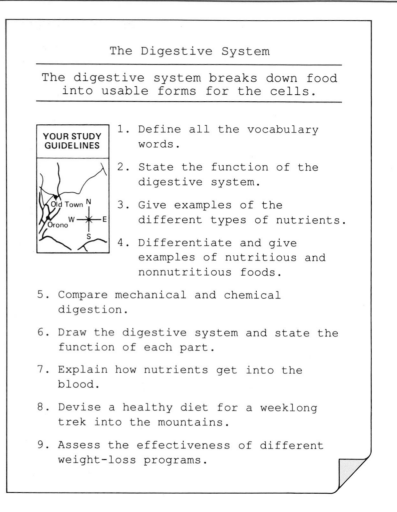

How to Use the Study Guidelines to Help Students Achieve

Step 1. The first time you give the students the assignment, explain to them why they are called "study guidelines." They are guides that you have prepared to help them complete the assignment. You want to be their guide and help them.

Step 2. Use the analogy of a map, program, agenda, or shopping list to explain the use of study guidelines. The study guidelines are to be presented as "user-friendly," not intimidating.

Step 3. Tell the students that the best way to use the study guidelines is to place them next to whatever they are studying out of, such as their textbook, worksheets, or notes. They are to use the study guidelines as their parents would use a map as a guide next to them on the car seat.

Step 4. Tell them that the central concept for the lesson is between the two black lines. They are to focus on this as the key idea for the assignment, as opposed to meaningless assignments like "Chapter 24," "Decimals," or "The Civil War."

Step 5. Point out the sentences on the study guidelines. There is no need to use the term *objectives* unless you choose to do so. Tell the students that these sentences are what they are responsible for. They must master these to understand the key idea.

Step 6. Tell the students that each sentence will be the subject of a series of questions on the exam. The students will be tested for their comprehension and mastery of each sentence or objective. (See Chapter 23.)

What About Students Who Need Additional Directions?

Objectives are fine for the average to above-average student, people who, when entrusted with a responsibility, will "take the ball and run with it." These students will grow up to be teachers, salespeople, or executives and will be able to translate a plan or a project into concrete results. **They are people who know how to solve problems and achieve on their own. They do not have to be told what to do!**

There are many students (and adults), however, who want to be told what to do. These students are not necessarily the below-average students. They may be students who have no background in your subject or face a linguistic or cultural barrier. For these students, write specific questions or procedures for each objective.

YOUR STUDY GUIDE FOR: <u>MAGNETISM</u>

"Nature of a Magnet"

    Your textbook has these four objectives at the beginning of the chapter.

1. *Explain how magnets are similar to objects with electric charges.*
2. *Use examples of the action of magnets to explain what magnetic poles are.*
3. *Explain how you can locate a magnetic field.*
4. *Use two magnets to demonstrate the effect of magnetic poles on each other.*

    I have prepared this Study Guide to help you learn these objectives. The following break the objectives into smaller questions or tasks. As you do the following, please:

■ Put the page number in the left margin where you found the answer. This will help you when you go back to study.

■ Note the number in the bracket. This tells you which objective it is matched to.

                              Thank you.

PAGE

(2) What is a magnetic pole?

(1) Three ways magnetic force and electrical forces are alike.

(4) Combinations for attracting and repelling.

       N with N _____

       S with N _____

       S with S _____

(2) What is a temporary magnet?

(2) What is a permanent magnet?

(2) Why does rubbing one end of a steel needle with a magnet magnetize it?

(3) What is a magnetic field?

(2) List five items that are attracted by a magnet.

(2) List five items that have no effect on a magnet.

(4) How can you show that a magnet has two poles?

    I hope this lesson does not repel you too much!

Example

Refer to objective 3 from the Study Guidelines on page 224.

Objective:

Give examples of the different types of nutrients.

Accompanying Questions:

1. Name the three kinds of nutrients.

2. Define and give examples of a protein.

3. Define and give examples of a carbohydrate.

4. Define and give examples of a fat.

5. Explain why proteins are important for your body.

6. Explain why carbohydrates are important for your body.

7. Explain why fats are important for your body.

Accompanying Task:

For students who really need lots of direction, next to each question, give the page number or location where the answer may be found.

Rather than giving the page number, have the students write the page number in the left margin after they complete the task or question. This way a student can quickly go back to the source of the answer for review.

The Key to Having Students Do Their Assignments

> **The Three Major Factors When Writing an Objective**
> 1. STRUCTURE: Use a consistent format.
> 2. PRECISENESS: Use succinct, clear sentences.
> 3. ACCOMPLISHMENT: Tell what is to be achieved.

To maximize the frequency with which the students will do their assignments and to maximize your effectiveness as a teacher:

1. Write assignments for accomplishment based on objectives, not coverage.

2. Write the objectives so succinctly and clearly that even outsiders such as parents can understand the assignment.

3. Give the students the objectives so that they know what they are responsible for accomplishing.

> *My teacher thought I was smarter than I was; so I was.*
>
> Quoted from a six-year-old

The Effective Teacher

1. Writes objectives that tell the student what is to be accomplished.

2. Knows how to write objectives at all levels of Bloom's taxonomy.

3. Writes assignments that will increase the rate of student success.

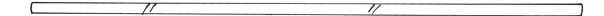

Key Idea: The purpose of a test is to determine if a student has mastered the objectives.

The Purpose of a Test

> **The major reason for giving a test is to find out if the students have accomplished the objectives of the assignment.**

Telling the students to read a chapter, story, or book involves no accomplishment. Nor does telling the students to read pages 222 to 235, complete a worksheet, or do a report on weather. Refer to Chapter 22 for the difference between teaching for accomplishment and just telling students what to do.

> **The students must have been given a list of criteria or objectives at the beginning of their assignment telling them what they are responsible for accomplishing.**

This chapter discusses the tests that are given at the end of an assignment to test for accomplishment of the objectives.

When to Write a Test

> **Both the assignment and the test are to be written concomitantly at the beginning of the assignment.**

The reason the assignment and the test must be written at the same time is that they are related and must correlate.

✓ **Grading Period.** Learning has nothing to do with the time interval of a grading period. Tests are not to be spaced according to time intervals, such as every two or three weeks because there is a six- to nine-week grading period or at the end of the third week because there is a deficiency notice due at the end of the fourth week.

Tests are used to monitor and evaluate learning, not because of a grading period. If grades are needed for report cards, structure the assignments, not the test, to fall within the grading period.

✓ **Period to Kill.** The number of questions on a test is not to be determined by the length of the class period. The length of a test is determined by the number and complexity of the objectives you are testing.

✓ **Points Needed for Curve.** It is a mistake to state arbitrarily, "I want each test worth 50 points so that I will have a sufficient point spread to grade the class on a curve."

The purpose of a test is not to get a point spread to compare one student against another. Tests are used to help the teacher determine what an individual student needs to learn, not to see who is smarter or dumber than someone else.

✓ **Sufficient Material Has Been Covered.** Tests are not to be written when sufficient materials have been covered. "We have covered enough materials, so let's have a test" is erroneous thinking.

THESE ARE NOT VALID REASONS FOR WRITING TESTS:
☐ Grading period about to end.
☐ To kill a period.
☐ Need points to grade on the curve.
☐ Sufficient material has been covered.

Some teachers will ask the class, "When did we have our last test?" When told, they exclaim, "Really, has it been that long? Then it's time we had another test to cover the material we've covered since the last test."

Tests are not to be used to test for teacher coverage of materials. **Tests are to be used to determine if the student has accomplished the stated objectives.**

Stop Covering and Start Accomplishing

One of the most misused and useless phrases in education is "I have so much to cover. How am I going to finish it by the end of the year?" Notice that the word *I* is used twice and the word *student* is never used.

> **Tests are given for the student's sake,**
> **not the teacher's sake.**

Many teachers, unfortunately, believe that their job is to cover a textbook, a collection of units or topics, or a set of worksheets. When a teacher "covers," that usually means that the teacher is going to go through the motions of telling (lecturing) and baby-sitting the students while they sit quietly and fill in a set of worksheets.

Getting the student to learn is the priority of the teacher. Teaching is not "coverage" because coverage has nothing to do with learning. The more quickly and the more superficially the teacher covers the material, the less the students learn.

Why? Because the students do not know what the teacher wants. Worse yet, the teacher probably does not know what he or she wants the students to know.

Learning has nothing to do with what you cover. Learning has to do with what you are able to get the student to accomplish. If you do not know what you want the students to accomplish, you cannot teach anything.

So stop covering and start getting the students to accomplish what you want them to accomplish. **Learning occurs only when the students demonstrate accomplishment.**

Show Examples of Your First Assignment and Test

One of the most frightening times for students is when the first assignment is due and the first test is to be taken. This is because the ineffective teacher never posts examples of what an ideal assignment or a typical test looks like. Students are lost because there are no models or examples.

They find out what should have been done or what should have been studied after the fact, and after an initial failure, many students are so disillusioned that they do not try again.

The following are ineffective instructions for assignments:

Complete the worksheet.
Answer all the questions at the end of the chapter.
Write a report on Amelia Earhart.
Do all the problems on page 57.
Write a summary of the chapter.

The following are ineffective instructions for tests:

The test will cover everything since the last test.
The test will cover everything we've covered this week.
There will be some multiple-choice questions, some true-false, and
    maybe some fill-ins.
The test will be worth about 50 points.

The effective teacher practices these techniques for assignments and tests:

■ Posts many examples of past assignments and tests so that the students can see what they are to do. Gives examples of ideal assignments that they can emulate.

■ Posts actual A papers written by past students and 100 percent tests they have taken. Not only do the students see excellent models, but by your encouragement, they recognize positive expectations on your part that everyone can achieve perfection.

The effective teacher posts examples of tests and explains how they are constructed. This way the students know how to study and what to expect.

Sample Spelling Pre-test

Spelling   Name #
Pre-test Unit 16-1   September 6, 19___

1 apple ✓   1 apple
2 school C   2 school
3 learns ✓   3 learn
4 neatness C   4 neatness
5 proofreld ✓ 5 proofread
6 quality C   6 quality
7 careful C   7 careful
8 homework C   8 homework
9 quietly C   9 quietly
10 proud ✓   10 proud

When to Give a Test

Call your assignments whatever you want to: lessons, chapters, units, or topics. To determine achievement for each assignment, there needs to be a test.

✓ Each assignment must have a set of criteria or objectives that state what the student is to demonstrate achievement in.

✓ Each assignment must have a set of questions written for each criterion or objective.

✓ The test must be written at the beginning of the assignment when the objectives were written.

✓ **The test must be given when the students finish the assignment.**

How to Write a Test

It is very easy to write a test. All you need to do is write a set of questions for each of the objectives.

> **The objectives govern what questions and how many questions are to be written for a test.**

Step 1. The basis of every test is the objectives for each assignment. Have these available as you write the test.

Step 2. Look at the first objective. Write a set of questions for the objective. Avoid writing only one question, because if the student guesses at the answer, you will not know if the student has mastered the objective.

Examples

OBJECTIVE:

List the steps of the scientific method.

QUESTION:

Which of the following are steps of the scientific method?

    A. observe, experiment, hypothesize

    B. experiment, study, conclude

    C. hypothesize, think, observe

    D. collect data, state principles, draw conclusions

OBJECTIVE:

Give reasons why paying attention is important in life.

QUESTION:

In the business world, your boss will want you to:

    A. conduct conferences.

    B. talk about the scientific process.

    C. pay attention to what you are doing.

    D. list the steps of the scientific method.

Step 3. Use any type of question. The questions do not even have to be on a written test. The questions can be of the oral or physical type whereby the teacher asks the student to perform a skill or produce a finished product.

Step 4. Repeat Steps 1 to 3 for each of the remaining objectives. When you have written a set of questions for each objective, you have finished writing the test.

On the next page is an example of a test that might have been written for a chapter or lesson on OBSERVATION. There are four key parts:

    1. Concept

    2. Objectives

    3. Questions

    4. Remediation

1. **Concept:** This is the key idea or major point of the lesson.

2. **Objectives:** These are the tasks the student is responsible for accomplishing.

3. **Questions:** Each question correlates with one of the objectives. Note the ( ) at the left of each question. The first number shows which objective the question correlates with.

4. **Remediation:** Look at the ( ) again. The second number indicates the part of the textbook in which the answer to the question may be found. (The next section, "The Test as a Corrective Tool," explains how to use this information to help the student study for mastery of the objective.)

This is an example only. Ignore the subject and focus on how the objectives and test questions correlate. Apply the example to your own subject matter.

Assignment: **Observation**

Lesson Concept:

Observing, or paying attention, is an important step in the scientific method.

Lesson Objectives:

1. Define all the vocabulary words.

2. Explain the importance in your life of studying biology.

3. List the steps of the scientific method.

4. State when and in what order the steps of the scientific method are applied.

5. Explain why the scientific method is useful in daily life.

6. Give reasons why paying attention is important in life.

Lesson Test:

1. Biology is the study of

    A. animals.
(1-1A) B. plants.
    C. living things.
    D. humans.

2. Science is

    A. the study of biology.
(1-1B) B. a method of thinking.
    C. paying attention.
    D. making observations.

3. Studying biology may be important to you because

    A. you may become a doctor.
(2-1B) B. you will learn about plants.
    C. you will find out what your body and your
       environment are trying to tell you.
    D. you will find out about animals.

4. Biology is important to you because

    A. you can learn about chemistry.
(2-1A) B. you can explain birth defects.
    C. plants and animals are important to study.
    D. life is the most precious resource on earth.

5. The first step in the scientific method is to

    A. state the problem.
(3-1B) B. collect data.
    C. conduct the experiment.
    D. make observations.

6. The following are some steps of the scientific method:

    A. observe, experiment, hypothesize
(3-1D) B. experiment, conclude, study
    C. hypothesize, think, observe
    D. collect data, state principles, draw conclusions

7. The steps of the scientific method can be

    A. used only with a scientific problem.
(4-1A) B. used at any time and in any order.
    C. used only in the proper order.
    D. used after much data has been recorded.

---

8. The scientific method can be used

    A. when you make observations.
(4-1B) B. when you experiment and collect data.
    C. when you state a conclusion.
    D. to accomplish all of the above.

9. The scientific method is used in daily life to

    A. solve problems.
(5-1B) B. make observations.
    C. make discoveries about the world.
    D. do all of the above.

10. Observations can be used in daily life to

    A. help you stay alive.
(5-1C) B. define science.
    C. explain the word *biology*.
    D. list the rules of the scientific method.

11. In the business world, your boss will want you to

    A. conduct experiments.
(6-1C) B. talk about science.
    C. pay attention.
    D. write about science.

12. When you don't feel well, your body is telling you

    A. to go to the hospital.
(6-1C) B. to work harder.
    C. to pay attention.
    D. to be careful.

13. Paying attention is a valuable life skill. It can help you to

    A. memorize the scientific method.
(1-Key B. appreciate life.
Idea) C. find a job.
    D. solve problems and make decisions.

14. Paying attention is an important step in

    A. the scientific method.
(1-Key B. the study of biology.
Idea) C. the study of science.
    D. causing problems.

The test you have just constructed in Step 4 is a **CRITERION-REFERENCED TEST**. The kind of test most teachers unknowingly write are **NORM-REFERENCED TESTS**. There is a major difference in the two types of tests:

✓ A **CRITERION-REFERENCED TEST** is a test in which each question is written to a prestated criterion. Since the students know what criteria they are responsible for, a percentage grade system should be used. The only person a student competes against in a criterion-referenced test is the student himself or herself. The student knows, for instance, that you have set your standard for an A at 92 percent.

✓ A **NORM-REFERENCED TEST** is a test used to determine placement on a normal distribution curve. Students are "graded on the curve" after a norm-referenced test. Norm-referenced tests are used to determine competitive ranking, such as for position on a team, entrance into a school, or placement on an organizational chart.

> **To teach for accomplishment, you use objectives and a criterion-referenced test.**

Norm-referenced tests have their place, as when you are trying to determine class rank or who will be on the first team. **When you are teaching a lesson, however, you are not teaching for rank. You are teaching for accomplishment, and you want everyone to succeed.**

When you have measurements, you have performance.

When you have no measurements, you have excuses.

Peter Drucker

You Already Know Before the Test Where Most of the Students Will Fall on a Curve

Benjamin Bloom noted the test scores of thousands of third graders and then followed them for several years. When the test scores of these students were examined in the seventh and the eleventh grades, he discovered that 90 percent received the same test scores they received back in the third grade.

When a teacher says, "I need points so that I can grade the class on a curve," this is not a valid reason for giving a test. According to Bloom, you already know where most of the students will fall on a curve.

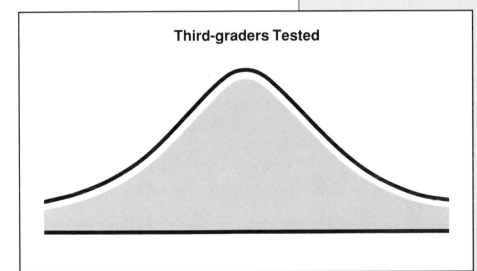

Third-graders Tested

The students whose test scores are in the shaded area in the third grade will receive the same test scores in the seventh and eleventh grades.

When students come into a class, most students already know who will be in the fast and who will be in the slow reading group, who will do well and who will do poorly, and who the teacher will treat as a winner and who will be treated as a loser. This is not what education is for, to peg people in holes at an early age and remind them with a succession of bell-shaped curves that they are either smart, average, or dumb.

A test should be used to do two things:

1. The TEACHER should use the results of each test item to remediate and correct for student mastery.

2. The STUDENTS should be graded on a percentage system. This way they are competing only against themselves to reach a level of achievement or success.

The main role of the teacher is to help every student reach the highest possible level of achievement.

The Test as a Corrective Tool

Assume that you have returned from a visit to the doctor. Your friend or spouse asks you, "What happened at the doctor's today?"

You say, "The doctor is running a test on me."

This does not mean that the doctor is going to grade you on the curve. It means that the doctor is awaiting the results of the medical tests. When the results are studied, the doctor then determines what needs to be done to correct your illness.

A criterion-referenced test is to be used in the same way, as a diagnostic instrument. **A test tells you if the student needs corrective help.**

Students who are lost or left behind have little chance of getting back on track.

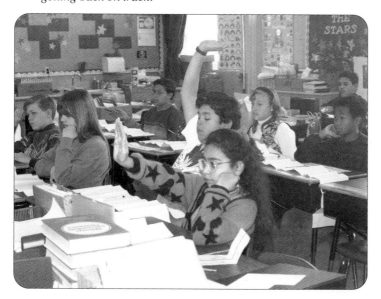

If the student **MASTERS** an objective, do not assign more work. Give the student enrichment materials or ask the student to help another student. Enrichment work could include puzzles, games, software, or leisure reading.

If the student **DOES NOT MASTER** an objective, give the student remediation or corrective help.

If you do not correct and remediate, learning gets worse and worse as the year progresses. It's no different from everything else in life. If you do not correct an illness or a bad habit, such as a cold, chain smoking, or drug abuse, your body or your life just gets worse and worse.

After some 10 chapters or units of study, many students have retained only 10 to 20 percent of what has been covered. The poor performance occurs because the ineffective teacher rolls through the school year, covering the chapters and giving tests because the teacher wants points to grade the class on a curve. After the test, the teacher blithely moves on to the next chapter without concern for students who do not comprehend the chapter.

If the Student Misses a Question

If a student should miss a question, remediate or give corrective action. Assume that the student answered question 6 incorrectly on the test shown on page 235.

> 6. The following are some steps of the scientific method:
>   A. observe, experiment, hypothesize
> (3-1B)   B. experiment, conclude, study
>   C. hypothesize, think, observe
>   D. collect data, state principles, draw conclusions

Note the information in the ( ). This gives you and the student information for remediation or correction.

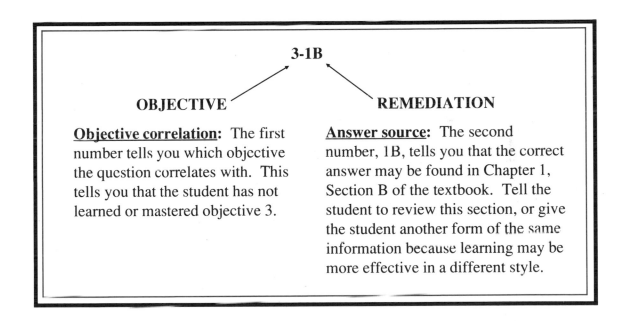

3-1B

OBJECTIVE   **REMEDIATION**

Objective correlation: The first number tells you which objective the question correlates with. This tells you that the student has not learned or mastered objective 3.

Answer source: The second number, 1B, tells you that the correct answer may be found in Chapter 1, Section B of the textbook. Tell the student to review this section, or give the student another form of the same information because learning may be more effective in a different style.

Tests are to be given for the student's sake, not the teacher's sake. The purpose of a test is not to accumulate points to grade the students on a curve. **The purpose of a test is to help the teacher identify what the student has or has not learned.**

Do You Grade All Tests?

There are two kinds of criterion-referenced and norm-referenced tests, FORMATIVE TESTS and SUMMATIVE TESTS.

✓ **FORMATIVE TESTS** are like drills and practice tests. They are given during the formative, developmental, or teachable period when the student is in the process of mastering an objective. You may not want to grade these tests. These simply let you and the students know how well you are doing at teaching and they at learning the objective.

✓ **SUMMATIVE TESTS** are given at the end of a unit when you want to sum up what the student has learned to determine a grade.

Formative tests are used to determine what remediation is needed for a student to master the content or skill (objective).

If it is determined that a student did not master a particular objective, a corrective activity must be given. A corrective activity is one that is given to the student in another form or with a different explanation so that the student can learn the objective through a different approach.

After the corrective activity is given, another formative test or a summative test should be given to determine mastery. **The test should be the same kind of test as first given, but the questions are asked in a different way.**

Some authorities, such as Bloom, believe that you should test and retest until mastery is attained. Others believe that testing twice is sufficient because much of the content covered in class is spiral and the student will come around to the content again later on in the school year.[1]

**Formative and Summative Tests
in Our Daily Lives**

Formative Tests:	Summative Tests:
Spring training	Opening day of the season
Dress rehearsal	Opening night
Training wheels on bike	Alone on two wheels
The bunny hill	The giant slalom
Drivers ed	Getting licensed from DMV
Student teaching	The first day of school

---

[1]Guskey, Thomas R. *Implementing Mastery Learning*. Belmont, Calif.: Wadsworth, 1985.

Beware of Publishers' Test Banks

There's a spate of test banks today. These are questions generated by publishers and even by school districts and stored so that you can just take and use questions from them. Some publishers will even send you a test from their bank if you tell them what kinds of questions and how many you want. **In practice, a test bank is a great time saver; in theory, it is bad test writing.**

The questions on a test must correlate with the known objectives, just as blood in a blood bank must correlate with the patient's blood type. All the blood stored in a blood bank is of no value if you do not know the patient's blood type. You would not administer a transfusion to the patient under such circumstances.

Likewise, if you and the students do not know what is to be accomplished, all the questions stored in a bank are of no value. Do not write a test or use a test bank under such circumstances.

A test bank should consist of questions written in light of prestated objectives. To produce a test bank of your own:

- Have the teachers in the department or at the grade level contribute objectives to a bank.

- Then write questions for the objectives. Be sure to include questions from all levels of Bloom's taxonomy. (See Chapter 22.)

- Now you have questions stored by objectives, as you have blood stored by type.

When you write a test:

- Look first at the objective you wish to test. Then select questions from the bank under that objective.

- If you are writing several formative tests, you test for the same objectives, but you have different questions on each test. In this way, you can even give the same class different forms of the same test.

The purpose of formative testing followed with corrective activities is not unique to education:

✓ A doctor does a laboratory test, prescribes medicine, and then repeats this procedure until the patient is cured.

✓ A baseball player watches a video of his or her swing, makes corrections at bat, and repeats this procedure until the batting average improves.

✓ A chef tinkers with a recipe, making changes until a perfect cake results.

The effective teacher tests and corrects, tests and corrects, because the teacher wants all the students to achieve.

The ineffective teacher delights in giving out only a few A's. Teachers do not give grades; students earn grades. Also, the ineffective teacher is satisfied with grading people on a curve and letting half the class know that they are below average or failures.

The purpose of teaching is to help all people succeed.

> **The purpose of teaching is to help all people succeed, not to remind people continually that they are failures.**

Through testing and correcting, the effective teacher is seeking 80 to 90 percent mastery for each assignment. If each assignment reaches 80 to 90 percent mastery, after some 10 chapters or units of studies, most students will have attained 80 to 90 percent mastery.

The students are successful and happy, and the teacher spends much of the time encouraging the students to do even better.

Your Students Can Outperform 98 Percent of the Regular Students

There are three basic methods of instruction.

1. **Conventional Instruction:** This is the ubiquitous textbook, lecture, worksheet, and test method. The chapters in the textbook constitute the assignment, and the tests are written to determine students' marks only.

2. **Mastery Learning:** The instruction is the same as in conventional instruction except the assignments are based on objectives the students are responsible for accomplishing and the tests are criterion-referenced tests. Many of the tests are formative tests used to determine what kind of corrective help the student needs before the summative test is given.

3. **Tutoring:** This is one-to-one instruction, frequently of the conventional form but preferably of the mastery learning form.

We all know that one-to-one tutoring is the most effective form of instruction, but this would be too costly, so Benjamin Bloom set out to find a comparable form of instruction that could be used in standard classroom group instruction. He found it! He discovered:

■ The average **TUTORED student outperformed 98 percent** of the students taught under a conventional form (within 2 standard deviations, if you are statistically inclined).

■ The average student taught under **MASTERY LEARNING outperformed 84 percent** of the students taught under a conventional form (1 standard deviation).

Based on what has been described about assignments (Chapter 22) and tests (Chapter 23), Steps 1 to 4 describe how a teacher could teach very effectively.

Step 1. Begin each assignment based on a set of objectives.

Step 2. Write each test based on the objectives; that is, criterion-referenced tests.

Step 3. Make the first test a formative test. You are teaching under a mastery learning format when you use Steps 1 to 3. You are now 84 percent more effective than the conventional teacher.

Step 4. After the tests are graded, you note, for instance, that the student has missed question 6.

Look at the information in the parentheses to the left of question 6. (See page 239 for an example.) With this information, determine what corrective activity you need to give to the student who has not mastered the objective. Even help the student with the corrective activity.

You have just changed from group instruction to individualized tutoring. You are now 98 percent more effective than the conventional teacher.

Mastery Learning + Individual Tutoring = High Student Achievement

---

Benjamin S. Bloom
"The Search for Methods of Group Instruction as Effective as One-to-One Tutoring."
Educational Leadership, May 1984, pp. 4-6.

The Effective Teacher

1. **Writes criterion-referenced tests.**

2. **Gives both formative and summative tests.**

3. **Uses formative tests to determine the appropriate corrective help.**

4. **Grades and encourages for percentage mastery, not on a curve.**

It's Simple to Record Your Grades

1. Using an alphabetical listing of students, assign each student a number beginning with 1 in your grade book.

2. When new students join the class, add their names to the bottom of your roll, and assign them the next available number.

3. On all tests, papers, projects, and reports turned in during the school year, students must write their unique number.

4. For consistency, choose one place on papers where this number must be written as a class procedure and routine.

5. For multiple-choice, true-false, and fill-in answers, give your students an answer form so that all answers are in the same place.

6. After the papers are collected, ask a student to arrange the papers in numerical order.

7. Do not grade tests one at a time, while watching the television and snacking. Spread the forms on a large table, perhaps 10 across, and correct the answers three to five questions at a time as you move across the forms.

8. Put the papers back in order ready to be recorded in your grade book. Then ask an aide or spouse to record the grades for you.

CHAPTER 24

Key Idea: The greater the time students work together and the greater the responsibilities students take for their work, the greater the learning.

What Is Cooperative Learning?

Cooperative learning is a win-win situation.

Everyone wins: students, teachers, administrators, community, and humankind.

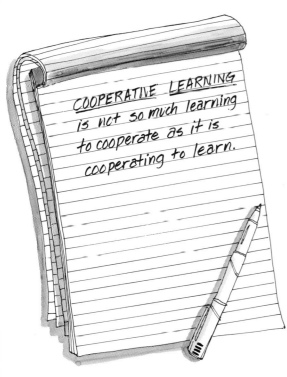

COOPERATIVE LEARNING is not so much learning to cooperate as it is cooperating to learn.

The students now know how to accomplish their assignments (Chapter 22), and they know how they will be tested (Chapter 23). Between the assignment and the test is what teaching is all about. Effective teachers spend their lifetime learning better techniques that will help students succeed in school and in life. This chapter will discuss one of those techniques: **COOPERATIVE LEARNING**.

Cooperative learning refers to a set of instructional techniques whereby students work in small, mixed-ability learning groups. The students in each group are responsible not only for the material being taught in class but also for helping their groupmates learn. In its simplest form:

✓ The teacher presents a lesson to the students.

✓ The student groups are given activities to master the objectives.

✓ The teacher teaches group and study strategies.

✓ The students work together to help one another master the objectives.

In cooperative groups, students help one another complete an activity the teacher has assigned. It is a structured situation. During the activity, the students clarify opinions, compare impressions, share solutions, and develop skills for leadership and teamwork.

Cooperative learning is a win-win situation. Everyone wins: students, teachers, administrators, community, and humankind.

> *The parents . . . see cooperative learning as a bonus because their children are getting the training in leadership, group decision making, and conflict management they'll need to be successful in later life.*

Roger Johnson
Educational Leadership,
November 1987, p. 16.

The reason cooperative learning is so successful is that the context of a work group is more important than the content of the group. If you have a group of people

Compete Only Against Yourself

If you must hang but two signs in your classroom, let this be one of them.

The message to your students is this:

■ There is only one person in the world you need to compete against, and that is yourself.

■ Strive each day to be the best person possible.

■ Your mission in life is not to get ahead of other people; your mission is to get ahead of yourself.

■ But while you are competing against yourself, you are expected to work with everyone else in this classroom cooperatively and respectfully.

■ You are responsible not only for your own learning but for the learning of your support buddies as well.

who care for and are committed to one another, they are going to achieve the goal of the activity much more quickly than if each were to attempt the task alone.

How to Divide Your Class into Groups

Factors of Success

1 – Using first day of school activities

6 – Enhancing positive expectations

7 – Involving the home

8 – Dressing for success

9 – Using invitational learning

10 – Using the five appropriate words

11 – Implementing effective classroom management strategies

12 – Having the classroom ready with a positive atmosphere

13 – Introducing yourself properly

14 – Arranging and assigning seating

15 – Posting and starting assignments immediately

16 – Taking roll quickly

18 – Investing time on teaching the discipline plan

20 – Rehearsing the class on procedures and routines

21 – Maximizing academic learning time

22 – Giving structured assignments with clear goals

23 – Explaining that tests are written to test for mastery

24 – Implementing strategies for cooperative learning

The question is not how to divide the class but rather how quickly and effectively the class will divide itself when the students are asked to do so.

Some teachers have no problems dividing their students into groups. When told to do so, the students do it quickly and quietly. Other teachers have problems getting their students to divide into groups. When told to do so, the students whine, complain, and even refuse to work with other people. Why?

Effective grouping is dependent on two major factors:

1. **The class climate**

2. **The explanation**

The Class Climate

Quite simply, if the students dislike the class or the teacher or are not successful, grouping will be difficult. **It is important that all the determinants of successful student cooperation be in place before the class is divided into groups.** The box to the left lists determining factors that may affect student cooperation. The number before the item indicates the chapter in this book where more information can be found.

When students do not cooperate, the ineffective teacher helplessly wonders, "What am I supposed to do?" and looks for a quick fix to resolve the crisis. There are no quick fixes in education. Implicit in the "Factors of Success" list on the previous page is the fact that it is the teacher who is responsible for the success of the classroom. The effective teacher knows this.

Telling the students to break up into groups is easy if the students are successful in class. It is the responsibility of the teacher to facilitate this success. In a successful classroom, the students respect the teacher's ability to move them quickly into groups for work.

✓ The teacher's job is to orchestrate all the classroom factors so that they function in harmony.

✓ The teacher is like the conductor of an orchestra, the captain of a ship, or the coach of a team.

✓ The teacher is a problem solver and a maker of decisions responsible for student success.

> The effective teacher has knowledge and control of ALL THE FACTORS related to the effective classroom that influence student success.

The effective teacher orchestrates all the factors for an effective classroom.

The Explanation

How quickly students move into groups depends on how explicitly the teacher explains how and why groups will be formed. "OK, divide into groups of four" is not how groups are set up. Vague directions like this are sure to provoke comments like these:

Can I work with Andrew?
Do I have to work with Charlotte?
How long do I have to stay in this group?

There is no need to solicit class input on grouping because there will be no permanent groups in the class. Simply tell your students the following:

✓ **Number of People in a Group:** *The class will be divided into groups many times. Each time there is a need for a group, the size of the group will depend on the nature of the activity. Some activities may take two people; others may take four, eight, or whatever. Whatever is the number needed, that will be the number of people in the group.*

Therefore, please do not ask if you can work with any particular person because the groups are not fixed.

✓ **Length of Time in a Group:** *Each time the class is divided into groups, the length of the group activity will depend on the nature of the activity. Some activities may take two minutes, others may take two days or two weeks.*

When the activity is finished, the group will be disbanded. Therefore, please do not ask how long you must be in a group. You will be in a group until the activity is finished.

Prepare yourself for the working world, where you will be working with many different combinations of people on committees, in groups, and on project teams for different lengths of time.

Cooperative learning is not something that will happen overnight. It occurs incrementally and requires time, patience, and constant reinforcement.

In the early grades, teachers should begin by teaching procedures and routines whereby the students move into groups quickly and quietly, speak softly, share the things they use, do their job, and take turns.

Younger children will ask the teacher when activity directions are not understood. Older students will often not ask because they do not like to admit that they do not know. Or if they do ask each other, they will frequently get a putdown response like, "What do you mean you don't understand? You stupid or what?" So rather than admit "stupidity," they withdraw and do not participate, misbehave to distract from their not understanding, or ask to work with someone who will not attack their self-esteem.

Older students inherently like to work together, so the problem is not student participation or interaction. It is poor teacher instructions. **When the directions, whether verbal or written, do not state what is to be done, and what is to be accomplished, the students will start to act up.** The teacher must structure and write the activity for maximum understanding.

They Knew the Names of Only Six Students

The following part of a letter was received by one us after presenting a workshop to a group of student teachers at a local college.

One of the student teachers tried something in her class to test out one of your ideas. She handed out a blank seating chart to her ninth-grade class and asked all the students to write in the seating chart, giving first and last names. Only about 80 percent of the kids seemed to have more than two-thirds of the names correct. Many of them only knew first names, and there were even a few students who could name only 6 or 8 students sitting right around them out of a class of 35.

The letter was dated May 20, so these student teachers were in a classroom that had been together for nine months. In addition, there were two teachers in the room, a cooperating teacher and a student teacher. Yet at the end of the year, few of the students really knew one another.

When you have a situation like the above, students are sure to misbehave, refuse to work cooperatively, and be reluctant to participate in group activities.

When students refuse to work together, the teacher may be to blame.

How quickly students move into groups depends on how explicitly the teacher explains the mechanics and responsibilities of the group assignment.

Who Is Placed in a Group?

Dividing the class into groups has nothing to do with the number in a group. The number of people in a group depends on the nature of the activity. What is important is who is placed in a group and why you want the grouping done accordingly.

> **Cooperative groups should be heterogeneous in terms of ability, sex, ethnicity, and other personal characteristics.**

Studies show that students are more positive about one another when they learn to work cooperatively, regardless of ability, ethnic background, or handicap.

Cooperative learning teaches the social skills necessary for success in a global economy.

✓ Students who have cooperative skills are more able to appreciate the viewpoint of others.

✓ They are more positive about taking part in controversy.

✓ They have better social skills.

✓ They have more positive expectations about working with others than students from competitive settings.

What you want for every student, especially for those with a lot of ability, is a cheering section urging and helping other students to work to maximum capacity. And you have the high, medium, and low kids in the same group, with the low kid cheering the high one on to boost the group score so that all can get a better grade. **The cooperative system encourages everyone, regardless of ability, background, or handicap, to work at top capacity.**

As students become more skilled in working together, they can practice more sophisticated skills, such as these:

✓ Asking for and giving help

✓ Showing that they are interested in what others are saying

✓ Talking about several solutions before choosing one

✓ Criticizing ideas, not people

✓ Looking for evidence before changing their mind

✓ Asking questions to try to understand another point of view

Over the years in school, learning experiences become richer and richer, and the students build a large repertoire of social skills that are essential in the global economy. The global economy is an economy of diversity. **It is only from working with a diversity of people that students will learn the skills needed in a world of diversity. These skills are learned when students are grouped heterogeneously.** There is nothing simple in such a process, but the results are worth it.

What About the Student Who Does Not Work?

> **The number of people in a group must equal the number of jobs in the group.**

Groups are to be divided by the number of jobs, not by the number of people. People do not go through life always working, say, in groups of four. The task always specifies the optimum number of people needed.

The reason some students do nothing or copy from other students is that they do not have specific tasks or jobs. Determine the number of students you need to accomplish an activity, divide the class accordingly, and then spell out the assignments.

For instance, in a group of four:

Student 1 is responsible for getting the materials and returning them to the appropriate place when the day or period is over.

Student 2 is responsible for seeing that the steps of the activity are followed.

Student 3 is responsible for making observations, recording data, and taking minutes as the activity progresses.

Student 4 is responsible for overseeing the writing of the group report.

Being responsible does do not mean that the student does all the work. Rather it means that the student is in charge of getting others to help in the task. For instance, it may take several people to get all the materials, everyone to help clean up, several to make observations, and certainly everyone to contribute to the group report.

✓ The teacher may not want to assign who does what job. If no assignments are made, the students are to choose who does which job.

✓ If the students may choose who does which job, you may want to specify that they are not to do the same type of job as they did in the last activity.

✓ Have group rules, responsibilities, and evaluation. (See the sample activity on page 262.)

What Are the Benefits and Results of Cooperative Learning?

> **Quite simply, all the research indicates that cooperative learning leads to higher achievement for all students. No research states otherwise.**

The research on cooperative learning is the oldest research practice in American social psychology. First done in 1897, a century of research has included hundreds of studies.

There is probably more evidence validating the use of cooperative learning than there is for any other aspect of education—more than for class size, lecturing, age grouping, reading readiness, departmentalizing, or the 50-minute period. And the research applies as much for teachers as it does for students.

> *The idea that people working together toward a common goal can accomplish more than people working by themselves is a well-established principle of social psychology.*

> Robert Slavin
> "Cooperative Learning and the Cooperative School."
> *Educational Leadership,* November 1987, p. 7.

These are some examples of the findings from research on cooperative learning:

✓ Many studies have shown positive effects for both high- and low-ability students, dispelling the myth that high-achieving students will not progress if they interact with students of lesser ability.

✓ On retention tests, cooperative learners score at least as well as high-achievers from competitive learning situations.

✓ Cooperative learners use higher-quality reasoning strategies, higher-level processing, and deeper thinking than isolated students.

You May Not Do the Same Job You Did Last Time

As the competitive global economy increases in complexity, the skills of cooperative learning and group problem solving may well become increasingly important for individual, corporate, and national success.

Scattered throughout the rest of this chapter are four stories where working cooperatively played an important role in the company's success. (See "The NUMMI Story," page 255; "The Diamond Star and Mazda Story" and "The Monsanto Story," page 256; and "The Honda Story," page 260.)

These stories validate the need to begin students at an early age to work cooperatively with one another. They will use the skill throughout their lifetime.

✓ Cooperative learners develop the skills of leadership, communication, decision making, and conflict management they need for future success in school and in a career.

✓ Cooperative learners develop a sense of interdependence. Students learn to care about and become committed to others' success as well as their own.

In a competitive classroom that lacks cooperative groups, students really have a stake in one another's failure. That includes making sure that the worse other students do, the better it is for them to get a higher grade. In an individualistic classroom, students have no stake in other students whatsoever. Each student works independently on his or her own agenda. What happens to others is irrelevant.

In cooperative groups, students have a vested interest in making sure that other people do well. Anything they can do to help their group or support buddies learn the material better, retain it longer, get a better grade on the test, or learn new skills benefits them all. They celebrate when other people learn.

✓ Cooperative learning produces committed relationships in which students really care about each other and provide assistance and help when needed. It promotes more positive peer relationships, better social skills, more social support, and, partly for that reason, higher self-esteem. Students like the class better, they're more interested in the subject, and they're more self-disciplined.

✓ In cooperative learning, students take more responsibility for helping each other with assignments and problems. That alleviates some of the stress on the teacher to maintain order and to keep the students on task.

✓ Cooperative learning improves self-confidence for many students. Because the teammates become responsible for one another's learning and have a vested interest in the others' success, all students tend to be more successful. Success builds self-confidence. By working together, the students find out that their ideas can be useful to others, and they become more self-confident.

The NUMMI Story

When the General Motors plant in Fremont, California, closed down in 1984, it had the highest absenteeism and lowest productivity of any General Motors plant.

It reopened in 1987 as the New United Motors Manufacturing, Inc. (NUMMI), a partnership between General Motors and Toyota. It is a union plant with many of the former union employees producing Chevrolets.

Its business style is vastly different, however:

■ It is based on participation, sharing of ideas, and problem solving together.

■ Groups of 7 to 12, under a group leader, are responsible for all the jobs in a given area on the production line.

■ All group members learn all the jobs and rotate among them.

Today this factory has the lowest absenteeism and the highest productivity of any GM plant—in fact, 25 percent better than any other GM plant.

The Diamond Star and Mazda Story

Two new automobile plants opened in 1988, Diamond Star Motors (owned by Chrysler and Mitsubishi) in Normal, Illinois, and Mazda Motor Company in Flat Rock, Michigan. The plants spent $42 million altogether to find and train the right workers.

Here is what their research revealed:

- Interpersonal skills are in. Rugged individualism is out. If you can't get along with others, you don't get in the door. And if you think that you can just do your job and go home, think again.

- To fit the bill, an applicant must show an aptitude for teamwork.

- Team participation is mandatory. Reward flows not so much from your personal performance as from your impact on the team and the company.

- They want employees who are not only good at their job but also have potential for growth. They want workers with high levels of skill and motivation and an aptitude for learning new methods.

Neither company spends much effort or money training for team participation in Japan, where the school system does much of the training and screening for them. **People who work together produce far superior products than people who are free spirits in an organization.**

"How Does Japan Inc. Pick Its American Workers?"
Business Week, October 3, 1988, pp. 84-88.

The Monsanto Story

Alvin K. Allison is a worker at the Monsanto Chemical Company in Greenwood, South Carolina. He leads a team of mechanics who divide the work and make key decisions themselves. There is no foreman peering over a worker's shoulder. The mechanics are involved in decision making and quality control.

"I knew 20 years ago that I could direct my own job," says Allison.

The result of cooperative work? Quality improvement and productivity is 47 percent higher than four years earlier.

"Monsanto Is Teaching Old Workers New Tricks,"
Business Week, August 21, 1989, p. 67.

How to Make Cooperative Learning Work

1. **Positive Interdependence.** Interdependence refers to the relationships that individuals have to others' success in a group. **For cooperative learning to be successful, the students really have to believe that they are in it together and to care for one another's learning.**

**The Four Basic Elements Needed
to Make Cooperative Learning Work**

1. Positive Interdependence
2. Social Skills
3. Individual Accountability
4. Group Evaluation

In cooperative groups, each student has a responsibility to the team. Goals or tasks are structured so that the students concern themselves with the performance of all members of the group, not just their own performance. When students understand that they are part of an interdependent group, they usually find ways to work together for the benefit of all.

2. **Social Skills.** The basis of cooperative learning is social skills that help students share leadership, communicate effectively, build trust, and manage conflict. Generally, the students do not come to the classroom with those skills; the skills must be defined clearly and taught in much the same way that academic subjects are taught.

Lots of verbal face-to-face interaction, explaining, arguing, resolving of conflicts, elaborating, consensus-forming, and summarizing will occur and should be encouraged.

3. **Individual Accountability.** Each member of the cooperative group is held accountable for the performance of all. It must be clear that every member of the group has to learn, that there's no free ride. No one can sit on the sidelines and let others do the work; everyone has to be in there, pulling equal weight.

The teacher can stress accountability by calling on one groupmate at random to give the group's report at the end of a task. If the student can report the group's conclusions, procedures, or solutions, the group has been successful. If the student called on cannot report the group's results, the group, not the individual, suffers. Therefore, it becomes the group's responsibility, not the teacher's, to ensure everyone's participation.

4. **Group Evaluation.** Periodically, the groups must assess how well they are working together and how they could do better.

How to Structure a Cooperative Learning Activity

Structure your lessons for cooperative learning. You can't just tell people to work cooperatively. The people at Diamond Star and Mazda (page 256) spent $42 million dollars to find and train people to work cooperatively.

> **How To Get the Students to Work Cooperatively on an Activity**
>
> 1. Specify the group **NAME**.
> 2. Specify the **SIZE** of the group.
> 3. State the **PURPOSE, MATERIALS, AND STEPS** of the activity.
> 4. Teach the **PROCEDURES**.
> 5. Specify and teach the **COOPERATIVE SKILLS** needed.
> 6. Hold the individuals **ACCOUNTABLE** for the work of the group.
> 7. Teach ways for the students to **EVALUATE** how successfully they have worked together.

1. **Specify the Group Name.** Want something better than calling your groups teams, squads, or groups?

> Consider calling the groups **support groups** and each member of the support group a **support buddy**.

Learning together is epitomized by the concept of a support group. There are support groups for people trying to lose weight, stop drinking, and learn parenting skills. There are support groups for single parents, senior citizens, abused children, battered wives, and war veterans. Power groups, or business support groups, exist to help such people as businesswomen to achieve leadership roles and secretaries to become executives.

A support group is formed by people, with like needs and goals, who join together to care for and help one another to solve problems and achieve success. Support groups in the classroom are formed for the same reason.

2. **Specify the Size of the Group.** The size of the group is a factor of how many jobs are needed to complete the activity. (See "What About the Student Who Does Not Work?" on page 252.)

3. **State the Purpose, Materials, and Steps of the Activity.** The students must be given an activity that is structured enough so that the students know what is to be done and how. (See the sample activity on page 262.)

4. <u>**Teach the Procedures**</u>. Here are four procedures for you to consider with your students. They should be posted, taught, modeled, rehearsed, and monitored. (See Chapter 20.)

1. **You are responsible for your own job and the results of the group.** (In the working world, you are responsible for your own job and the results of the people you work with.)

2. **If you have a question, ask your support buddies. Do not ask your teacher.** (In the working world, you do not raise your hand for help. You seek, ask, and research because you are being paid a salary to perform.)

3. **You must be willing to help if a support buddy asks you for help.** (In the working world, you are expected to apply teamwork skills.)

4. **If no one can answer a question, agree on a consensus question and appoint one person to raise a hand for help from the teacher.** (In the working world, negotiating and reaching agreements are the keys to success.)

5. <u>**Specify and Teach the Cooperative Skills Needed**</u>. Teach, model, and monitor the group rules for the sample activity on page 262.

6. <u>**Hold the Individuals Accountable for the Work of the Team**</u>. The teacher acts as consultant to the group after setting the objectives, assignments, and procedures. Problems are turned back to the group for resolution. That aspect of cooperative learning is often difficult at first, but it is crucial to the success of cooperative learning in the classroom.

PROCEDURES DURING GROUP WORK

1. You are responsible for your own job and the results of the group.
2. If you have a question, ask your SUPPORT BUDDIES. Do not ask your teacher.
3. You must be willing to help if a SUPPORT BUDDY asks for help.
4. If no one can answer a question, agree on a single question and appoint one person to raise a hand for help from the teacher.

The support groups are to write reports cooperatively and give team presentations. Students must control the process as well as the content of the lesson.

The support group will get a group grade, and that grade will be each individual's grade, so it is important that each member of the support group support the others to achieve.

7. **Teach Ways for the Students to Evaluate How Successfully They Have Worked Together.** Tell your students to write down the group rules. (See page 263.) After each rule, state whether their support group followed the rule most of the time, sometimes, or not at all.

For each rule, have the support groups discuss how they can improve their cooperative skills. The rules that truly need to be discussed are those that received a rating of "most of the time." By being aware of why they followed the rules most of the time, they can review and apply the success of how they worked together to improving the rules rated lower.

Learning is an individual activity but not a solitary one.

It is more effective when it takes place within a supportive community of learners.

The Honda Story

Honda has a factory in Marysville, Ohio. The company employs more than 10,000 "associates" (not workers).

The associates work in groups. The procedure is for each group to submit complaints and suggestions to management at the end of each shift. In the United States, management does not want to hear about problems, and workers do not want to get involved with problems.

The Honda procedure requires answers to three questions:

1. What was the problem?
2. What did you do about the problem?
3. What is your suggestion for long-term solution of the problem?

Honda works on quality through empowering workers, within groups, to achieve excellence.

Overall, the average Japanese employee submits 24 suggestions a year, compared with 0.14 per U.S. worker (That's the same as $24 vs. 14 cents, no comparison in a competitive environment).

Thomas Peters
San Antonio Light,
February 7, 1989.

The Benefits of a Structured Cooperative Activity

✓ Peer pressure severely limits achievement in many schools. Students who do not do well scorn those who do well, and these students join together, socially, to limit each other's success. In cooperative classrooms, by contrast, **students encourage their teammates to do well because they all benefit.**

✓ **All members of the group share leadership responsibilities.** Each member has a job to do, and the group has no formal leader.

✓ In their groups, **the students focus on both the academic assignments and the skills they need to work together.** They review the success of their assignment and their cooperation, and they try to improve both.

✓ The teacher benefits from cooperative learning because **the students take more responsibility for classroom management.** Hands-on participation requires that the students interact with the materials, and cooperative learning is structured so that the students, not the teacher, manage the materials.

Quake Teaches Us the Virtue of Cooperation

Now, don't get me wrong. I believe in competition. I'm an unabashed fan of capitalism. Yet I do believe that there are limits to competition. I find the idea of "killing," "crushing," "destroying" and "annihilating" to be a disgusting and counterproductive approach to life and business.

I can't imagine the average bank teller or lending officer will be inspired by an exhortation to kill, crush, destroy and annihilate. The bank will get back and keep customers only if it serves them well. That, in turn, will occur only when the people inside the bank treat each other well.

Helping others to succeed and competing with ourselves (albeit with a keen eye aimed at excelling at something) is likely to get you and me—and our organizations—further than acting out some primitive urge to kill, crush, destroy and annihilate. A. P. Giannini (bank president) knew it. Coach Walsh (Super Bowl winner) knew it. After watching the San Francisco Bay Area respond to the quake, so do I.

Thomas Peters
San Jose Mercury News,
November 6, 1989.

**The greater the time students work together
and the greater the responsibilities
students take for their work,
the greater the learning.**

The following is an example of a cooperative learning activity. Substitute your own activity. Begin by rewriting sections: background, problem, materials, and activity steps. Apply the example to your own subject matter.

Sample Assignment

In this activity you will be working in **support groups** of four. Your teacher will choose the members of the support group. The reason you work in support groups is because when you discuss new ideas with your classmates, you understand the ideas better.

Sometimes you will work with your friends, and sometimes not. No matter who your support buddies are, your responsibility is to help one another understand and complete the activity. This is why you are called **support buddies.**

Your teacher will explain what jobs need to be done. Either the teacher will choose or you will be asked to choose who does which job.

You need to work together and talk about your assignment so that each member of the support group understands what your group has done and why. When it is time for your support group to report to the class, your teacher will call on only one member of your group. That member will explain the support group's results, so make sure that you all know what is happening before you get called on. When your support group looks good, you look good!

How Do Propellers Work?

Background

Some airplanes and helicopters fly because of propellers. As the shape and pitch (angle) of the blade change, different results are obtained.

Problem

How many different ways can you design a propeller blade?
How does each design perform?
What is your evaluation of each design?

Support Group Jobs

Equipment Manager: Your job is to obtain the materials needed for the activity and to make sure that they are returned to the appropriate place at the end of the designated time.

Facilitator: Your job is to make sure that the group is following each step of the activity carefully and correctly.

Recorder: Your job is to observe, take minutes, and record data. You need to see that the support group has the proper forms to record the results of the activity as they occur.

Reporter: Your job is to coordinate the writing of the group report.

Materials

Binder paper, scissors, and a paper clip.

Activity Steps

1. Cut a piece of binder paper across its width into 2-inch strips.
2. Cut and fold the paper as shown. (Fig. 1)
3. Hold and release the paper as shown. (Fig. 2)
4. Try different versions of the helicopter.
5. Observe and record each result.

Fig. 1

Support Group Rules

Move into your groups quickly and quietly.
Stay with your group in your area.
Do your job.
Help each other.
Follow the procedures.

Support Group Responsibilities

Fig. 2

1. The **facilitator** needs to make sure that everyone has read and discussed the activity before beginning to work. Do not start until everyone knows the purpose of the activity, what needs to be done (activity steps), and what everyone needs to do (support group rules and responsibilities).

2. The **equipment manager** needs to see that the materials are collected.

3. The **recorder** needs to see that a record page is set up on which to record what is to be observed. This can be a form for taking minutes, a table for recording numbers, or a chart for writing observations. Do not start until the record page has been set up.

4. The **facilitator** takes the group through the activity steps, as a moderator would take a meeting through its agenda.

5. At all times the members of the **support group** must cooperatively and respectfully help each other by following the procedures and the support group rules.

6. The **support group** must help the recorder record the results of the activity.

7. The **reporter** coordinates the writing of the group. Make sure that everyone in the support group can explain the activity: its purpose, steps, and results.

When everyone can explain the purpose and results of the activity, all the members of the group should sign their name to the group report.

Thank You

Applying Cooperative Learning to Teachers and Administrators

Cooperation is especially important for teachers because much of what they learn is procedural. This is similar to learning how to play bridge or how to perform surgery. Procedural learning differs from the simple learning of facts and acquiring knowledge. It relies heavily on receiving feedback about performance and modifying one's implementation until errors are eliminated.

Cooperation must start at the classroom level because that determines the organizational climate in the school. There are teachers who spend five to seven hours a day advocating a competitive, individualistic approach, telling students:

"Do your own work."	"Don't care about each other."
"Don't talk to your neighbors."	"Just try to better yourself."
"Don't share; don't help."	"Think for yourself."

These are the values the teachers are going to have in their relationships with colleagues and administrations.

Conversely, there are teachers who spend five to seven hours a day saying:

"Help each other."	"Figure it out together."
"Share."	"Put your minds together."
"Work together."	"You're responsible not only for your
"Discuss the material in groups."	own learning, but for the learning of
"Explain things to each other."	your support buddies as well."

These are the values the teachers will have and hence will look at their colleagues as potential cooperators. What you want are teachers supporting one another so that if a teacher has a particular strength or plans a new unit or comes in with new materials, the other teachers will provide support and encouragement.

Staff-development Support Groups

Form **staff-development support groups** to help you implement success. Collegial support groups offer a formal structure for learning from colleagues. This is called **collegial learning**. Consisting of small groups of teachers and perhaps administrators, the goal of the support group is to improve one another's professional competence and ensure the professional growth of all.

The Cooperative School

Whatever happens in the classroom with students will hold true at the building level with teachers. **The most effective schools are those where there is a cooperative staff that pulls together.**

School A for Apathetic

■ Teachers do not discuss with each other their practice of teaching, nor do they help each other to improve their skills.

■ Teachers pay no attention to evaluations which point out areas for improvement, but they will be quick to point out to their students areas for improvement.

■ When new programs or ideas are suggested, teachers respond with apathy and indifference.

■ The faculty seldom unites around any effort to improve the school.

School C for Cooperative

■ Teachers are working toward a common goal of school improvement.

■ Teachers observe one another's teaching and strive to help one another improve.

■ Experienced teachers regularly share with new colleagues the practices that have worked effectively for them.

■ The principal provides the support teachers need to work together, and the teachers point to one another as resources for solving problems.

■ The teachers are proud to take part in decision making.

After Stuart C. Smith
"The Collaborative School."
Educational Leadership, November 1987, p. 4.

Members of collegial support groups serve many functions:

✓ They discuss new teaching practices and problems connected with their implementation.

✓ Together they plan, design, prepare, and evaluate curriculum materials.

✓ They observe one another's teaching and offer helpful feedback.

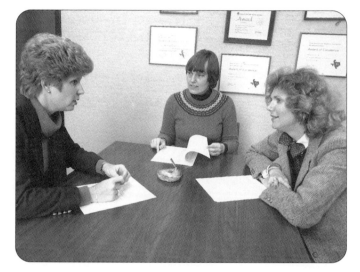

A support group for collegial learning.

The support groups consist of dedicated, caring, and knowledgeable colleagues willing to share techniques for beginning the first days of school and continued teaching in the most effective ways.

The quality of education is largely determined by what happens at the school site. Cooperation is needed at the professional level among everyone at the school site. Without cooperation, teaching cannot be a profession.

Medicine is a profession because doctors invite their colleagues to evaluate their techniques. When they develop a new surgical technique, for example, colleagues are invited to watch and provide suggestions for improvement.

✓ **If support groups of teachers and administrators at schools can operate in this way, then, and only then, can teaching be called a profession.**

✓ For education to be a profession, its members must learn and grow together and ON THEIR OWN without constant prodding from the administration or the public. When that happens, collegial learning is taking place.

> **Education is a helping profession.**
> **There are professionals out there willing to help.**
> **Help each other, and we all profit.**

The Effective Teacher

1. Applies all the factors discussed in Chapters 1 to 23 to set a cooperative class climate.

2. Writes structured cooperative activities.

3. Works cooperatively and shares with colleagues.

4. Applies the evaluation method taught to students to their own professional life.

To be successful is to achieve an objective.

But, to be a success is always to have yet another objective in mind after you've achieved the last one.

UNIT E

Future Understandings— The Professional

The teacher who constantly learns and grows becomes a professional educator.

UNIT E

Future Understandings — The Professional

The teacher who constantly learns and grows becomes a professional educator.

◆◆

Key Idea: How a person chooses to behave will greatly determine the quality of that person's life.

What Do You Want from Life?

> **You can have anything you want from life.**

You Can Have Anything
You Want from Life

The first 24 chapters contain information to help you begin school successfully. Turn back to these pages frequently to help you during your daily work. This chapter and the next are written to help you with the rest of your life. **Chapters 25 and 26 are designed to help you prepare for your career as a professional educator.** You have choices:

✓ You can be a *worker* or a *leader*.

✓ You can have a *job* or a *career*.

✓ You can become a *teacher* or an *educator*.

Depending on your choices, you can have anything you want from life. What do you want?

Are You a Worker or a Leader?

There are two kinds of people: **WORKERS** and **LEADERS**. They each have their distinctive characteristics, and these characteristics will give a person certain results in life. **You can predict your life as a teacher 10, 20, even 30 years from now on the basis of these characteristics.**

Worker

| The two things that matter the most to a worker are time and money. |

Workers are concerned about time and money.

Workers are preoccupied with time for breaks, holidays, overtime, and work hours. They will do everything to negotiate for longer breaks and shorter work hours. There are teachers and teacher organizations who will negotiate away in-service meetings, negotiate the number of minutes allotted to in-service, or negotiate to have in-service on a Friday before a three-day weekend. Time and money, not learning or growing, are the primary concerns of a worker.

A worker will agree to put in more hours or agree to in-servicing if there is additional pay or some form of perk. **Money or tangible rewards are understood by workers.**

Workers have jobs and can earn more money by either putting in more time, such as teachers who moonlight, or they can increase their skills to be placed in a higher job category.

| Workers Have No Future |

Workers who do not increase their skills run the risk of being the first to be laid off or fired because they have failed to stay abreast of changing job skills in a technological society. Thus workers have no future. There is no future for a person who has a job, such as a teacher who knows how to teach but one subject, one way, and that one way may be suspect.

Teaching is used by many teachers as a way to earn money to pay the bills and support the family. Their commitment to teaching stops at the dismissal bell, with no time and little desire to partake of growth and learning opportunities.

In reality, the worker-teacher has already been fired from within the system. These are the teachers who retired in their own classrooms and have fired themselves from life. These are the teachers to whom early retirement is offered or who are transferred from school to school or job to job so that they will do the least amount of damage or, at least, spread the damage evenly and as thinly as possible throughout the district. These are the teachers the parents have fired because they complain long and hard to have their children placed with another teacher elsewhere.

The worker profile is not unique to teachers in education. There are many worker-administrators. It is unfortunately too common to see worker-administrators sitting out in the hall or in the back row while the teachers are attending in-service, too many administrators whose attitude is, "I'll sit by the door so that I can get out of here quickly."

Leader

Educational leaders have a variety of careers from which to choose.

The two major concerns of a leader are enhancement and cooperation.

Like workers, leaders have a job and put in time to earn money. But leaders are willing to put in additional time to improve themselves, the people they work with, and the environment in which they work. As a result, leaders also make more money. They make more money not because they put in more time on the job but because they put in more time to improve and enhance their life. **Life rewards the competent, not the clock-watchers.**

Leaders also have the ability to work with other people and can lead or get other people to work cooperatively and productively. **Anyone who can work cooperatively and productively is always rewarded to a greater extent.**

Leaders have careers. People who are constantly enhancing their lives have careers rather than jobs.

> **Whereas a job is something a person does specifically, a career is what a person pursues as a lifework.**

A person who has a career can do many jobs because through constant learning and growing, a person acquires many talents and skills.

Anyone who has talents and skills is valuable as a thinker, a problem solver, and a decision maker. These people, of course, are more valuable to a community, school, or organization and are rewarded accordingly.

Leaders are professionals. A person who has a career, who has many talents and skills, who is a thinker, a problem solver, and a decision maker is a professional. **The professional teacher recognizes that the classroom is a complex environment; the most successful teacher is the one who is capable of making decisions and solving problems in that environment.**

People with careers can do many jobs and, should they lose a job, can move to another job because they are qualified to do several things. Therefore, leaders are not concerned with time and money; they have their mind set on growing and working cooperatively with others.

A WORKER is concerned with **time** and **money**.
A LEADER is concerned with **enhancement** and **cooperation**.

A WORKER has a **job**.
A LEADER has a **career**.

A WORKER is a **hired hand** to do a job.
A LEADER is hired to **think, make decisions,** and **solve problems**.

A WORKER is an hourly **laborer** with a skill.
A LEADER is a **professional** with talent.

A WORKER **can** be fired from a job.
A LEADER **cannot** be fired from a career.

A WORKER **cannot** find another job because of training in only one job.
A LEADER **can** always find another job because he or she possesses versatile skills.

A WORKER has **no future** in having a job.
A LEADER has a **great future** because he or she is oriented toward a career.

Job Titles Do Not Reflect Worker or Leader Status

A teacher wrote:

I work on our intermediate professional development committee and as a leader in my local education association, I'd like to purchase two sets of your tapes to share with the staff to enjoy after our in-service meeting with you.

> Michelle Averill
> Houghton Lake Community Schools
> Houghton Lake, Michigan

A president said:

The in-service went five minutes over. You owe me five minutes.

> President
> Local (N.J.) Education Association

More Characteristics of Workers and Leaders

<u>You Can Recognize Workers</u>	<u>You Can Recognize Leaders</u>

You see them in the morning. They're tired.

You see them in the morning. They're helping someone.

They manage by crisis.

They manage by leadership.

They are full of excuses.

They have plans, goals, and vision.

They dress like laborers.

They dress for success.

You see them at lunch. They're tired.

You see them at lunch. They're on their way to a meeting.

They sit at the back of meetings.

They sit where they can learn.

They complain about why they have to be in-serviced.

They enjoy being part of a meeting.

They complain about other people, places, and things.

They compliment people, places, and things.

You see them after school. They're tired.

You see them after school. They're waiting for a parent.

They blame other people, places, and things.

They work cooperatively with people, places, and things.

They are frequently late.

They are prompt and have their materials ready.

They chitchat.

They pay attention.

You see them at a meeting. They're tired.

You see them at a meeting. They have a report ready.

They are always asking, "What am I supposed to do?"

They are able to make decisions and help solve problems.

They do not subscribe to journals.

They subscribe to and read the professional literature.

They do not belong to professional organizations.

They belong to professional organizations.

They seldom, if ever, go to conferences and even complain about district in-service meetings.

They attend and may even contribute academically at conferences.

They love to say "have to" or "ought to," as in "Do I have to do this?" "Must I do this?" "I'm only doing this because I've got to."

They know to say "want to" and "choose to," as in "I want to go to the conference" and "It is my choice to do a workshop and share my unit with others at a meeting."

They talk about not getting respect.

Their success earns them respect.

They decide to do what others do.

They choose to do what they have determined is best.

They worry about their jobs and their job conditions.

They have a career and have options to choose from.

They are victims.

They have power and are in control.

They are unwilling to learn or turn elsewhere for help.

They are knowledgeable and can turn elsewhere for help.

You see them while shopping. They're tired.

You see them while shopping. They're smiling!

Their outlook on life is, "Another day, another dollar."

Their outlook on life is, "You strive to be a peak performer and pursue life, love, and happiness."

> **What counts is not the number of hours you put in but how much you put into those hours.**

Which Will You Be?

Now that you know the difference between a worker and a leader, which will you be?

Will you DECIDE to be a WORKER?
or
Will you CHOOSE to be a LEADER?

If I Didn't Read This, I'd Go Broke

Al Sisson ran the corner service station and was my mechanic for over 20 years. He was outspoken and often brusque but unafraid to do what he believed was right. He was both admired and disliked for these very attributes. He was good at fixing cars and honest to boot.

I got some insight into why he was so good when I was in his waiting room one day. There was a melange of automotive magazines, mostly filled with ads from automotive parts houses, strewn on a table.

I said to Al, "You read this stuff?"

He said, in his brusque voice, "I wish they would stop sending me that garbage." But then he looked at me over his glasses and said authoritatively, like a mentor who knew what was right, "You bet I read it. If I didn't, I'd go broke!"

Al Sisson was a professional. He enhanced his own life without anyone telling him what he had to do.

When you walk into teachers' homes, look at the end tables or the coffee table. More often than not, not a single education magazine or journal will be in sight. Ask them to produce one from their home-office, and they cannot. Ask them the last time they read *Educational Leadership, Teacher,* or some similar journal, and you get a look that seems to say, "What are those magazines? I've never heard of them."

In many a teacher's lounge you will find duplicating machines, vending machines, a bulletin board of notices, and teacher mailboxes but not a single professional journal.

This is why lots of teachers are already bankrupt and the Al Sissons are not. Knowledge is power.

Will You Decide or Will You Choose?

Decide

Look at the two parts of the word *decide*. There is a prefix, *de*, as in *defeat, destroy, denigrate*, and *deemphasize*. It is a negative prefix. There is a stem *cide*, as in *suicide, pesticide, insecticide*, and *herbicide*. *Decide* is a negative, killing word.

Many people make decisions by deciding. Have you ever dined with someone at a restaurant who cannot **decide** what to order from a menu? While everyone at the table waits for this person to place an order, someone impatiently barks out, "How long does it take you to decide? When will you decide? Can't you decide?"

When you study a menu, do you choose or do you decide?
Workers let other people make their decisions.

And does the person order? No. Instead the person asks everyone at the table what they plan to order, and based on what others order, they will decide to do the same.

Oh, you're going to have a turkey sandwich? I'll have the same. No mayonnaise? Oh yes, make mine the same way. I'll have the same thing.

Monkey see, monkey do, just as the kids tease.

And what happens to people who decide? **Deciders become victims because they allow other people to make decisions for them.**

> **VICTIMS are people who are suffering because they
> have no control over their own lives.**

Many teachers are victims:

✓ You don't stand at the door to greet the students? I don't have to either.

✓ You take roll at the beginning of the day or period? I'll do it that way, too.

✓ You write tests that equal 50 points, three times a grading period? If everyone else is doing it that way, so will I.

✓ I see that almost everyone is coming to school dressed in a sweatshirt and jeans. I'll decide to come to school looking like that, too.

✓ Look at all the people who sit at the back of the in-service meeting. None are taking notes; many are reading magazines, knitting, or grading papers; and several are talking and reading the morning paper. Since most of the teachers are sitting in the back doing these things, I'll decide to do the same.

If you listen to enough people bemoan the fact that they are tired and underpaid and get no respect, you will believe that you, too, are tired and underpaid and have no respect.

If you listen to enough people who vilify administrators, parents, and students, you will believe that administrators, parents, and students are the cause of your being a victim.

> **When you see in a given situation what everyone else
> sees, you become so much a part of that situation that
> you become a victim of that situation.**

Choose

Leaders CHOOSE! Leaders do not decide.

Leaders have control over their own lives. They know that life comes from what they earn for themselves. They generate their own happiness, and much of that comes from serving and sharing with others. Leaders enjoy problems and challenges.

Leaders are achievement-oriented. They have visions that help them see beyond their task or job. They know what the word *choose* means and how to use it.

✓ *Choose* means that I am responsible for my choice.

✓ *Choose* means that I am accountable for my choice.

✓ *Choose* means that I have control over what I do.

✓ *Choose* means that I accept the consequences that accompany my choice. If it fails, blame me. But if it succeeds, reward me.

Workers-deciders-teachers do not strive for success, happiness, money, or respect. This is why they never receive anything in life.

Leaders-professionals-educators are rewarded with whatever they are striving for—be it happiness, success, money, achievement, popularity, or respect as a professional. **Leaders are people who strive, reach for excellence, and seek achievement.**

Leaders control their own lives and are achievement-oriented. Leaders seek their own means to reach a goal.

> Some people go through life adding years to their life.
>
> Others go through life adding life to their years.

Workers Decide	Leaders Choose
Life comes from what others get for me.	Life comes from what I earn for myself.
I expect others to bring me happiness.	I will generate my own happiness.
Life comes from some other source.	Life comes from within me.
Life will be better when I get a new x or more y.	Life is better when I share or serve others.
Life will be better if I didn't have to do all these things.	Life is fine because I want to or choose to do these things.
All I want is some peace and quiet.	I enjoy challenges; they are the elixirs of life.
I can't do this. You know I have to go home and cook.	I can't wait to go home and have a candlelight dinner with my family.
I can't wait for the weekend.	I can't wait for the reading conference.

Now that you know the difference between deciding and choosing, what will you decide or choose to do?

Life Begins When You Make a Choice

Laura was a worker-teacher. She was typical of the countless number of sweet, kind, average people who teach. Laura was a maintainer, a survivor. She did her work: taught class, gave assignments, wrote tests, showed movies, passed out worksheets, supervised lunch, attended faculty meetings, and baked cookies for the textbook selection committee she was on for the year. She had a family and even sang in the church choir.

She took early retirement at 53, having "put in" 30 years. During that time she all but never read a journal, belonged to a professional organization, or attended a conference.

During her 30 years Laura never caused any problems, did not abuse her sick leave, and seldom said a word at faculty meetings. She always sat at the back of meetings and knitted. She didn't really harm any children, but then she never really lit any fires under any of them either. She did her job and felt, as workers are prone to tell you angrily, "I did my job, didn't I? What more do you want me to do? I wish they would end this meeting. I have to go home and take care of the kids."

One day several years after Laura's retirement, I ran into her in a shopping mall. It was a nice reunion. After all, she was sweet and kind and generally well liked by the staff. I certainly liked her. She was not one of the staff turkeys or agitators that I couldn't stand. I asked her what she had been doing and she said, "Well, I go to see my grandchildren, watch television a lot, and walk the malls. Walking is good for me, and the malls are safe. That's about all. I've been taking it easy."

Then she asked, "And what are you doing?"

I said, "I'm teaching part-time with students but seemingly full-time with preservice and in-service teachers. In addition I have a book coming out later this year, did a workshop at the regional International Reading Association conference, and for my fifty-fifth birthday, my family surprised me with a raft trip down the Colorado River."

We sat down on a nearby bench, amid passing shoppers, and she looked into my eyes, with her eyes glistening, and said to me, **"When does life begin?"**

I wanted to say to her, **"Laura, life begins when you start making choices,"** but I could not bring myself to say it.

The Choices We Make That Determine the Quality of Our Lives

> **What a person decides or chooses to do will greatly determine the quality of that person's life.**

A **person's behavior will determine what choices that person will make.** The normal distribution curve, the bell-shape curve, will be used to explain this concept. The normal distribution curve describes, graphically, how events or things occur. **The tall part of the curve in the middle says that more things or events are average in occurrence.**

For instance, if the heights or shoe sizes of people are measured and plotted on a graph, the results state that most people have average heights or shoe sizes. Fewer people have small or large shoe sizes or are short or tall; their results are shown at the two ends of the curve. This is how people are normally distributed on a graph when it comes to comparing shoe size or heights.

The phenomenon of a normal distribution curve holds true for countless other examples in life:

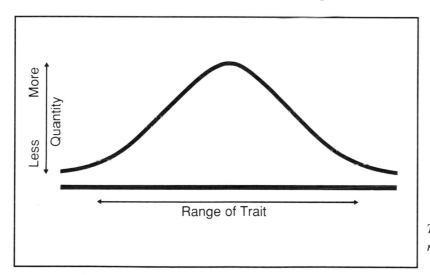

✓ Speed of cars on the highway—some go fast, some go slow, most travel at the speed limit.

✓ Length of recitals—some are too long, some are too short, most are of tolerable length.

✓ Week in which the snow first falls—sometimes early, sometimes late, mostly predictable.

✓ Grades students receive in class—some A's, some F's, mostly C's.

Traits in nature do not occur in equal proportions. The shape of a bell more accurately describes how traits are normally distributed.

Protective Behaviors

Protective people spend most of their time complaining or rationalizing to protect themselves.

The normal distribution curve can be used to describe the behavior of people. People normally fall into three categories, according to the behaviors they exhibit:

1. **Protective Behaviors**

2. **Maintenance Behaviors**

3. **Enhancement Behaviors**

People who use protective behaviors are full of excuses and are prone to complain about people, places, and things. They are good at explaining, rationalizing, or even lying to justify their position. When they talk about others, they never dignify people or groups with their appropriate names. It's typically, "these people" or "those administrators." "These, them, and those" is how they usually refer to others. **By complaining, rationalizing, or putting others down, they avoid doing what is expected of them, and they divert your thoughts from the task at hand.**

Protective people are easy to spot. They frequent the teachers' lounge more than others and can be heard complaining and moaning about everything on the school grounds. And if anyone tries to do something positive, they are convinced that the only reason is to make them look bad or create more work for everyone.

The surest path to decline is to blame others for your problems.

Maintenance Behaviors

Maintenance people spend most of their time coping and hoping that life and work will improve.

People who use maintenance behaviors are the great survivors of life. They even tell you, "I'm a survivor." They don't complain, rationalize, lie, or put people down (well, most of the time). Instead, they hope, cope, and survive. They hope that the lottery will pay off or that they will receive an inheritance from a heretofore unknown relative. They are primarily concerned with themselves and their own survival, safety, health, and welfare.

Maintenance people are the hardworking backbone of society. They work to pay the bills, feed the mouths, and clothe the children. They wonder where the college tuition will come from, and if only, if only Ed McMahon would knock on their door with the $10 million sweepstakes award, their worries would be over.

Maintenance people do a lot of wishing. They wish for a new car, a new husband, four fewer kids in class, and the day to go by faster. They like to fantasize, so their day is preoccupied with watching the soaps, reading the tabloids, playing the lotteries, and consulting their horoscope.

Because they are maintainers and survivors, they do nothing to rock the boat. They are pleasant and unassuming people who get along fine with others. Some of their favorite phrases are "Go with the flow," "*Que sera sera*," and "Whatever you guys want to do will be fine with me."

> **The surest path to stagnation is to do nothing or just get by.**

Enhancement Behaviors

Enhancement people spend most of their time participating and growing.

People who use enhancement behaviors are "we" people. They enjoy participating, so they go to conferences, conventions, and meetings. They go to meetings because they know that they can learn by interacting with, sharing with, and listening to other people.

These are the people the protectors and the maintainers wish would just sit down, rest, and smell the roses, right? Every time you look up, there they are on some committee, going to some conference, getting some award, or having their picture taken.

It's easy to identify the people with enhancement behaviors. You keep hearing them use the word *we*, as in "We need to find a solution to reduce the dropout rate;" "Do we have some people who would like to volunteer to answer the phones at the educational television station pledge night campaign?" or "We can do it; I know that we can do it; so let's all go out and give it the best try we have ever given."

People who use enhancement behaviors are leaders and professionals. Enhancement people are easy to spot. They are the active people at school and in the community. They get the work done, and they make contributions to society. They are achievement-oriented and have vision. They are called enhancement people because they enhance the life of everyone around them.

> **The surest path to success is with an attitude of enhancement and cooperation.**

The Most Vulnerable Teachers

The most vulnerable people on the staff are the maintenance people, the middle 60 percent of the curve. They know that they should be enhancing lives, first their own and then those of the people they teach. They know that they should work cooperatively with the enhancement people of the staff.

But at the faculty meetings, the protective people stand up and start to shout about the pay, the conditions, the parents, the publishers, and the crummy administrators (remember, protective people need to blame others to protect themselves). The needs of the people with a maintenance behavior to survive are so great that they decide to follow the protectors.

Because maintainers do not choose, they go through life vacillating, one day deciding to follow the enhancers and the next day deciding to follow the protectors. Which group should they follow?

If only they would make a choice!

How to Succeed with a Minimum of Effort

Teachers

80 percent are affiliation-oriented.
20 percent are achievement-oriented.

Research has shown us that 80 percent of teachers are affiliation-oriented. That is, they join organizations, specifically the teacher's organization or union (fine groups, please), and expect the affiliation to get their rewards for them. Their happiness, money, fringe benefits, and parties are all gotten for them by the dues they pay. Their attitude seems to be, "Let others get my rewards for me."

They even expect the teacher organization to write newspaper releases and run television commercials about the good deeds being done by teachers and the schools. "Let others bring me respect."

Twenty percent of the teachers are achievement-oriented. Teachers who are achievement-oriented do more than belong to a teacher's organization. They may attend workshops or conferences or serve on an education committee. Their dues are the opportunities they look for in life. They derive great satisfaction from getting their own rewards in life.

Why 20 Percent of the Teachers Achieve Much from Life

Maintenance

Protective

Enhancement

Eighty percent of people spend most of their lives complaining or just trying to survive.

Twenty percent of people spend most of their lives improving their quality of life.

Since 80 percent of the teachers are affiliation-oriented, it is fairly simple for the 20 percent who are achievement-oriented to succeed without too much effort.

People who are successful are people who put in effort and have an achievement-oriented attitude.

The Choices We Make That Determine the Quality of Our Lives

NORMAL DISTRIBUTION OF HUMAN BEHAVIORS

20 Percent	60 Percent	20 Percent
PROTECTIVE BEHAVIORS	MAINTENANCE BEHAVIORS	ENHANCEMENT BEHAVIORS
Rationalize and complain	Cope, hope, and survive	Participate and grow
HAVE TO	WISH TO	WANT TO
They	Me or I	We or Us
SELF-DEFEATING PEOPLE	GETTING-ALONG, COPING PEOPLE	SELF-ENHANCING PEOPLE

EXAMPLES OF TYPES OF BEHAVIORS

The kids can't read.	If only I could make it through the week.	May I share this article with you?
The administration is not supportive.	I need a raise, newer materials, less work, more help, ...	What can I do to contribute? I volunteer.
The young (old) teachers don't know anything.	I wish I had a new principal, different coworkers, ...	Let's work on this project together.
In-services are boring. They are a waste of time.	End this meeting; I have to shop, cook, and go to aerobics class.	Let's go to the conference together.
The new program will never work. I tried it years ago.	I wish I had the materials to follow this program properly.	Tell me about your new idea.
Where does it say that in the contract?	I'll just go with the flow and do what the group wants to do.	We need constantly to strive for excellence.
I'll sit on the fringe, in the back, alone, or not come at all. I'll do my own thing.	Where will you sit? I'll sit with you and knit and read to pass the time.	I'll sit with and work with involved people.
I'm taking early retirement.	My problems are unique.	I believe in opportunities.
People bother me.	People don't understand or appreciate me.	People are our most precious resource.

RESULTS OF THE THREE BEHAVIORS

HAPPIER →
SUCCESSFUL →
PRODUCTIVE →
WELL-LIKED →
PROFESSIONAL →
MONEY →

Now that you know the difference between people who use protective, maintenance, and enhancement behaviors, which one do you choose to be?

Why It Is Easy to Succeed in Life

Have you determined which kind of behavior you exhibit most of the time? If not, here's another way of telling. People with similar behaviors or values tend to group themselves.

✓ **Protective people** form their own group at school, although they will deny it. They can usually be found sitting in the back row of meetings, in the lounge complaining, or at association meetings filing grievances.

✓ **Maintenance people** form their own cliques also, although they will not recognize it. They are characterized by being tired much of the time. They hope that they can make it through the week, always seeking sympathy.

✓ **Enhancement people** form their own group also. Whereas the protective and maintenance people will not recognize or accept the fact that they are in a group, enhancement people acknowledge and give their groups names.

They say things like this:

"We have this support group organized to help each other."
"We go out once a month to a power breakfast and share our successes and problems."
"We have this self-help group, and our purpose is to help mentor the beginning teacher."
"We need to work together with the administrators, the classified staff, the community, and the business sector."
"Jan is my support buddy."

Because of their behavior:

✓ **Protective people are self-defeating people.** Because their behavior can spread, they can cause an organization to defeat itself also.

✓ **Maintenance people are coping people.** They do not destroy an organization, like protective people do, but it is necessary to light a bonfire under these people to get them to contribute to an organization.

✓ **Enhancement people are self-enhancers.** They are self-motivated, self-disciplined people who contribute to the quality of life, first their own and then that of the organization.

As a result, enhancement people are happier.

✓ They are more productive.

✓ They achieve higher status.

✓ They make more money.

✓ They earn more rewards.

✓ They are more professional.

✓ They have greater respect.

✓ They get whatever else they strive for.

On a normal distribution curve, the percentages are represented as follows:

✓ People with protective behaviors: 20 percent

✓ People with maintenance behaviors: 60 percent

✓ People with enhancement behaviors: 20 percent

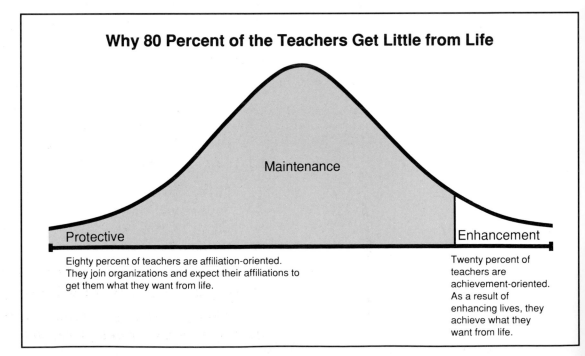

Why 80 Percent of the Teachers Get Little from Life

Maintenance

Protective

Enhancement

Eighty percent of teachers are affiliation-oriented.
They join organizations and expect their affiliations to
get them what they want from life.

Twenty percent of
teachers are
achievement-oriented.
As a result of
enhancing lives, they
achieve what they
want from life.

The protective and the maintenance people make up 80 percent of the teaching population. Since 80 percent of the teachers are self-defeaters and survivors, they forfeit their happiness and success to others. **The enhancers are successful not because they are such great strivers but to a great extent because 80 percent of their colleagues are not striving, seeking, or growing.**

The Prado Principle

20 percent of the people own 80 percent of the wealth;
80 percent of the people own 20 percent of the wealth.

Vilfrado Prado
Italian economist

A coach will tell you that a winning team does not necessarily win a game. Most often, a losing team botches itself into defeat from all the mistakes they make. Look at the statistics for a football game. The team with the greater number of turnovers (errors such as fumbles and intercepted passes) is usually the loser. The team with the greater number of takeovers (fumble recoveries and interceptions) is usually the winner.

Vic Braden, the tennis teacher, tells his class, "Just lob or dink the ball over the net. You don't have to smash, and you don't need top spin. Just lob or dink the ball over the net. Why? Because the average player on the other side of the net will hit the ball back into the net or out of bounds 70 percent of the time. Do not beat yourself when playing tennis. The odds are that your opponent will do that for you."

Such is life with teachers. Eighty percent of the teachers are turning over their lives because of their protective and maintenance behaviors, whereas 20 percent of the teachers easily walk away with the opportunities life offers them because of their enhancement behaviors. These teachers just keep lobbing the ball back into play.

That's the way the ball bounces. By keeping the ball in play, you keep striving, growing, and enhancing your life.

That's life in this profession. If you stay focused, you will consistently develop your career as a professional educator.

1. **Chooses rather than decides.**
2. **Practices enhancement techniques.**
3. **Practices cooperative skills.**

KEY IDEA: The rewards in education and life go to the person who is a professional.

CHAPTER 26

The Rewards Go to the Professional Educator

> **A profession is defined not by the business
> a person is in but by the way that person
> does his or her business.**

The Rand Corporation reports that teacher reform still leaves a major question unanswered: "Are teachers full-fledged professionals or merely semiskilled workers who constantly need supervision and regulation?"[1] It can be argued late into the night as to whether teaching is a profession or not. We maintain that it is, but only for those teachers who perform as professionals.

As with any group, the competence of the people in the group will range from inept to masterful. There have been good and bad presidents, prima ballerinas, television evangelists, auto mechanics, teachers, and administrators.

The debate over whether teaching is a profession will be resolved when everyone, or at least a significant number of teachers, are professional in their own lives.

---

[1]Darling-Hammond, Linda, and Barry Barnett. *The Evolution of Teacher Policy*. Santa Monica, Calif.: Rand Center for the Study of the Teaching Profession, 1988.

A professional is someone who, without supervision or regulation:

✓ Is a responsible person

✓ Has a continuing growth plan to achieve competence

✓ Strives continuously to raise the level of each new group of students

All some teachers want is a job. They want a job working 180 days, 8 A.M. to 3 P.M., closed in a room with no worry of a supervisor, reluctant to be in-serviced, and free to belittle people (children, administrators, and parents) to cover their ineffectiveness. Making money to pay bills is the primary concern of such a worker-teacher.

The totally inept go in one of two directions. They either leave the profession of teaching or develop a repertoire of defense mechanisms that protect their fragile self-concepts. These teachers become bitter blamers, constant critics, despondent despots, and managers of monotony. Worst of all, they stay in the classroom and believe they are doing a good job.

Douglas Brooks
Kappa Delta Pi Record,
Summer 1986, p. 99.

The truth is some people who teach do not want to be professionals. It takes work and effort to be a professional. It takes time to go to conferences, read the journals, work actively on committees, and give extra help after school to students who need it. **But the rewards go to the professionals.**

Are you a worker or a leader?

> **The rewards go only to the professionals. They are the happiest, make the most money, have the most respect, and are the most successful.**

The Thin Margin for Success

The margin for success is so thin and easy that it is frightenly simple.

Take baseball as one example. The difference between being an all-star and an average player in baseball is so thin that it makes baseball almost seem like a silly game.

Consider the difference between a great year and a rotten year.

The season is 26 weeks long. A player gets 500 at-bats between April and September. That's about 20 at-bats per week, or 5 games per week.

The difference between a .300 average and a .250 average is ONE hit per week—ONE more every 20 times you bat.

At the end of the season there will be fewer than 20 players in each league (National and American) batting above .300. From about 400 players playing full-time on all the teams, only 10 percent, 40 out of 390, will be batting .300.

If you bat .300 per year, you are in an elite crowd that is able to earn millions more per year. **And all you have to do is get ONE more hit per week!**

Likewise, for any team, the difference between a miserable season with a 66–96 record and a terrific season with a 92–70 record is ONE more victory per week.

In the same way, success in life is simple. Try one or two new ideas or techniques each year:

- Go to a conference.
- Move up six rows at an in-service.
- Share an idea with another teacher.
- Welcome students at the classroom door with a smile.

Notice the active verbs of successful people: *go, move, share,* and *welcome.* It takes just as much effort and you use exactly the same amount of energy to perform these activities:

- Sit in the faculty lounge with the negative people who moan, complain, and belittle.
- Sit in the last rows.
- Hide from people who may ask you to do something.
- Gaze at your watch wondering when the day will be over.

Notice the sedentary type verbs of unsuccessful people: *sit, hide, gaze.* Which verbs best describe your attitude toward life?

The difference between a great year and a rotten year is so thin!

Life is no different. **All that separates a person from SUCCESS or FAILURE is one word: *ATTITUDE.***

Fourteen players batted above .300 during the 1990 season.

National League
Batting
(Minimum of 502 plate appearances.)

	Avg	AB	R	H	HR	RBI
Willie McGee, St.L . . .	.335	501	76	168	3	62
Eddie Murray, LA	.330	558	96	184	26	95
Dave Magadan, NY . .	.328	451	74	148	6	72
Lenny Dykstra, Phi . . .	.325	590	106	192	9	60
Andre Dawson, Chi . .	.310	529	72	164	27	100
Bip Roberts, SD	.309	556	104	172	9	44
Mark Grace, Chi	.309	589	72	182	9	82
Tony Gwynn, SD	.309	573	79	177	4	72
Brett Butler, SF	.309	622	108	192	3	44
Ryne Sandberg, Chi . .	.306	615	116	188	40	100
Lonnie Smith, Atl	.305	466	72	142	9	42
Ron Gant, Atl	.303	575	107	174	32	84
Barry Larkin, Cin	.301	614	85	185	7	67
Barry Bonds, Pit	.301	519	104	156	33	114
Kal Daniels, LA	.296	450	81	133	27	94
Tim Wallach, Mon	.296	626	69	185	21	98

The Rewards Go to Those Who Continue to Learn

The first days of school may be history for you now, but the school year continues. What does the teacher do after the first days of school?

The worker-teacher will do nothing except read stories, cover the basal text, hand out worksheets, lecture, show movies, and give tests—a pattern to be repeated decade after boring decade.

The professional educator is always learning and growing. The professional educator is constantly on an endless journey of looking for new and better ideas, new information, and improved skills to succeed with students. These are some specifics to learn.

The Professional Educator Learns How to Promote Student Growth

Seeing that students perform at or above expectations
Solving problems so that students receive the best possible services
Using recent research and technological advancements
Applying higher-order learning skills
Applying information processing strategies
Applying increasingly complex learning tasks
Using cooperative learning
Using invitational learning
Applying classroom management research

My students work their buns off! Yes, I have high expectations, but I've never been disappointed. Discipline is not a problem; neither is incomplete work.

We've walked the Freedom Trail together; students have flown to Washington, D.C., with me. I've sat in dentist offices with them, gone to court with them, even figured out how to get underwear (no, not Frederick stuff) under a tree because that's what a little girl wanted from Santa but was too poor.

Yes, I've laughed with and cried with my students, but they have learned. I love teaching.

Donna Fournier
Fifth-grade teacher
New Haven, Vermont

This is _Not_ Teaching.

There is no research to support this model of teaching...
- Read the assigned chapters.
- Answer the questions at the end of the chapter.
- Sit and take lecture notes.
- Watch a movie.
- Complete the worksheet.
- Take a test.

The Professional Educator Learns How to Make Good Use of Instructional Time

Positive Expectations	**Procedures & Routines**
Concept Learning	Home Relationship
SQ3R	
Love	**TEACHING TECHNIQUES**
ALT	
Prescriptive Learning	Credibility
Cooperative Learning	Critical Thinking Skills
Classroom Management	First Days

(The diagram reads:)

Positive Expectations | Procedures & Routines | Self-Esteem & Achievement
Concept Learning | Home Relationship | Direct Teaching
SQ3R | | OBI
Love | **TEACHING TECHNIQUES** | CRT
ALT | | TESA
Prescriptive Learning | Credibility | Para-Professionals
Cooperative Learning | Critical Thinking Skills | Learning Style / Teaching Style
Classroom Management | First Days | Discipline Plan

These are some general areas to learn.

Following lesson plans
Focusing student attention
Communicating purpose of lesson
Applying modeling behaviors
Applying study guidelines
Using guided practice
Using materials, media, and technology appropriately
Planning according to types of students
Planning instructional strategies
Optimizing time on task
Studying and demonstrating the subject being taught
Maintaining smooth flow and momentum of events
Being aware of class activities
Managing several events simultaneously
Articulating information clearly
Giving effective directions for activities
Providing logically sequenced instruction
Revising and augmenting instruction on the spot
Managing aides, tutors, and parents
Evaluating and improving classroom instruction

Knowledge is power. Knowledge, like money and status, is a form of power. Power is not force but rather the ability to do things. For instance, the more money a person has, the more a person can do. The more horsepower in a car, the easier it is to climb a hill. The more knowledge and the smarter a person, the more the person is able to accomplish. **Thus the ability to achieve and accomplish comes to those with the knowledge.**

Knowledge gives a person options. A person with no options is helpless in life. You can see this in the ineffective teachers. Because they do not read the literature or attend conferences, their fund of knowledge is minimal. People with a poor knowledge background are not aware of the options they have to solve problems. They repeatedly run into brick walls and then helplessly yell into the world seeking specific answers.

Options give a person the power of choice. Professional educators have no brick walls. Their life is spent adding the fuel of knowledge to a power cycle. As more knowledge is added, more learning takes place, more options are generated, and more power to accomplish is unleashed.

Knowledge to help you become a more effective teacher is at your fingertips—waiting to be accessed.

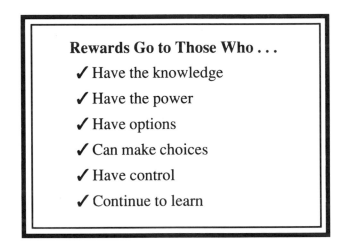

Rewards Go to Those Who . . .

✓ Have the knowledge

✓ Have the power

✓ Have options

✓ Can make choices

✓ Have control

✓ Continue to learn

Thank You for Expanding My Awareness

Professional persons, leaders, are always alert, searching for opportunities, and looking for ways to move forward in life. They may not agree with everything they hear or see. They will even look for information not in their present realm of influence. However, their attitude is always, "Thank you for expanding my awareness."

The worker-teacher is not interested in any expansion of awareness. Awareness means looking ahead, beyond, and into the future. Beware of worker-teachers who try to prevent you from expanding your awareness. They sit at meetings belittling and ridiculing the proceedings. They are no different from the problem students who belittle the teacher, the subject, and the students who do well.

Worker-teachers expend energy to prevent you from learning. If you expand your realm of awareness, you threaten their existence. They have trapped themselves, like lobsters, in a cage. Their goal each day is to drag others into the cage with them. And if you get caught and try to escape, they will reach up with their claws and pull you back down.

Do not allow people who cannot control their own lives to control your life. Rather, proceed through life expanding your awareness, searching for opportunities, working and sharing with the professionals who are also expanding their awareness.

The Basics for a Beginning Teacher

The most crucial years in a new teacher's life are the first one to three years. During this time, some 40 percent of the teachers will decide to leave teaching. But regardless of the reasons they give, the fact is that no one quits who is successful. The professional accepts the responsibility of personal growth and invests time to nurture his or her competence.

The Fundamentals for a Teacher:
People and Programs You Need to Know

People

Jack Canfield on self-esteem
Barbara Coloroso on discipline
Art Costa on higher-order thinking skills
Madeline Hunter on effective teaching
David and Roger Johnson on cooperative learning
Harry K. Wong on classroom management

Tapes and Videos

Classroom Management, Association for Supervision and Curriculum
    Development
How You Can Be a Super Successful Teacher, Harry K. Wong
I Choose to Care, Harry K. Wong
Reducing and Preventing Discipline Problems, Harry K. Wong
Teaching Strategies Library, Association for Supervision and Curriculum
    Development

Books and Magazines

Fuery, Carol L. *Winning Year One.* 1986. Sanddollar Publications,
    P.O. Box 461, Captiva Island, FL 33924.
Jones, Fredric H. *Positive Classroom Discipline/Instruction.* 1987.
    Fredric H. Jones and Associates, Inc., 103 Quarry Lane,
    Santa Cruz, CA 95060.
Williamson, Bonnic. *A First-Year Teacher's Guidebook for Success,* 1988.
    Dynamic Teaching Company, P.O. Box 276711, Sacramento, CA 95827.
Zike, Dinah. *Classroom Organization, K-6.* 1989. Dinah-Might Activities,
    Inc., P.O. Box 39657, San Antonio, TX 78218.
Educational Leadership, the journal of the Association for Supervision and
    Curriculum Development
Journal from your own discipline or area of responsibility

The Rewards Go to Those Who Share

Professionals consult and help one another. Physicians who have difficulty diagnosing an illness routinely consult with other physicians. Lawyers who are stumped by a case get help from colleagues in their firm. Athletes seek advice from coaches. Most teachers, sad to say, seldom seek or get help from anyone. **Though the essence of a teacher's work is helping others to learn, teachers are the worst learners when it comes to improving their own performance.**

<u>**Join or Organize a Support Group.**</u> Find the effective and professional teachers. Chapter 25 describes how to recognize these teachers. The effective teachers are well respected in professional circles. In turn, they are regarded with great jealousy by the worker-teachers.

The most effective support group strategy is known as coaching. Attend a seminar or have your district contract with a group to teach coaching techniques. In coaching each person helps others to grow. Work and socialize with the professional teachers. You will not only learn much from them, but you will learn a professional ethos that will bring you much respect too.

Support groups are common outside of school, but they are normally not formalized in schools. You will have to look for pockets of successful teachers. You may find them at your school, at another school, or at conferences. Conferences are the best places to find the superprofessional teachers, the ones who are educational leaders. Make these people your support group. They already have their own support groups, so adding another professional will be easy.

Your support groups are your best source of information and emotional support from which you can learn and gather strength to be an effective teacher.

<u>**Listen to Others.**</u> **Listen to your support group.** These are teachers and administrators with years of experience and are active in professional circles. They are well read, know people, have contacts, can suggest references, and know about future conferences.

<u>**Listen to Tapes and Watch Videos.**</u> Buy your own; borrow from your mentor; check out the media center in your district or local educational service center; inquire what the school of education has; and see if your district subscribes to a satellite in-service program (such as TI-IN Network).

To Be a Professional Educator

✓ Join or organize a support group.

✓ Listen to others.

✓ Read the literature.

✓ Observe other effective teachers.

✓ Participate in conferences.

✓ Use the research.

<u>Read the Literature</u>. Subscribe to at least one professional journal. This is the easiest way to know how, who, and what is happening in education. There is nothing more disconcerting than a teacher who does not know what is happening in the profession.

It can be downright embarrassing when you mention Madeline Hunter, William Glasser, outcome-based education, hemisphericity, or learning styles and get a glazed look. Would you tolerate this lack of knowledge from your doctor, pharmacist, or accountant?

Be knowledgeable. **Knowledge is power, and knowledge gives professionals options on which to base decisions.**

<u>Observe Effective Teachers</u>. Observe other teachers. The effective teacher can be the best source of knowledge because you will be able to observe a strategy being implemented in a classroom. They are easy to spot and have much to share. Ineffective teachers have nothing to share and will be reluctant to have you visit. They will even negotiate to prevent or greatly regulate supervision.

Free samples are only part of the fun of going to conferences.

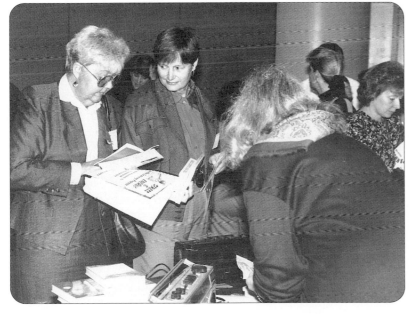

Effective teachers welcome visitors and are not afraid of evaluations. Effective teachers do not regard evaluations as supervision; rather, they regard evaluation sessions as a way of finding out how they can improve.

> *Though I have been appraised as a clearly outstanding teacher by my district, I am not satisfied with my students' success rates and I am looking forward, thanks to the help I get, to a far better year for them.*
>
> Chris Ann Dorgan
> Elementary school teacher
> Bastrop, Texas

Effective teachers exist right in your own building or district. Start by observing the effective teachers in your own support group. Consult with your administrators, supervisors, and coordinators. Many were outstanding teachers when they were in the classroom. There is plenty of talent in your own building.

<u>**Participate in Conferences**</u>. **Go to conventions, conferences, seminars, and workshops.** National, state, and local groups have their meetings near you. These conferences typically have speakers, workshops, seminars, exhibits, sample materials, parties (yes, parties), socials, and field trips. You will return to school with bags of free samples, papers other teachers have shared at workshops, and pages of notes on how to be a more effective teacher.

Give a paper or conduct a workshop and share your materials. Don't just attend a conference; be on the program and participate or serve on the convention committee. Become an officer and contribute to the profession. Join the organization and receive its magazine and materials. **Professionals share.**

<u>**Use the Research**</u>. Learn how to use ERIC, the Educational Research Information Center. ERIC is an electronic library of all educational research and papers in the United States. It is available in over 2,000 locations, each able to access the main terminal where educational information is stored.

Without having to spend hours in a library tracking down information, you can ask an ERIC librarian to search the literature for you electronically and provide you with a printout. Ask your nearest university or educational service center if it has access to ERIC. Many districts have it in their central office. Ask the ERIC librarian to show you how to use ERIC. The service is provided at nominal cost, but the information you receive will be priceless.

Before You Start Your First Day of School

1. **Listen** to the tape series *How You Can Be a Super Successful Teacher* before you begin your first day of school. Thousands of people have bought them, listened to them, and given them as presents to others. These tapes are the most popular tapes on classroom management.

2. **Read** "The First Day of School" by Douglas Brooks in *Educational Leadership*, May 1985.

3. **Participate** in a workshop or a college class that will stress classroom management skills.

4. **Find** a mentor, support buddy or a support group of experienced professional educators, not a fellow new teacher, who can share with you.

5. **Hope** that your district has an induction or in-service program to help new teachers with classroom management. If not, ask why not. You have every right to expect a program to help you succeed.

6. **Believe** in yourself. Regardless of who you are or what you have been, you can be what you want to be!

The Greatest Civil Right Is the Right of Equal Opportunities

Professional educators or teachers in the process of becoming professional educators do not sit in the back at a meeting.

The back of an auditorium is the worst place to sit.

- It is the hottest location.

- It is the most crowded.

- It is the most uncomfortable.

- You can't see or hear well.

- You will be distracted by every movement around you.

- You will be surrounded by all the negative people who do not want to be at the meeting to learn and cooperatively participate.

- The handouts will run out before they reach you.

It is common knowledge that the students with the poorest attitudes and grades, if allowed open seating, will sit at the back of the room. Moreso, they will sit at the back corners, nearest the doors. Their body language is telling you that they do not want to be in class and are anxious to get out first and fastest.

Being at the back is the same in life as being at the end of the line, the back of the pack, the rear of the group, the last in class, the bottom of the league.

There was a time in history when certain groups of people were forced to sit at the back of the bus, the back of the meeting, and the back of

church. Why? Because if you want to discriminate against a group, you put them at the back, where you reduce their chances of partaking or achieving.

Thanks to one little lady, Rosa Parks, who refused to sit at the back of a bus in Montgomery, Alabama, all people are now free to sit where they choose to sit.

The worker-teachers who do not want to learn decide to sit in the back with all the other worker-teachers.

The leaders and professional educators choose to sit nearer the front, where they can see, hear, pay attention, not be distracted, and receive handouts. It's also a lot more comfortable because people are not packed in.

TESA research has discovered that the best students sit in class in the shape of an inverted T—that is, across the front and down the middle. If you plot this on a graph, you get a bell-shaped curve. The worst students sit at the far corners. Note this of your students; note this of your colleagues.

The next time you go to a conference, a place where professionals go to enhance their lives, notice the teachers who arrive early at workshops, sit up front, and badger workshop leaders for handouts. These are the people you want for role models.

Thanks to Rosa Parks, we now have equal access to all the opportunities that are available in a free society. Professionals understand and make use of this concept.

Rosa Parks

The Rewards Go to Those Who Take Risks

There can be no accomplishment without taking some risk. The professional educator understands the concept of taking risks. Risk taking is not the same as gambling.

Gamble **is a dangerous word.** *Gamble* means that the odds are against you but you are taking a chance that the odds will roll in your favor. Betting on a game, playing the lottery, and smoking cigarettes are examples of gambling. You know that the odds are against you, but you are betting that you will beat the odds.

Risk **is a safe word.** Before you try something in your class, you do these things:

1. Identify what you need to resolve.
2. Read to see what technique is available.
3. Observe other teachers using the technique.
4. Ask questions about the technique.
5. Discover that many others are using the technique.
6. Observe that the technique is a common technique.
7. Determine that the technique is a commonsense approach supported by research.

After careful consideration of items one through seven above, you choose to implement a new technique. This is because in risk taking, the odds are in your favor. **Accomplishment and rewards go to those who take risks.**

There is one thing perhaps more dangerous than gambling, and that thing is doing nothing.

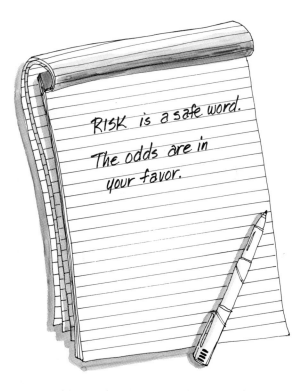

RISK is a safe word.

The odds are in your favor.

> **Nothing will ever be accomplished by sitting around doing nothing, making butt prints in the sands of time.**

One of the hardest things about your life when you're over a half century, as I am, is to realize what you should have done 20 years earlier. I blew it.

Dustin Hoffman
Newsweek,
December 11, 1989.

Rollie Fingers, a future Hall of Famer who earned millions playing baseball, is broke at age 43. When asked if there was anything he would wish for Christmas, he replied:

Yeah, to be 10 years younger and know what I know now.

San Jose Mercury News,
December 2, 1989.

Your Chances of Success Are One to One

Your odds of winning a state lottery are 14 million to 1.

Your odds of jumping out of an airplane with two parachutes and not having both open are 1.2 million to 1.

Your odds of getting hit by lightning are 600,000 to 1.

Your odds of success in whatever you choose to do are better than winning a lottery or getting hit by lightning.

Your odds of succeeding are 1 to 1. There is only one person you ever need to compete against, and that is yourself.

Reward Yourself with a Career Risk Plan

If you put money into an investment or savings plan that has an interest rate of 10 percent, compounded semiannually, you will double your investment every 7.2 years. For instance, if you save $2,000 each year, at the end of seven years you would have not $14,000 but $20,000.

At the end of 14 years, you would have not $28,000 but $56,000.

And at the end of 28 years, you would have not $56,000 but $260,000, over a quarter of a million dollars. Investment people call this a compound growth curve. At the beginning nothing seems to accumulate, but as the years progress, the sums jump forward in leaps and bounds.

The professional educator invests in his or her career. After three years of investing in your own life, you can be 33 percent better than you were when you started. After four years, you can be some 45 percent better than you were when you started.

After three to five years, growing 10 percent each year, you should be in the top 20 percent of the teaching profession. Why? Because 80 percent of your colleagues will have been sitting, doing nothing. Some are even regressing and destroying the organization they are in.

✓ The research shows that 80 percent of the teachers have not been to a conference on their own time and money for an average of 10 years.

✓ Forty percent of the teachers have not been to a conference for an average of 16 years.

✓ Simply put, the great majority of teachers refuse to learn and grow, yet they expect their students to do so.

The rewards in education and in life go to the professionals. The rest get paid a salary for putting in time.

A Professional Educator's Career Risk Plan

✓ Each year try two or three new ideas or techniques.

✓ Start with one, perhaps one from this book.

✓ A few months later, try another one.

✓ A few months later, try another one.

✓ Each year try two or three new ideas.

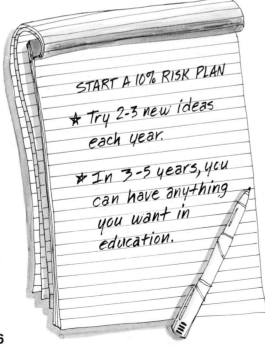

START A 10% RISK PLAN

★ Try 2-3 new ideas each year.

★ In 3-5 years, you can have anything you want in education.

How to Be at the Forefront of Your Profession

I first heard you speak five years ago. I had just transferred from a nice, small Catholic school to a much larger Detroit public elementary school. I also went from teaching 21 fifth graders to running a library and seeing over 500 students a week, including Special Ed.

I was overwhelmed, discouraged, and unsure of myself as a teacher.

When I first heard you at Seaholm High School in Birmingham that year, I felt recharged, inspired, and understood. I immediately bought your tapes and listened to them frequently. I used your discipline plan and modified it for my situation, and it worked wonderfully. I had my diploma framed and hung it in my library.

*But the one message that helped me the most was when you said, **"Every year do one thing that is different, above and beyond your job. If you do this, in five years you will be at the forefront of the profession."***

I began that year to dress up as a book character from the story "Miss Nelson Is Missing." I posed as Viola Swamp, the meanest, oldest, and ugliest substitute teacher in the world.

A year later, my supervisor started asking me to speak at reading conferences and in-services in Detroit. Two years later, I was speaking around the state. Last year I spoke in Texas, Indiana, Alabama, and Washington, D.C. I was asked back a second time to Houston to be the keynote speaker at the Greater Houston Reading Council. This summer I will be speaking in Atlanta, Arkansas, and again in Alabama.

Because I dared to be different, I am at the forefront of my profession. But far more important, I am happy with myself. I love teaching. I know I am a great teacher. And like you, I know I can inspire other educators to be innovative, loving, humorous, and proud of themselves.

Sincerely,

Mary Kay Stark

The Rewards Go to Those Who Implement a Risk Plan

You can have anything you want in education in three to five years:

✓ The school of your choice

✓ The district of your choice

✓ The job of your choice

✓ A salary greatly improved from what you have now

✓ Happiness, success, and respect

You can have it all in three to five years—and with no effort to boot. This is how and why.

The scope of this book has been restricted to a small but very significant part of a teacher's life, the first days of school. The book does not pretend to be a comprehensive textbook, nor should it be used to evaluate a teacher. There is still much for a professional educator to learn.

Since there is no scope or sequence to the content, nor does the information represent a model, there is really no beginning or ending to this book. Plunge in wherever you may need help, just as you would use a cookbook or a repair manual. As for an ending, the professional educator never stops learning.

A woodsman who has been lost in the forest for several weeks has been rescued. Tired and hungry, he is taken to a restaurant featuring an eat-all-you-want buffet.

Staring at his first sight of food in weeks, a rescuer asks, "You seem puzzled. Do you not know what to do?"

The woodsman replies, "Oh, I know what to do. I just don't know where to begin."

The professional educator says, "What do I need to know in order to do what I need to do?"

> **The Biggest Secret for Professional Growth in Education**
>
> **If you invest 10 percent into your life each year, you will go zooming by most of your colleagues and be an accomplished professional educator in three to five years.**

Begin by asking yourself what you need to do. Are you having problems with discipline, roll taking, seating assignments, homework, collecting papers, or what? Until you know what you need to do, you will never do anything.

After identifying what needs to be done, turn to the appropriate chapter for the information and begin.

Just begin! Begin anywhere, but take a risk and begin.

Which one of you will be the next great teacher? If not you, someone else will.

The rewards go to those who implement a risk plan.

✓ The rewards go to the professional educators.

✓ The rewards go to those who continue to learn.

✓ The rewards go to those who share.

✓ The rewards go to those who take risks.

✓ The rewards go to those who implement a career risk plan.

Risk

To laugh is to risk appearing the fool.
To weep is to risk appearing sentimental.
To reach out for another is to risk involvement.
To expose your feelings is to risk exposing your true self.
To place your ideas, your dreams, before a crowd is to risk their loss.
To love is to risk not being loved in return.
To live is to risk dying.
To hope is to risk despair.
To try is to risk failure.

But risks must be taken, because the greatest hazard in life is to
    risk nothing.
Persons who risk nothing do nothing, have nothing,
    and are nothing.
They may avoid suffering and sorrow, but they cannot learn,
    feel, change, grow,
      love, or live.
Chained by their attitudes, they are slaves, for they have forfeited
    their freedom.

Only a person who risks is free.

The Effective Teacher

1. Implements a career risk plan.
2. Can document annual professional growth.
3. Is able to explain why he or she is a professional educator.

I touch the future . . .
I teach.

Christa McAuliffe

Although we have taught in American schools, our many speeches and workshops have taken us to schools worldwide in Canada, Asia, Europe, South America, and Africa. The ideas and techniques used in this book may have come primarily from American schools, but our message is applicable to the children of the world.

We ask our friends in Canada and abroad to take a serious look at the crisis in America, a nation that went in a few short years from being the world's leading creditor nation to the world's leading debtor nation, a nation of scientific and technological giants but ethical and moral midgets. If you suspect that the same crisis is looming on the horizon for your country, this closing epilogue applies to you also.

Our Children Are an Endangered Species

✓ Each year 700,000 students drop out of school, equivalent to the school population of Minnesota. At this rate, 40 percent of our population in the year 2000 could consist of citizens who dropped out of school.

✓ Each night 100,000 children are homeless, and this does not include children who have run away from home or have been kicked out of the house.

✓ The intact family, of responsible parents who teach values, seldom exists. Only 4 percent of families in America consists of a married couple with two children.

✓ An estimated 25 million Americans are illiterate. The business world knows that the next generation of workers will not be as qualified as this generation.

✓ Children are caught in a maelstrom of cultural and social problems: drugs, permissiveness, poverty, teenage pregnancy, broken homes, and falling academic standards.

✓ Never before in the history of a country have so many children been raised by strangers. First the parents transfer their responsibility to a care person or care center; later they transfer it to the schools. The result is that schools are struggling to deal with the increasing numbers of at-risk youth.

✓ Whereas each generation has had a better life than each past generation, the next generation in America could quite possibly be the first generation to be worse off than the previous generation.

It doesn't make sense. The teachers of today are better than the teachers of yesteryear. So are the administrators, the schools, and the curriculum. Yet the product is worse than ever before. **The reason is societal.**

The schools are being blamed, incorrectly, for the ills of society. Why do certain nations succeed while others fail? It is a complex question with many answers, but there is one common answer—*culture*. Countries that create wealth (economically, socially, and politically) stress education, freedom to create, delayed gratification, mutual trust, and hard work. Those that don't stay poor, remain in debt, or head toward bankruptcy.

Within the American culture, groups whose culture stress hard work and learning succeed in disproportionate numbers to those who do not. It isn't a lack of talent but the lack of values and culture that too often results in failure. Culture overcomes discrimination and poverty if it sends the right signals.

We are blaming the schools for faults that lie deeper within our society. In the long run, the habits, values, and behavior of citizens determine national strength. The truth is that culture, not politics, money, or skin color, determines the success of a society.

America did not become strong by eating junk food, watching TV, or by crowing "We're number one." **America became strong with its cultural values: hard work, effort, and integrity.** One of the causes for the current problems with youth is the inability of the culture to pass on its values.

The family is the bulwark of culture. Schools merely help the family to pass on culture. But when you no longer have intact families, a family dinnertime, or a visible set of societal values, the next generation will never acquire culture.

Our children—America's most precious resource—are an endangered species. They are our most precious resource because they are our future. We need leaders-teachers, professional educators who will begin this revitalization of our culture and values.

For many of our students, we play an extraordinarily important role:

✓ We may be the only stable adult in their lives.

✓ We may be the only people able to pass on culture.

✓ We may be their only hope and dream for a brighter tomorrow.

Teachers Create Their Own Culture

By the year 2000 there will have been an 80 percent turnover of the teachers.

✓ **This is a challenge, a charge, a mission for the veteran teachers to leave a legacy of positive expectations with the new teachers.**

✓ **This is a challenge, a charge, a mission for these new teachers to create a revolutionary change in the cultural attitude of teachers.**

It is not money, class size, or a new textbook that determine the success or respect of a group of teachers. It is culture.

People tend to look at each other's wallets instead of each other's eyes and heart. You can't buy a look into someone's heart. The best things in life are not things.

Money can't buy health, and it cannot buy hope. Money can't buy a nice conversation around the family dinner table. Money cannot buy freedom, time, peace of mind, equality, justice, love of your children, or an end to loneliness.

Teachers play a dramatic role in the life of a child.
Are you up to the part?

When I Look at Them...

When I look at them,
When I smile at them,
When I hold them,
I realize that I have
*   the universe in my hands.*

They are the light of my life.
They are the love of my life.

They are life.

Money cannot buy integrity or respect.

A principal thanked a teacher for sending her transcript, but needed her vita also. Her response was telling and a reflection of the attitude of many teachers.

"I don't have a vita," she said. "What would I put on it? I'm just a teacher."

The TRUTH About Teachers

✓ Only 22 percent of the general population have a college degree, but all teachers have one. We are an intelligent group of people.

✓ The teaching profession is the ONLY profession in which over half of its members have voluntary advanced degrees. As of 1989, some 51.4 percent of the teachers had degrees beyond a bachelor's degree. Teachers are the intellectual elite of America.

✓ Every tenured teacher has a teaching credential. Teachers are an intelligent, certified, licensed, and competent group of people.

Just a teacher. Indeed. The lack of integrity or respect we have for ourselves is a reflection of the cultural attitude teachers have toward themselves.

Teachers see themselves as "just teachers." The fact is that teachers express the worth of their work humbly, modestly, and apologetically. The learned helplessness of some teachers is pitiful.

The reflection of people toward the work they do is a reflection of their own worth. Teachers need a different set of values from which to construct their self-worth. Teachers need to construct a whole new culture for themselves, not one where the public only knows us as a group of people forever whining about raises in pay.

We are not against better pay; rather, we are appalled that teachers view themselves as a group of people who are poor and forlorn. Walk out to the parking lot and see if any teachers are driving old wrecks; go to the homeless shelters and see if any teachers are bedded down; go to the rescue mission and see if any teachers are in line for a meal.

The truth is far rosier. Sadly, you would never know this by looking at many teachers. Some come to school dressed like they have just finished cleaning the house or repairing the car. Even more complain about getting an education, such as attending in-services, conferences, and college classes. Then you look around their classrooms and their diplomas and credentials are nowhere to be seen.

When you walk into a doctor's office, you see degrees, certificates, and licenses framed and neatly hung on the wall in columns and rows. The same is true in the offices of accountants, pharmacists, and even mechanics, with their Mr. Goodwrench certificates.

Effective teachers display their diplomas with pride.

Members of every profession display their diplomas, licenses, and certificates—every profession but teaching. The tragedy is that teachers are in the diploma business. On Graduation Day, the student receives a diploma, the only tangible proof of years of schooling. Yet teachers are reluctant to hang up their product, a diploma that says to the world, "Look at me; I am an educated person." Why? Because teacher culture has taught teachers to practice learned helplessness, planned pitifulness.

One of our teachers really zeroed in on your "diploma" comments and has arranged for all her Chapter 1 students to spend a day at our local university. They will attend classes, eat lunch, visit with one of the university administrators, and then get a "diploma" with the future date of their graduation indicated. In the students' individual goal conference, they will refer to their goal of graduation from college and so on.

Trish Marcuzzo
Omaha, Nebraska

How often I have looked at my college degrees sitting in a box in my attic gathering dust. And just to think about the years and time spent in earning them. Thanks to you mine are in the process of getting framed to be displayed with pride like those of people in other professions.

Sandra Knecht
Marion Center,
Pennsylvania

All of our national problems, from international competitiveness to improving our standard of living to the future of our children, ultimately rest on one important word: *education*.

Through the history of civilization, the concept of education has remained stable. Colors fade, temples crumble, empires fall, but education endures. Societies that succeed respect their teachers, and the teachers respect themselves.

We must begin with ourselves.

Leaders Begin with Themselves

Leaders begin with respect for their own worth. Society needs models of leadership. What better models of leaders than the teachers of a community.

✓ Teachers can be compared productively with business executives in that teachers, like executives, develop, manage, and evaluate the work and productivity of a relatively large number of individuals on a daily basis.

✓ When comparing teachers and doctors, teachers make more complex decisions than doctors do, and make them far more frequently.

✓ More teachers go into teaching because of the influence of another teacher. This is not true for other professions. Teachers have influence.

✓ Teaching is the profession that makes all other professions possible.

✓ We are the only profession dedicated to making the world a better place for our future generation. They are our legacy.

✓ We are the only profession concerned with all youth and the realization that our children today are our most precious resource, that through them we will realize a better tomorrow.

✓ We realize that the degree of civilization of any nation is equivalent to the civilization of its youth.

Our mission is to teach students the important skills, knowledge, and values necessary to be a success in tomorrow's world. What better way to teach these important skills, knowledge, and attitudes than to have ourselves as models?

Our children need models of success. Teachers who are considered successful work at being successful. There is no other way. There is no simple, foolproof, teacherproof, easy way—not even in this book. Every suggestion in this book must be worked at and worked at. Having a disciplined class, a class of academic achievers, a class of students who perform well at the annual musical, a team of students who are perennial league champions, requires constant work.

You are their hope and dream for a brighter tomorrow.

Commitment, dedication, and hard work make a person a leader. Ability and talent are not enough. Leadership is not created; it is achieved. It is the product of ability and talent combined with relentless practice and tempered by years of training. But even then, leaders give more. They give their heart and soul.

Accomplishment begins with teachers who are leaders. You do not want someone else's accomplishments, and you cannot give your accomplishments to someone else. What you can do is share how you achieved those accomplishments so that others may work toward and have pride in achieving their own successes. And that is why we are teachers.

The best results are the results you earn, own, look back on, and take pride in. You have to compete only against yourself to achieve the results you want from your life. The very second you commit yourself to work on a goal, you are a success.

Success of any kind requires you to take responsibility. In the final analysis, the one quality that all successful people have is the ability to take on responsibility.

The effective teacher knows that all children are capable of success.

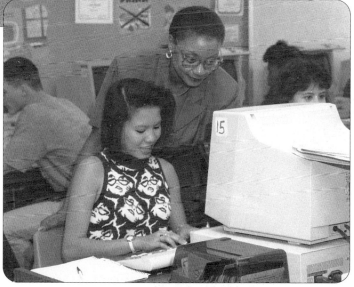

Some people can give thousands of reasons why they cannot succeed at something when all they need is one reason why they can succeed. Knowing that any person can succeed is the responsibility and spirit of a leader.

You are a leader, a professional educator. Your challenge is to change the image and culture of the teaching profession. Your challenge is to revitalize the culture and restore the values of this nation.

> **With desire and commitment the leader builds a fire inside that catches others on fire. No matter what the odds, the leader knows that any task can be accomplished.**

Never be satisfied with even a good job, because good is not good enough. You need to be brilliant, to excel, to go beyond, to be preeminent.

Going far beyond the call of duty, doing more than what others expect—this is what the children need from our teachers.

Striving, maintaining the highest standards, looking after the smallest details, and going after that extra mile—these are the values our nation needs from the leadership of its professional educators.

You can do it.

The ultimate joy, happiness, nourishment, and reward lies within yourself. Get in touch with your own magnificence.

✦ ✦ ✦ ✦ ✦ ✦ ✦ ✦ ✦ ✦ ✦ ✦

One hundred years from now it will not matter

What kind of car I drove,
What kind of house I lived in,
How much I had in the bank account,
Or what my clothes looked like.

But the world will be a better place because
I was important in the life of a child.

Photo Credits

American Library Association, p. x;

Reavis Z. Worthum, Communications Department, Garland Independent School District, Garland, Texas, pp. 7, 32, 47, 49, 53, 74, 78, 82, 86, 98, 117, 119, 130, 194, 201, 205, 207, 220, 242, 266, 280, 312, 315, 318, 319, 321;

Santa Cruz Seaside Company, The Giant Dipper, p. 13;

Aaron Rosander, p. 58;

Robert Messick, p. 83;

Little Fort Media, p. 297;

A/P World Wide Photos, p. 303.

Acknowledgments

Grateful acknowledgment is made to the following people and institutions for permission to use their pictures, illustrations, or facilities:

Alicia Escobar, p. iv;

Mary Ellen King, p. vi;

American Library Association, p. x;

Jane H. Smith, p. 10;

Eric Abrams, p. 26;

Flowing Wells School District, Tucson, Arizona, pp. 26, 39, 45, 67, 87, 159, 165, 187, 268, 317;

Elouise Bettis, p. 27;

Oklahoma City Public Schools, p. 37;

Phil Grant, p. 56;

Luisa Velasco, p. 58;

Yokota High School, Japan, pp. 72, 107, 202;

Alice Waters, p. 83;

Aaron Rosander, p. 88;

Yokota East Elementary School, Japan, p. 92, 124;

Sherry Sather Braaten, p. 104;

Shirley Lanham Elementary School, Japan, p. 107;

James Teslow, p. 113;

Lauri McCaffrey, p. 113;

LaContenta Junior High School, Yucca Valley, California, p. 117;

Cummings Elementary School, Japan, pp. 121, 158;

Shirley Bert Lee, p. 125;

Merle J. Whaley, p. 139;

Jim Dohr, p. 151;

Laura LaNotte-Hays, p. 183;

Cindy Wong, p. 186;

Janelle M. Tynan, p. 225;

Yokota West Elementary School, Japan, p. 251;

Elayna Tami Grant, p. 278;

Brian Colbert, p. 278;

Jerry Peterson, p. 317.

About the Authors

Who Are Harry and Rosemary Wong?

They are teachers.

INDEX

W

Z

The First Days of School

Full color cover
Two color print
352 pages
10 x 8 inches
128 illustratrions
103 photographs

My daughter did everything you suggested and was rated by her principal as one of the best first-year teachers.

Karen Willis
Sulphur Springs, Texas

THE FIRST DAYS OF SCHOOL
How to Be an Effective Teacher
by
Harry K. Wong
Rosemary Tripi Wong

There is overwhelming evidence that the first two to three weeks of school are critical in determining how well students will achieve for the remainder of the year. What the teacher does on the first days of school will determine the teacher's success or failure for the rest of the school year.

✓ If you had to buy only one book in education to help you become a successful teacher, **The First Days of School** is the book you want.

✓ If you are having trouble with your students and you are not getting the results you want, **The First Days of School** is the book you want.

✓ If you are a staff developer or an administrator and you want to help your teachers be the best that they can be, **The First Days of School** is the book you want.

✓ If you are a college professor and you want to help your preservice teachers be the best that they can be, **The First Days of School** is the book you want.

Order direct from Harry K. Wong Publications. Call for immediate shipment at sale prices. Quantity discounts available.

Produced by:
Harry K. Wong Publications
1030 W. Maude Ave., Ste. 507
Sunnyvale, CA 94086
TEL (408) 732-1388
FAX (408) 732-2206

I choose to CARE

60 minutes
1/2" VHS format
Studio quality cameras
Studio quality production
Unconditionally guaranteed against
  manufacturer's defects

*Dr. Wong, now I know why
you are the most sought after
speaker in the country. I have
invited and listened to a number of
speakers in the last 12 years and
you rank number one. You are not
only a master teacher, but an
exciting and dynamic speaker.*

Dante Thurairatnam
Bowling Green (Ohio) University

I choose to CARE
with
Harry K. Wong

I choose to CARE is a one-hour motivational video tape that stirs and renews the professional soul of teachers. It offers concrete, practical, and applicable classroom suggestions that teachers can use. Recorded live before an audience of 3,200 district employees, Harry K. Wong will make you laugh and make you cry. When it's over, you leave determined to strive for excellence.

Harry K. Wong brings out the best in educators. His in-service and convention speeches are legendary. Although he is a coveted conference keynote speaker, he's at his very best in the trenches, at in-service meetings. He has done thousands of them, all over the United States, Canada, and the world, to some half-million people. No one is better than Harry K. Wong as an educational speaker. He is in a class by himself—world class.

The video is produced for maximum personal and staff development. The content of *I choose to CARE* is solid, research-based, classroom effectiveness material. Add to this the charisma of Harry K. Wong and you know why he is considered the most exciting and motivating speaker in education.

CONTENTS OF *I choose to CARE*

A. The Four Beliefs of Effective Teachers
  ✓ The teacher makes a difference.
  ✓ The teacher is competent.
  ✓ The teacher is a good classroom manager.
  ✓ The teacher uses research-based practices.

B. Effective Teachers Use Research-based Practices To Ensure Student Success
  ✓ Questions for comprehension
  ✓ Maximizes time on task
  ✓ Uses procedures and routines
    for efficiency
  ✓ Teaches to objectives
  ✓ Teaches responsibility
  ✓ Has a discipline plan

C. Effective Teachers Teach Leadership
  ✓ Leaders make choices.
  ✓ Leaders are risk takers.
  ✓ Leaders have curiosity.
  ✓ Leaders work cooperatively.
  ✓ Leaders have a work ethic.
  ✓ Leaders care.

Contact Harry K. Wong Publications for additional information, current prices, or quantity discounts.

Produced by:
Harry K. Wong Publications
1030 W. Maude Ave., Ste. 507
Sunnyvale, CA 94086
TEL (408) 732-1388
FAX (408) 732-2206

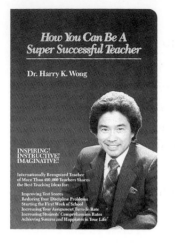

How You Can Be a Super Successful Teacher

Four audio tapes, 4½ hours
Vinyl case
Lifetime replacement guarantee

I recently took over a class that had somewhat poor discipline. This being the first class I could call my own, I have found the information and advice contained in your tapes to be invaluable. In just three days I have managed to gain some semblance of order where before chaos had reigned supreme. Thank you for having produced these tapes.

Jim Orth
Wendell, Idaho

HOW YOU CAN BE A SUPER SUCCESSFUL TEACHER
with
Harry K. Wong

How You Can Be a Super Successful Teacher is the most widely used set of tapes on classroom management, discipline, and self-esteem. Some 50,000 tapes have been sold and they continue to inspire and help teachers. No bull, all beef. Little theory, all substance. Harry Wong has been called "Mr. Practicality." Invest in these tapes for your own success.

How to Achieve Maximum Success in the Classroom (tapes 1 & 2)
Dozens of immediately useful techniques to achieve maximum success with your students. All techniques are proven, tested, and easy to implement. You will learn how to:
- ✔ begin a class with success
- ✔ increase the homework turn-in rate
- ✔ increase student's test scores, reading and retention rates
- ✔ teach students to teach themselves
- ✔ be a caring and loving teacher

Once and for All You Can Solve Your Discipline Problems (tape 3)
Here is a simple three-part plan to help you greatly reduce your discipline problems, reduce your stress level, and increase the achievement level of your students. You will learn how to:
- ✔ reduce 80 percent of your discipline problems
- ✔ discipline those who break your rules
- ✔ reward those who obey your rules
- ✔ reduce your stress level
- ✔ include other teachers in your discipline plan
- ✔ increase students' academic learning time

You Are a Marvel (tape 4)
Listen to this tape when you need a shot-in-the-arm to remind yourself of your importance, dignity, and respectability as a teacher and a human being. This tape explains how to move from being an ordinary teacher to becoming a super successful teacher. You will learn why:
- ✔ every person is unique
- ✔ people make excuses
- ✔ some people are always happy and fulfilled
- ✔ some people can't decide, while others make good choices
- ✔ YOU, as a teacher, are so important!

Contact Harry K. Wong Publications for additional information, current prices, or quantity discounts.

Produced by:
Harry K. Wong Publications
1030 W. Maude Ave., Ste. 507
Sunnyvale, CA 94086
TEL (408) 732-1388
FAX (408) 732-2206

Please Share with Us

Every 20 years education cycles itself. There are really no new ideas in education. Newer ideas are refinements of older ideas.

Everything we have shared in *The First Days of School*, we have acquired from years of research, visiting schools and classrooms, and interacting with teachers, administrators, and college professors. Teacher-specific ideas and techniques are given to us and mailed to us after our in-service meetings. We thank these professional educators for their contributions.

Please share with us your ideas, your techniques, your strategies.

Please share with us your:

✓ worksheets

✓ assignments

✓ criterion-referenced tests

✓ study guidelines

✓ discipline plans

✓ procedures and routines

✓ invitational messages

✓ school and classroom pictures

We'd like to hear from:

✓ Teachers - your personal stories of success

✓ Staff Developers - your professional development programs

✓ Administrators - your beginning teacher induction programs

✓ College Professors - your preservice class experiences

Send to:

Harry and Rosemary Wong
1030 W. Maude Ave., Ste. 507
Sunnyvale, CA 94086

Thank you for sharing and enhancing our profession.

Sharing

If you have a dollar and I have a dollar and we exchange dollars, we still each have a dollar.

But if you have a teaching technique that works and I have a teaching technique that works and we exchange these techniques, you still have your technique, but you have mine also, and I still have my technique, but have yours also.

We are now 100% better off than before because we shared.

◆ ◆